Java EE 7 Development with WildFly

Leverage the power of the WildFly application server from JBoss to develop modern Java EE 7 applications

Michał Ćmil

Michał Matłoka

Francesco Marchioni

BIRMINGHAM - MUMBAI

Java EE 7 Development with WildFly

First published: June 2013

Second edition: December 2014

Production reference: 1241214

Published by Packt Publishing Ltd.
Livery Place
35 Livery Street
Birmingham B3 2PB, UK.

ISBN 978-1-78217-198-0

www.packtpub.com

Cover image by Michael Jasej (milak6@wp.pl)

Credits

Authors
Michał Ćmil
Michał Matłoka
Francesco Marchioni

Reviewers
Dustin Kut Moy Cheung
Adam Dudczak
Maxime Gréau
Bartosz Majsak
Jakub Marchwicki

Commissioning Editor
James Jones

Acquisition Editor
James Jones

Content Development Editor
Mohammed Fahad

Technical Editors
Indrajit A. Das
Rohit Kumar Singh

Copy Editors
Gladson Monteiro
Adithi Shetty

Project Coordinator
Akash Poojary

Proofreaders
Ting Baker
Simran Bhogal
Ameesha Green

Indexers
Rekha Nair
Priya Sane

Production Coordinator
Shantanu N. Zagade

Cover Work
Shantanu N. Zagade

About the Authors

Michał Ćmil is a Java developer with experience in web and desktop application development. In the past, he has worked for the e-commerce sector. Currently, he is developing manufacturing execution systems for industry clients. He has been a volunteer at GeeCON. Michał works as a software designer/developer for PSI Poland.

Michał Matłoka is a Java developer with experience in both Java EE and Spring technologies. He is a JBoss community contributor, focusing mainly on Arquillian and ShrinkWrap, and is also a winner of the JBoss Community Recognition Award in 2013 for his contributions to ShrinkWrap. He has spoken at Poznan Java User Group and volunteered at GeeCON. Michał is currently one of the 20 CEOs at SoftwareMill, a fully distributed company with no main office and a completely flat organization structure.

Francesco Marchioni is a Sun Certified Enterprise architect employed for an Italian company based in Rome. He started learning Java in 1997, and since then he has followed the path to the newest Application Program Interfaces released by Sun. In 2000, he joined the JBoss community when the application server was running the 2.x release.

He has spent many years as a software consultant, where he has envisioned many successful software migrations from vendor platforms to the open source products such as JBoss AS, fulfilling the tight budget requirements of current times.

For the past 5 years, he has been authoring technical articles for O'Reilly Media and also runs an IT portal focused on JBoss products (http://www.mastertheboss.com).

In December 2009, he authored *JBoss AS 5 Development*, *Packt Publishing*, which describes how to create and deploy Java Enterprise applications on JBoss AS.

In December 2010, he authored his second title, *JBoss AS 5 Performance Tuning*, *Packt Publishing*, which describes how to deliver fast and efficient applications on JBoss AS.

In December 2011, he authored yet another title, *JBoss AS 7 Configuration Deployment Administration*, *Packt Publishing*, which covers all the aspects of the newest application server release.

In August 2012, he coauthored the book, *Infinispan Data Grid Platform*, *Packt Publishing*, with Manik Surtani, which covers all aspects related to the configuration and development of applications using the Infinispan data grid platform.

I'd like to thank Packt Publishing for sharing the vision of this new book and for all the effort they put in it. I'd also like to thank my family for being always on my side, particularly, my wife for allowing me to follow my book author ambitions, and my father for buying me a C-64 instead of a motorcycle when I was young.

About the Reviewers

Dustin Kut Moy Cheung was born and raised in the island of Mauritius. His interest in computers was sparked when he got his first computer at the age of nine. He went on to study Electrical Engineering at McGill University in Montreal, Canada. Dustin is currently working as a productization engineer in the JBoss productization team at Red Hat.

> I would like to thank the authors for giving me the opportunity to be one of the reviewers for this book. Java EE 7 has certainly made web development in Java easier and more elegant. Using the Wildfly application server will enable users to fully unlock all the capabilities that Java EE has to offer while providing easy administration, configuration, deployment, clustering, and much more!

Adam Dudczak is an experienced software engineer working with Java and related technologies since 2004. He is interested in the creation of lightweight, bulletproof, and scalable applications. He has a strong background in information retrieval and text mining. Currently, he is working on a better search experience in one of the major east European e-commerce portals. He is one of the leaders of Poznań JUG (http://www.jug.poznan.pl) and a co-organizer of the GeeCON conference (http://geecon.org). Adam is a father and husband and occasionally blogs at http://dudczak.info/dry. His Twitter handle is @maneo.

Maxime Gréau has been building software professionally for about 12 years, mostly for the Web and most of it with Java. He wrote a French book about Apache Maven 3 in 2011. He currently works as a Java EE architect.

Maxime is a speaker at conferences on Java and web technologies such as DevNation and DevFest. He is also a technical reviewer.

He blogs at `http://mgreau.com/blog/` and can be found on Twitter and GitHub at `@mgreau`.

Bartosz Majsak works as a software developer at Cambridge Technology Partners, based in Zurich. He is passionate about open source technologies and testing methodologies. He is a proud JBoss Community Recognition award recipient for 2012 and 2013. He's also an Arquillian team member and the lead for two modules: Persistence Extension (makes writing database-oriented tests easier) and Spock Test Runner (gives your Arquillian tests some BDD and Groovy love). One thing that perhaps proves Bartosz is not a total geek is his addiction to alpine skiing.

Jakub Marchwicki has been in the software development industry for the past 10 years—wearing multiple hats, getting his hands dirty in multiple environments, and securing both technical as well as the business side of *The Thing*, which is an engineer with a human-friendly interface. Additionally, he has worked with a variety of languages and frameworks.

Jakub has always considered programming a tool to solve real-life problems in a pragmatic way. He has always stayed close to the business side of the solution, focusing on the technology. He combines his daily job of managing a horde of software engineers at Young Digital Planet with lectures, technical trainings, and commitment to Gdańsk Java User Group.

www.PacktPub.com

Support files, eBooks, discount offers, and more

For support files and downloads related to your book, please visit www.PacktPub.com.

Did you know that Packt offers eBook versions of every book published, with PDF and ePub files available? You can upgrade to the eBook version at www.PacktPub.com and as a print book customer, you are entitled to a discount on the eBook copy. Get in touch with us at service@packtpub.com for more details.

At www.PacktPub.com, you can also read a collection of free technical articles, sign up for a range of free newsletters and receive exclusive discounts and offers on Packt books and eBooks.

https://www2.packtpub.com/books/subscription/packtlib

Do you need instant solutions to your IT questions? PacktLib is Packt's online digital book library. Here, you can search, access, and read Packt's entire library of books.

Why subscribe?

- Fully searchable across every book published by Packt
- Copy and paste, print, and bookmark content
- On demand and accessible via a web browser

Free access for Packt account holders

If you have an account with Packt at www.PacktPub.com, you can use this to access PacktLib today and view 9 entirely free books. Simply use your login credentials for immediate access.

Instant updates on new Packt books

Get notified! Find out when new books are published by following @PacktEnterprise on Twitter or the *Packt Enterprise* Facebook page.

Table of Contents

Preface

WildFly, the newest release of the JBoss Application Server, provides developers with a full implementation of the Java EE 7 platform. It is built on solid foundations of the modular architecture introduced with JBoss AS 7, but it has grown in terms of flexibility and performance. The newest version of the Enterprise Java focuses on developers' productivity, and so does WildFly.

This book will introduce Java developers to the world of enterprise applications. We will use modern development techniques and tools that are battle-tested in real-life projects. We'll also utilize the features provided by the WildFly platform, such as security, caching, testing, and clustering. Finally, you will learn how to manage your server using dedicated tools, created specifically for WildFly.

The learning process will be concentrated around a ticket booking application, which is a sample project that will get more features (and sometimes completely different user interfaces) with every chapter.

What this book covers

Chapter 1, Getting Started with WildFly, is an introduction to the Java EE platform and new Java EE 7 version specifications. It also focuses on presenting WildFly's new features, the developer environment setup, and basic server management.

Chapter 2, Your First Java EE Application on WildFly, describes the basics of the WildFly server usage, presenting information required to deploy your first application.

Chapter 3, Introducing Java EE 7 – EJBs, introduces Java EE business objects called Enterprise Java Beans. In this chapter, we create the foundations of the ticket booking application.

Chapter 4, Learning Context and Dependency Injection, covers the CDI technology that connects the building blocks of your applications.

Chapter 5, Combining Persistence with CDI, is a look into the database world and object mapping in Java EE.

Chapter 6, Developing Applications with JBoss JMS Provider, is a dive into HornetQ and enterprise system integration using JCA.

Chapter 7, Adding Web Services to Your Applications, discusses not only the old-style SOAP web services but also the modern and popular approach based on JAX-RS (REST). We'll also take a look at how to integrate a Java EE 7 backend with an AngularJS browser application.

Chapter 8, Adding WebSockets, introduces a completely new asset to the Java EE 7 platform: WebSockets. We will look at them in our sample AngularJS application.

Chapter 9, Managing the Application Server, discusses WildFly management features.

Chapter 10, Securing WildFly Applications, focuses on security-related aspects of the server and your application.

Chapter 11, Clustering WildFly Applications, discusses making Java EE applications highly available and scalable.

Chapter 12, Long-term Tasks' Execution, describes the new area of enterprise Java batch applications and concurrency management on the server.

Chapter 13, Testing Your Applications, demonstrates how we can write integration tests for for our applications using Arquillian after covering the most important Java EE technologies.

Appendix, Rapid Development Using JBoss Forge, covers the JBoss Forge tool. It shows how you can use this application to speed up your work with its code generation features on starting Java EE-based projects.

What you need for this book

This book is a code-oriented guide into the Java EE and WildFly worlds. To fully benefit from this book, you will need access to an Internet connection in order to download all the required tools and libraries. Knowledge of Java is required. We will also use Maven as a build automation tool, but thanks to its verbosity, the examples provided in this book are self-explanatory.

Although we will use AngularJS, additional JS knowledge is not required. All examples for the framework will be showcase-based, and their aim is to show how different parties can interact with Java EE in typical scenarios.

Who this book is for

If you are a Java developer who wants to learn about Java EE basics or if you are already a Java EE developer who wants to learn what's new in WildFly or Java EE 7, this book is for you. This book covers basics of the described technologies and also ensures to bring some more interesting, advanced topics for those who already have some knowledge.

Conventions

In this book, you will find a number of styles of text that distinguish between different kinds of information. Here are some examples of these styles and an explanation of their meaning.

Code words in text, database table names, folder names, filenames, file extensions, pathnames, dummy URLs, user input, and Twitter handles are shown as follows: "After an MDB instance's onMessage() method returns, the request is complete, and the instance is placed back in the free pool."

A block of code is set as follows:

```
<jms-destinations>
    <jms-queue name="TicketQueue">
        <entry name="java:jboss/jms/queue/ticketQueue"/>
            <durable>false</durable>
    </jms-queue>
</jms-destinations>
```

When we wish to draw your attention to a particular part of a code block, the relevant lines or items are set in bold:

```
@Stateless
public class SampleEJB {

    @Resource(mappedName = "java:/ConnectionFactory")
    private ConnectionFactory cf;
}
```

Any command-line input or output is written as follows:

```
CREATE DATABASE ticketsystem;
CREATE USER jboss WITH PASSWORD 'jboss';
GRANT ALL PRIVILEGES ON DATABASE ticketsystem TO jboss;
```

New terms and **important words** are shown in bold. Words that you see on the screen, in menus or dialog boxes, for example, appear in the text like this: "For example, the Eclipse's **File** menu includes an option **JPA Entities from Table** that (once a connection has been set up to the database) allows reversing your DB schema (or part of it) into Java entities."

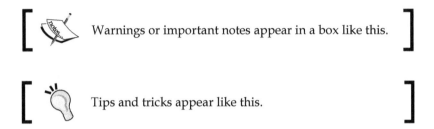

Warnings or important notes appear in a box like this.

Tips and tricks appear like this.

Reader feedback

Feedback from our readers is always welcome. Let us know what you think about this book—what you liked or may have disliked. Reader feedback is important for us to develop titles that you really get the most out of.

To send us general feedback, simply send an e-mail to feedback@packtpub.com, and mention the book title via the subject of your message.

If there is a topic that you have expertise in and you are interested in either writing or contributing to a book, see our author guide at www.packtpub.com/authors.

Customer support

Now that you are the proud owner of a Packt book, we have a number of things to help you to get the most from your purchase.

Downloading the example code

You can download the example code files for all Packt books you have purchased from your account at http://www.packtpub.com. If you purchased this book elsewhere, you can visit http://www.packtpub.com/support and register to have the files e-mailed directly to you.

Errata

Although we have taken every care to ensure the accuracy of our content, mistakes do happen. If you find a mistake in one of our books—maybe a mistake in the text or the code—we would be grateful if you could report this to us. By doing so, you can save other readers from frustration and help us improve subsequent versions of this book. If you find any errata, please report them by visiting http://www.packtpub.com/submit-errata, selecting your book, clicking on the **Errata Submission Form** link, and entering the details of your errata. Once your errata are verified, your submission will be accepted and the errata will be uploaded to our website or added to any list of existing errata under the Errata section of that title.

To view the previously submitted errata, go to https://www.packtpub.com/books/content/support and enter the name of the book in the search field. The required information will appear under the **Errata** section.

Piracy

Piracy of copyright material on the Internet is an ongoing problem across all media. At Packt, we take the protection of our copyright and licenses very seriously. If you come across any illegal copies of our works, in any form, on the Internet, please provide us with the location address or website name immediately so that we can pursue a remedy.

Please contact us at copyright@packtpub.com with a link to the suspected pirated material.

We appreciate your help in protecting our authors, and our ability to bring you valuable content.

Questions

You can contact us at questions@packtpub.com if you are having a problem with any aspect of the book, and we will do our best to address it.

Getting Started with WildFly

1

Java Enterprise Edition provides a standard to develop enterprise software, but allows the developers to choose its specific implementation. For every technology that is included in the Java EE (Enterprise Edition) specification, there is a reference implementation; an open source library or component that fulfills all of the requirements. Companies and organizations can create their own versions of the components, which means that there is no central Java EE platform that everybody uses. In place of that, we get multiple approaches on the implemented specification, with improvements and optimizations for specific cases. At the time of writing this, there are about 20 certified (full) implementations of Java EE 6 and three implementations of Java EE 7.

An application server is a runtime environment that provides applications with all the Java EE components. Glassfish is the reference implementation sponsored by Oracle, but beginning from Version 4 (created for Java EE 7), there is no longer commercial support for it. In this book, you will learn how to develop applications on the WildFly Application Server, previously known as the JBoss Application Server.

JBoss is a division of Red Hat, which seeks to provide a developer-friendly open source ecosystem for enterprise development. Currently, the company supports multiple projects (around 100), and some of them are implementations of Java EE specifications. The enterprise elements are combined in JBoss's own application server, WildFly.

It is worth noting that the name change from JBoss AS to WildFly was made to separate the application server from the company and other subprojects. The name was chosen in a public vote (more information on this is available at http://jbossas.jboss.org/rename/vote).

The new release features a scalable and high performing web server called Undertow, which supports the HTTP upgrade mechanism and WebSocket protocol. What's more, the new version of the container is even faster than JBoss Application Server 7, and offers a unified configuration mechanism. However, the main essence of the latest release is the Java EE 7 compliance, which allows developers to use technologies from the newest version of the Java EE specification.

The focus of this book is on application development; therefore, we will first need to gather all resources required to deliver our applications. In this chapter, we will cover the following topics in detail:

- An overview of Java EE and WildFly
- Preparing your environment for the installation of software
- Downloading and installing WildFly
- Verifying the WildFly installation
- Installing other resources needed for development

An overview of Java EE and WildFly

Java EE (formerly called J2EE) is an umbrella specification embracing a standard set of technologies for server-side Java development. Java EE technologies include Java Servlet, **JavaServer Pages (JSPs)**, **JavaServer Faces (JSFs)**, **Enterprise JavaBeans (EJB)**, **Contexts and Dependency Injection (CDI)**, **Java Messaging Service (JMS)**, **Java Persistence API (JPA)**, **Java API for XML Web Services (JAX-WS)**, and **Java API for RESTful Web Services (JAX-RS)**, among others. The newest version of Java EE extends the range of available technologies even further by providing support for Batch Applications, Concurrency Utilities, **JSON Processing (JSON-P)** and WebSocket. Several commercial and open source application servers exist, which allow developers to run applications compliant with Java EE; WildFly (formerly known as JBoss AS) is the leading open source solution adopted by developers and, although this is difficult to measure in exact terms, it is likely to be the most widely used application server in the market.

As with all application servers compliant with Java EE, WildFly ships with all the required libraries to allow us to develop and deploy Java applications that are built on the Java EE platform.

WildFly and Enterprise Application Platform

WildFly and previous JBoss Application Servers were freely available for the community in the form of downloadable binary packages (for major releases) or buildable source code (for bug fixing releases). These versions are called community releases and are free to use for development and production.

JBoss also releases more stable and hardened versions of software of the community builds, which are called **Enterprise Application Platform (EAP)**, a commercial product with support service from Red Hat. Red Hat calls this kind of relationship between projects as upstream/downstream. The community builds are the source of changes and innovations for the downstream, the code is downstream. The commercial version numeration differed from the community line, but it was an extended variant of the community releases (for example, EAP 6.1.0 was built on JBoss 7.2.0, which was available only on GitHub in the form of buildable source code; the same goes for EAP 6.2.0 and JBoss 7.3.0). EAP builds have a more complex licensing system; the usage terms depend on the maturity of the build and are as follows:

- **EAP Alpha** is free for the developers and production use, as they are an equivalent of the standard community version with optional fixes included. The corresponding community binaries may not be available for download, as they would be similar to the EAP Alpha version.

- **EAP Beta** is available to developers for free (after registration to a subscription program), but cannot be used in production.

- **EAP Final** is also available to developers for free, but additionally, new security patches are available only in the paid subscription.

The distribution model proposed by JBoss allows the developers to work for free on the same version as the one used in production. This is a huge benefit, especially since the competitive solution from Oracle (Glassfish: the reference implementation of a Java EE compliant server) no longer has a version with commercial support.

Welcome to Java EE 7

Java EE 7 includes several improvements and additions to the existing version. The new version is focused on three themes: developer productivity, HTML5, and providing new features required by enterprise applications. The following sections list the major improvements to the specifications that are of interest to enterprise application developers.

If you are starting your adventure with Java EE, feel free to skip this section. The technologies described in the following sections will be covered in future chapters in more detail.

JavaServer Faces 2.2 – JSR 344

Java EE 7 includes a new version of the JSF specification, which is not so revolutionary as 2.0, but still provides some appealing additions for developers. The key features delivered by JSF 2.2 are as follows:

- The HTML5 markup is now supported by the usage of pass-through elements and attributes. Earlier, custom attributes would have to be supported by an extended renderer for every component. The new constructs allow the developer to pass additional HTML attributes to the markup generated by JSF components.

- The flow scope has been introduced with @FlowScoped, which makes the creation of wizards (dialogs with multiple steps) easier.

- The Ajax-based file upload is now supported out of the box.

- Also, stateless views have been presented as a way to improve performance.

Enterprise JavaBeans 3.2 – JSR 345

Compared to EJB 3.1, the Version 3.2 is a minor update of the existing version. It concentrates mainly on marking some older features as obsolete (they are now optional, which means that not every Java EE 7-compliant application server will support them). The optional features are connected with persistence to web services based on EJB 2.1 and JAX-RPC. The main enhancements provided by the new specification are as follows:

- Life cycle methods for stateful session beans can now be transactional.

- The Timer Service API, now allows you to access all active timers in the current EJB module.

- A new container provided role (**) has been introduced. It can be used to indicate any authenticated user (without taking his or her actual roles into account).

- Passivation of stateful session beans can now be disabled.

Transactional parts of the EJB specification have been extracted and reused in other parts of the Java EE platform (the transaction support has been placed in the JTA 1.2 specification). For instance, the transactional behavior can now be used in CDI beans, thanks to the introduction of the @Transactional annotation.

Java Persistence API 2.1 – JSR 338

JPA was introduced as a standard part of Java EE in Version 5 of the specification. JPA was intended to replace entity beans as the default object-relational mapping framework for Java EE. JPA adopted ideas from third-party object-relational frameworks, such as Hibernate and JDO, and made them a part of the standard version.

JPA 2.1 is an improvement over JPA 2.0 as it provides several facilities for developers, which are as follows:

- It provides a standardized schema generation mechanism, thanks to an extended set of annotations and `persistence.xml` properties
- It adds support for type conversion, by the introduction of the `@Converter` annotation
- Stored procedures are now supported by the Entity Manager API, so that the use of the SQL query mechanism for them is no longer required
- Criteria API has been extended by bulk updates and deletes
- Injection is possible into entity listener classes along with the usage of life cycle callback methods
- Named queries can now be created during runtime
- The **JPA Query Language (JPQL)** has been extended with new database functions

Additionally, Java EE 7-compliant containers must now support preconfigured data sources (along with other resources), which can be instantly used by JPA entities.

WildFly uses Hibernate as its JPA provider and is shipped with a ready-to-use H2 in-memory database. The default data source points to the H2 instance hosted inside of the application server.

Contexts and Dependency Injection for Java EE 1.1 – JSR 346

Version 1.1 of **Contexts and Dependency Injection (CDI)** provides improvements for the issues identified in CDI after its introduction in Java EE 6. The process of simplifying the programming model started in Version 1.0 and is now being continued. The areas covered by the update are as follows:

- CDI is now enabled by default (without the need to add the `bean.xml` file to the deployment), with the possibility to specify the desired component scanning mode.

- More fine-grained control over the bean discovery mechanism is now available for the developer, thanks to the use of the `@Vetoed` annotation and class or packages filters in `beans.xml`. Interceptors, decorators, and alternatives can now be globally enabled for the whole application using the `@Priority` annotation, instead of enabling every module.

- Event metadata can now be examined when a CDI event is handled.

- Interceptors have been enhanced with the possibility to be executed around constructor invocation.

- Finally, the new version contains a significant number of enhancements for the development of portable extensions.

Weld is the CDI implementation internally used in WildFly.

Java Servlet API 3.1 – JSR 340

The new version of the Java Servlet API has a clear focus on new features. The most important of them is the HTTP upgrade mechanism, which allows the client and server to start a conversation in HTTP 1.1, and negotiate another protocol for subsequent requests. This feature was used to implement the WebSockets mechanism in Java EE 7. Other features of the new version of specification are as follows:

- Non-blocking I/O API for Servlets has been provided to improve scalability of web applications

- Multiple security improvements have been introduced; the most notable of them is the possibility to set the default security semantics for all HTTP methods

JAX-RS, the Java API for RESTful Web Services 2.0 – JSR 339

In Java EE 7, the JAX-RS specification has been enriched with some long-awaited features. The version has changed from 1.1 to 2.0 because of the major impact of the improvements that came with the new specification. The most important features are listed as follows:

- The client API is now part of the specification, so the usage of third-party libraries is no longer needed. The implementation of the specification is required to provide a REST client that conforms to the common API.

- Asynchronous requests are now supported so that the client does not have to passively wait for the completion of the task.

- Filters and handlers have been introduced as a common mechanism to provide extension points for the developer. They can be used for cross-cutting concerns, such as auditing and security.

- Bean Validation has been integrated into JAX-RS, making constraint annotations usable for request parameters.

WildFly comes bundled with RESTEasy, an implementation of JAX-RS 2.0.

Java Message Service 2.0 – JSR 343

The JSR 343 is the first update for the JMS specification in over a decade. Once more, the main theme of the update is the simplification of the API. The new API dramatically decreases the amount of boilerplate code that has to be written by the programmer while still maintaining backwards compatibility. Other new features are listed as follows:

- Asynchronous message sending is now supported, so the application does not have to be blocked until an acknowledgment from the server is received

- Messages can now be sent with a scheduled delay for the delivery

HornetQ is the JMS provider used and developed by JBoss. It is possible to use it outside of WildFly as a standalone message broker.

Bean Validation 1.1 – JSR 349

The process of updating the Bean Validation in Java EE 7 concentrates on two main features:

- Methods validation, which allows the developer to validate parameters and return values
- Tighter CDI integration, which changes the life cycle of the elements of the validation framework, allowing the developer to use dependency injection in his or her own `ConstraintValidator` implementations

Concurrency utilities for Java EE 1.0 – JSR 236

Concurrency utilities is a new feature pack to use multithreading in Java EE application components. The new specification provides `ManagedExecutorService` (a container-aware version of `ExecutorService` known from Java SE), which can be used to delegate the execution of tasks to a separate thread. These managed tasks could use most of the features that are available for application components (such as EJBs or Servlets). It is also possible to schedule cyclic or delayed tasks using new `ManagedScheduledExecutorService`. These new additions to the platform are filling a functional gap for Java EE, which was very hard to overcome within its architecture earlier on.

Batch applications for the Java Platform 1.0 – JSR 352

Batch jobs were another area of enterprise application development, which was not covered by earlier versions of Java EE. The new batch processing framework is used to provide a common solution to run tasks that are executed without user interaction. Java EE provides the developer with the following options:

- Batch runtime for the execution of jobs
- A job description language (based on XML)
- The Java API for the implementation of the business logic for the batch tasks
- jBeret, which is the batching framework used in WildFly

Java API for JSON Processing 1.0 – JSR 353

Java EE 7 now comes with out-of-the-box JSON processing, so the developer is no longer forced to use external libraries for this task. The new API allows JSON processing to use two approaches: object model (DOM based) and streaming (event-based).

Java API for WebSocket 1.0 – JSR 356

To fully support the development of applications based on HTML5, Java EE 7 requires a standardized technology for two-way communication between the server and the user's browser. The WebSocket API allows the developer to define server-side endpoints, which will maintain a TCP connection for every client that will connect to them (using, for instance, a JavaScript API). Before the new specification, developers had to use vendor-specific libraries and not portable solutions to achieve the same goal.

New features in WildFly

The eighth release of WildFly is based on modular architecture introduced in the previous release named JBoss AS 7. It has improved on several key points, including areas of performance and management. The most important change for the developers is that this release implements the Java EE 7 standard completely. Some of the most notable improvements include the following:

- WildFly 8 implements all standards presented by Java EE 7 specifications, which are also described in this chapter.

- The web server module was completely rewritten under the name Undertow. It supports both blocking and non-blocking operations. Early performance tests (for example, `http://www.techempower.com/benchmarks/#section=data-r6&hw=i7&test=plaintext`) show major performance improvements in HTTP request handling. Undertow is also available as a separate project and is possible to be used without WildFly.

- The final WildFly release has reduced the number of used ports. Now, it uses only two of them, one (`9990`) for management, JMX, and web administration, and the second one (`8080`) for standard services, including HTTP, WebSockets, remote JNDI, and EJB invocations.

- Now, it is possible to limit a user's management permissions using the Management **role based access control** (**RBAC**). All configuration changes can be tracked using the audit log.

- For previous releases, any upgrade operation requires a completely new server installation. WildFly brings the patching feature, allowing to install and rollback modules using management protocols.

In the next section, we will describe all the required steps to install and start a new application server.

Installing the server and client components

The first step in learning about the application server will be to install all the necessary components on your machine in order to run it. The application server itself requires just a JDK environment to be installed.

As far as hardware requirements are concerned, you should be aware that the server distribution, at the time of writing this, requires about 130 MB of hard disk space, and allocates a minimum of 64 MB and a maximum of 512 MB for a standalone server.

In order to get started, we will need to go over this checklist:

- Install JDK where WildFly will run
- Install WildFly
- Install the Eclipse development environment
- Install the Maven build management tool

At the end of this chapter, you will have all the instruments to get started with the application server.

Installing Java SE

The first mandatory requirement is to install a JDK 8 environment. The Java SE download site can be found at http://www.oracle.com/technetwork/java/javase/downloads/index.html.

Choose the latest version of Java SE 8 and install it. If you don't know how to install it, please take a look at http://docs.oracle.com/javase/8/docs/technotes/guides/install/install_overview.html.

Testing the installation

Once you have completed your installation, run the `java -version` command from a command prompt to verify that it is correctly installed. Here is the expected output from a Windows machine:

```
C:\>java -version
java version "1.8.0_11"
Java(TM) SE Runtime Environment (build 1.8.0_11-b12)
Java HotSpot(TM) 64-Bit Server VM (build 25.11-b03, mixed mode)
```

Installing WildFly

The JBoss WildFly application server can be downloaded for free from `http://wildfly.org/downloads/`.

As you can see in the following screenshot, at the moment of writing this book, the latest stable release of WildFly is 8.1.0.Final, which features a Certified Java EE 7 full profile:

Once you have chosen the appropriate server distribution, you will then be warned that this download is part of a community release and, as such, is not supported.

> If you need Enterprise support for your applications, you can opt for the Red Hat Enterprise Application Platform.
>
> Compared to the community version, the EAP has gone through different quality tests and might be different in terms of features/packaging. More information about the differences between EAP and the community version can be found at the beginning of this chapter. However, at the time of writing this book, EAP does not yet support Java EE 7, and no road map is publicly available.

Installing WildFly is a piece of cake; it does not require anything else besides unpacking the `wildfly-8.1.0.Final.zip` archive.

Windows users can simply use any uncompressing utility, such as built-in compressed folders (in newer Windows releases), WinZip, WinRAR, or 7-Zip taking care to choose a folder name that does not contain empty spaces and white spaces. Unix/Linux should use the `$ unzip wildfly-8.1.0.Final.zip` unzip shell command to explode the archive.

> **Security warning**
>
> Unix/Linux users should be aware that WildFly does not require root privileges, as none of the default ports used by WildFly are below the privileged port range of `1024`. To reduce the risk of users gaining root privileges through WildFly, install and run WildFly as a non-root user.

Starting WildFly

After you have installed WildFly, it is wise to perform a simple start up test to validate that there are no major problems with your Java VM / operating system combination. To test your installation, move to the `bin` directory of your JBOSS_HOME (the path to which you have unzipped your application server) directory and issue the following command:

```
standalone.bat      # Windows users
$ ./standalone.sh    # Linux/Unix users
```

The following is a screenshot of a sample WildFly start-up console:

```
16:57:11,706 INFO  [org.wildfly.extension.undertow] (ServerService Thread Pool -- 47) JBAS017527: Cr
eating file handler for path C:\DevTools\wildfly-8.1.0.Final/welcome-content
16:57:11,701 INFO  [org.wildfly.extension.undertow] (MSC service thread 1-5) JBAS017525: Started ser
ver default-server.
16:57:11,812 INFO  [org.jboss.as.connector.deployers.jdbc] (MSC service thread 1-7) JBAS010417: Star
ted Driver service with driver-name = postgresql
16:57:11,832 INFO  [org.jboss.as.connector.subsystems.datasources] (ServerService Thread Pool -- 27)
 JBAS010403: Deploying JDBC-compliant driver class org.h2.Driver (version 1.3)
16:57:11,814 INFO  [org.wildfly.extension.undertow] (MSC service thread 1-6) JBAS017531: Host defaul
t-host starting
16:57:11,856 INFO  [org.jboss.as.connector.deployers.jdbc] (MSC service thread 1-4) JBAS010417: Star
ted Driver service with driver-name = h2
16:57:11,899 INFO  [org.jboss.as.server.deployment.scanner] (MSC service thread 1-7) JBAS015012: Sta
rted FileSystemDeploymentService for directory C:\DevTools\wildfly-8.1.0.Final\standalone\deployment
s
16:57:11,905 INFO  [org.jboss.as.connector.subsystems.datasources] (MSC service thread 1-8) JBAS0104
00: Bound data source [java:jboss/datasources/PostgreSqlDS]
16:57:12,045 INFO  [org.wildfly.extension.undertow] (MSC service thread 1-7) JBAS017519: Undertow HT
TP listener default listening on /127.0.0.1:8080
16:57:12,104 INFO  [org.jboss.as.connector.subsystems.datasources] (MSC service thread 1-3) JBAS0104
00: Bound data source [java:jboss/datasources/ExampleDS]
16:57:12,232 INFO  [org.jboss.ws.common.management] (MSC service thread 1-6) JBWS022052: Starting JB
oss Web Services - Stack CXF Server 4.2.4.Final
16:57:12,258 INFO  [org.jboss.as] (Controller Boot Thread) JBAS015961: Http management interface lis
tening on http://127.0.0.1:9990/management
16:57:12,259 INFO  [org.jboss.as] (Controller Boot Thread) JBAS015951: Admin console listening on ht
tp://127.0.0.1:9990
16:57:12,259 INFO  [org.jboss.as] (Controller Boot Thread) JBAS015874: WildFly 8.1.0.Final "Kenny" s
tarted in 1879ms - Started 190 of 239 services (81 services are lazy, passive or on-demand)
```

The preceding command starts up a WildFly standalone instance, which is equivalent to starting the application server with the run.bat/run.sh script used by earlier JBoss AS releases. You will notice how amazingly fast the new release of the application server is; this is due to the modular architecture introduced in Version 7 of JBoss AS, which only starts up necessary parts of the application server container needed by the loaded applications.

If you need to customize the start-up properties of your application server, open the standalone.conf file (or standalone.conf.bat for Windows users), where the memory requirements of Wildfly have been declared. Here is the Linux core section of this file:

```
if [ "x$JAVA_OPTS" = "x" ]; then
    JAVA_OPTS="-Xms64m -Xmx512m -XX:MaxPermSize=256m
       -Djava.net.preferIPv4Stack=true"
    JAVA_OPTS="$JAVA_OPTS
       -Djboss.modules.system.pkgs=$JBOSS_MODULES_SYSTEM_PKGS
       -Djava.awt.headless=true"
else
    echo "JAVA_OPTS already set in environment; overriding default
settings with values: $JAVA_OPTS"
```

So, by default, the application server starts with a minimum memory requirement of 64 MB of heap space and a maximum of 512 MB. This will be just enough to get started; however, if you need to run more robust Java EE applications on it, you will likely require at least 1 GB of heap space or 2 GB or more, depending on your application type. Generally speaking, 32-bit machines cannot execute a process whose space exceeds 2 GB; however, on 64-bit machines, there is essentially no limit to the process size.

You can verify that the server is reachable from the network by simply pointing your browser to the application server's welcome page, which can be accessed from the well-known address, `http://localhost:8080`. The welcome page of WildFly is shown in the following screenshot:

Connecting to the server with the command-line interface

If you have been using previous releases of the application server, you might have heard about the twiddle command-line utility that queried MBeans installed on the application server. This utility has been replaced by a more sophisticated interface named the command-line interface (**CLI**); it can be found in JBOSS_HOME/bin.

Just launch the jboss-cli.bat script (or jboss-cli.sh for Linux users), and you will be able to manage the application server via a shell interface. This is shown in the following screenshot:

```
                                    C:\WINDOWS\system32\cmd.exe                          _ □ x
You are disconnected at the moment. Type 'connect' to connect to the server or 'help' for the list o
f supported commands.
[disconnected /] connect
[standalone@localhost:9990 /] help
Usage:

  jboss-cli.sh/jboss-cli.bat [--help] [--version] [--controller=host:port]
                     [--connect] [--file=file_path]
                     [--commands=command_or_operation1,command_or_operation2...]
                     [--command=command_or_operation]
                     [--user=username --password=password]
                     [--no-local-auth]
                     [--timeout=timeout]
```

We started an interactive shell session that can also use the command-line completion (by pressing the *Tab* key) to match partly typed command names. No more searches are needed to find the exact syntax of commands!

[In the previous screenshot, we connected to the server using the connect command; it uses the loopback server address and plugs into port 9990 by default.]

The command-line interface is discussed in depth in *Chapter 9, Managing the Application Server*, which is all about server management interfaces; we will, however, get an initial taste of its basic functionalities in the next sections to get you accustomed to this powerful tool.

Stopping WildFly

The easiest way to stop WildFly is by sending an interrupt signal with *Ctrl + C*.

However, if your WildFly process was launched in the background or, rather, is running on another machine, you can use the CLI interface to issue an immediate shutdown command:

```
[disconnected /] connect
Connected to localhost:9990
[standalone@localhost:9990 /] :shutdown
```

Locating the shutdown script

There is actually one more option to shut down the application server that is pretty useful, if you need to shut down the server from within a script. This option consists of passing the -- connect option to the admin shell, thereby switching off the interactive mode as shown in the following command line:

```
jboss-cli.bat --connect command=:shutdown        # Windows
./jboss-cli.sh --connect command=:shutdown         # Unix / Linux
```

Stopping WildFly on a remote machine

Shutting down the application server that is running on a remote machine is just a matter of providing the server's remote address to the CLI, and for security reasons, a username and password, as shown in the following code snippet (see the next chapter to learn more about user creation):

```
[disconnected /] connect 192.168.1.10
Authenticating against security realm: ManagementRealm
Username: admin1234
Password:
Connected to 192.168.1.10:9990
[standalone@192.168.1.10:9990 / ] :shutdown
```

However, you have to remember that you need access to a given port because often, it may be blocked by a firewall.

Restarting WildFly

The command-line interface contains many useful commands. One of the most interesting options is the ability to reload the AS configuration or parts of it using the reload command.

When issued on the root node path of the AS server, the reload command can reload the services' configuration:

```
[disconnected /] connect
Connected to localhost:9990
[standalone@localhost:9990 /] :reload
```

Installing the Eclipse environment

The development environment used in this book is Eclipse, which is known by Java developers worldwide, and it contains a huge set of plugins to expand its functionalities. Besides this, Eclipse is the first IDE that is compatible with the new application server.

So, let's move to the download page of Eclipse, which is located at http://www.eclipse.org.

From here, download the latest Enterprise Edition (at the time of writing this book, it is Version 4.4 and is also known as Luna). The compressed package contains all the Java EE plugins already installed. This is shown in the following screenshot:

Eclipse IDE for Java EE Developers 259 MB
Downloaded 1,027,442 Times

Tools for Java developers creating Java EE and Web applications, including a Java IDE, tools for Java EE, JPA, JSF, Mylyn...

Windows 32 Bit
Windows 64 Bit

Once you have unzipped the previously downloaded file, you will see a folder named eclipse. In this folder, you will find the Eclipse application (a big blue dot). It is recommended that you create a shortcut on the desktop to simplify the launching of Eclipse. Note that, just as with WildFly, Eclipse does not have an installation process. Once you have unzipped the file, you are done!

Installing JBoss Tools

The next step will be installing the JBoss AS plugin that is a part of the suite of plugins named JBoss Tools. Installing new plugins in Eclipse is pretty simple; just follow these steps:

1. From the menu, navigate to **Help | Install New Software**.

2. Then, click on the **Add** button, where you will enter JBoss Tools' download URL (along with a description), `http://download.jboss.org/jbosstools/updates/development/luna/`. This is shown in the following screenshot:

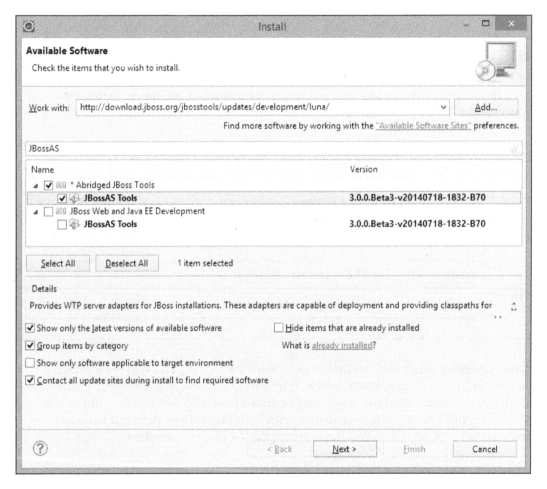

3. As you can see in the preceding screenshot, you need to check the **JBossAS Tools** plugin and move forward to the next option to complete the installation process.

Enter JBossAS into the filter field to quickly find the JBoss AS Tools plugin among the large set of JBoss Tools.

4. Once done, restart the process when prompted.

 You can also download JBoss Tools as individual zip files for an offline installation. See JBoss Tools Downloads at http://tools.jboss.org/downloads/.

5. Now, you should be able to see WildFly listed as a server by navigating to **New | Server** from the upper menu and expanding the **JBoss Community** option, as shown in the following screenshot:

Completing the server installation in Eclipse is quite straightforward as it just requires pointing to the folder where your server distribution is; we will therefore leave this to you to implement as a practical exercise.

Alternative development environments

Since this book is all about development, we should also account for some other alternatives that might suit your programming style or your company standards better. So, another valid alternative is IntelliJ IDEA, which is available at `http://www.jetbrains.com/idea/index.html`.

IntelliJ IDEA is a code-centric IDE focused on developer productivity. The editor exhibits a nice understanding of your code and makes great suggestions right when you need them and is always ready to help you shape your code.

Two versions of this product exist—Community edition and Ultimate edition—that require a license. In order to use Java EE and the WildFly plugin, you need to download the ultimate edition from `http://www.jetbrains.com/idea/download/index.html` and then simply install it using the installation wizard.

Once you have installed the Ultimate edition, you will be able to get started with developing applications with WildFly by going to **File | Settings** and choosing the **IDE Settings** option. Here, you can choose to add new application server environments. This is shown in the following screenshot:

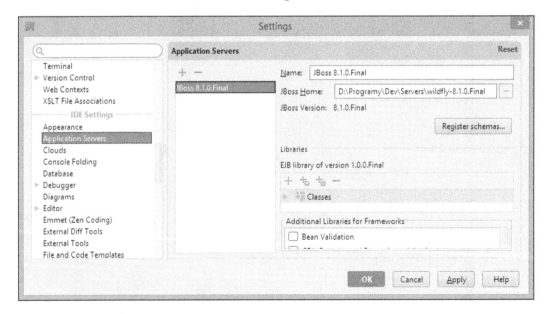

Another development option that is quite popular among developers is NetBeans (http://netbeans.org), which has support for WildFly in its releases 7.4 and 8.0, but requires installation of additional plugins available in the NetBeans plugins registry.

Installing Maven

Besides graphical tools, you are strongly encouraged to learn about Maven, the popular build and release management tool. By using Maven, you will enjoy the following things:

- A standard structure for all your projects
- A centralized and automatic management of dependencies

Maven is distributed in several formats, for your convenience, and can be downloaded from http://maven.apache.org/download.html.

Once the download is complete, unzip the distribution archive (for example, apache-maven-3.1.1-bin.zip for Windows) to the directory in which you wish to install Maven 3.1.0 (or the latest available version), for example, C:\\Programs\ apache-maven-3.1.1. Some operating systems such as Linux or OS X offer Maven packages in their application repositories.

Once done, add the M2_HOME environment variable to your system so that it will point to the folder where Maven has been unpacked.

Next, update the PATH environment variable by adding the Maven binaries to your system path. For example, on the Windows platform, you should include %M2_HOME%/bin in order to make Maven available on the command line.

Some additional Maven learning materials are available on the Sonatype website in the form of free books; refer to http://www.sonatype.com/resources/books.

Testing the installation

Once you have completed your installation, run the mvn version to verify that Maven has been correctly installed. Refer to the following code snippet to verify the correct installation:

```
> mvn -version
Apache Maven 3.1.1 (0728685237757ffbf44136acec0402957f723d9a; 2013-09-
17 17:22:22+0200)
Maven home: C:\Programs\Dev\apache-maven-3.1.1
```

```
Java version: 1.8.0_11, vendor: Oracle Corporation
Java home: C:\Programs\Java\jdk1.8.0\jre
Default locale: en_US, platform encoding: Cp1250
OS name: "windows 8.1", version: "6.3", arch: "amd64", family: "dos"
```

Summary

In this chapter, we ran our first mile on the track to application server development. We introduced the new features of the application server and had an overview of the Java Platform Enterprise Edition in Version 7, also known as Java EE 7.

Next, we discussed the installation of the WildFly AS and all the core components that include JDK and a set of development tools, such as Eclipse and Maven, which will be your companions on this journey.

In the next chapter, we will summarize all the application server features with a special focus on the components and commands needed to deliver an application, which is the main aim of this book.

2
Your First Java EE Application on WildFly

This chapter will provide you with a crash course in the new application server so that you will be able to create a deployable skeleton of our first Java EE 7 application in the next chapter. More specifically, we will cover the following topics:

- An introduction to the WildFly 8 core concepts
- The anatomy of the WildFly 8 filesystem
- An introduction to the available management instruments
- Deploying your first Hello World application

WildFly 8 core concepts

Now that we have downloaded and installed WildFly 8, it is worth spending a few minutes familiarizing ourselves with some basic concepts. The architecture and most of the core ideas are taken straight from JBoss AS 7; although, there are some new mechanisms that were introduced with the newest version (for example, role-based security for the management system, reduced number of used ports, and a new patching system). Just like JBoss AS 7, WildFly can be run in two modes: the standalone mode and domain mode.

In the **standalone** mode, each WildFly instance is an independent process (similar to the previous JBoss AS versions, such as Version 4, Version 5, Version 6, and the standalone mode in Version 7). The standalone configuration files are located under the `standalone/configuration` directory of the application server.

In the **domain** mode, you can run multiple application servers and manage them from a central point. A domain can span multiple physical (or virtual) machines. On each machine, we can install several instances of WildFly that are under the control of a Host Controller process. The configuration files in the domain mode are located under the `domain/configuration` folder of the application server.

From the process point of view, a domain is made up of three elements:

- **Domain Controller**: The domain controller is the management control point of your domain. A WildFly instance running in the domain mode will have at the most one process instance acting as a domain controller. The domain controller holds a centralized configuration, which is shared by the node instances that belong to that domain.

- **Host Controller**: This is the process that is responsible for coordinating the life cycle of server processes and the distribution of deployments from the domain controller to the server instances.

- **Application server nodes**: These are regular Java processes that map instances of the application server. Each server node, in turn, belongs to a server group. Domain groups are explained in detail when we will discuss the domain configuration file.

Additionally, when starting a domain, you will see another JVM process running on your machine. This is the Process Controller. It is a very lightweight process whose primary function is to spawn server processes and Host Controller processes, and manage their input/output streams. Since Process Controller is not configurable, we will not discuss it any further.

The following diagram depicts a typical domain deployment configuration:

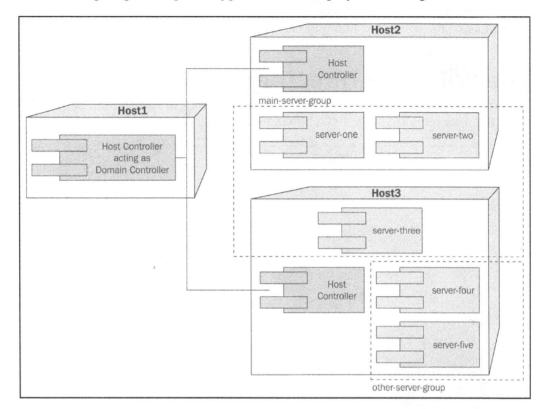

As you can see in the preceding diagram, one host (**Host1**) acts as a dedicated domain controller. This is a common practice adopted in domain-managed servers in order to logically and physically separate the administration unit from the servers where the applications are hosted.

The other hosts (**Host2** and **Host3**) contain the domain application servers, which are divided into two server groups: **main-server-group** and **other-server-group**. A server group is a logical set of server instances that will be managed and configured together. Each server group can, in turn, be configured with different profiles and deployments; for example, in the preceding domain, you can provide some services with **main-server-group** and other services with **other-server-group**.

This has some advantages. For example, when you don't want to shut down your application for a new version, you can start by redeploying only one server group at a time. When one server is not fully operational, requests can be handled by the second one.

Getting into the details of the domain configuration is beyond the scope of this book; however, by the end of this chapter, we will see how to deploy application units in a domain using the command-line interface available in WildFly.

The WildFly 8 directory layout

The difference between standalone and domain reflects in the directory layout of the application server is shown in the following diagram:

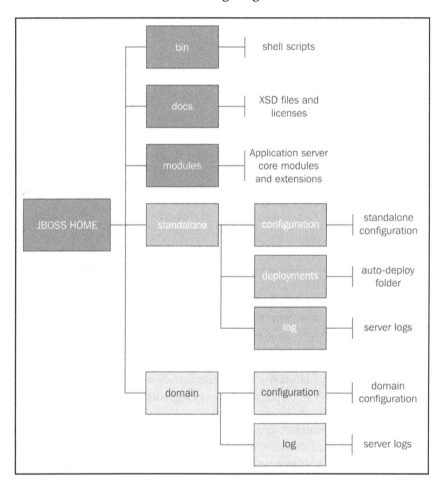

As you can see in the preceding diagram, the WildFly directory layout is divided into two main parts: the first one is pertinent to a standalone server mode and the other is dedicated to a domain server mode. Common to both server modes is the modules directory, which is the heart of the application server.

WildFly is based on the `JBoss Modules` project, which provides an implementation of a modular (nonhierarchical) class loading and an execution environment for Java. In other words, rather than a single class loader that loads all JARs into a flat class path, each library becomes a module, which only links to the exact modules it depends on and nothing more. It implements a thread safe, fast, and highly concurrent delegating class loader model, coupled with an extensible module resolution system. This combines to form a unique, simple, and powerful system for application execution and distribution.

The following table details the content of each folder present in the `root` folder of `JBOSS_HOME`:

Folder	Description
bin	This folder contains the startup scripts, startup configuration files, and various command-line utilities, such as vault, add-user, and Java diagnostic reports available for Unix and Windows environments
bin/client	This folder contains a client Jar for use by the remote EJB and CLI and clients not using any build systems with automatic dependency management such as Maven, Ant with Ivy, or Gradle
bin/init.d	New in WildFly, this folder contains scripts for Red Hat Linux and Debian, which registers WildFly as a Linux service
bin/service	New in WildFly, this folder contains a script that allows to register WildFly as a Windows service
docs/examples	This folder contains some sample standalone configurations such as a minimal standalone configuration (`standalone-minimalistic.xml`)
docs/schema	This folder contains XML schema definition files
domain	This folder contains the configuration files, deployment content, and writable areas used by the domain mode processes run from this installation
modules	This folder contains all the modules installed on the application server
standalone	This folder contains the configuration files, deployment content, and writable areas used by the single standalone servers run from this installation
appclient	This folder contains the configuration files, deployment content, and writable areas used by the application client container run from this installation
welcome-content	This folder contains the default Welcome page content

Digging into the standalone mode tree, we can find folders that are pertinent to standalone independent processes. If you have experience with earlier server releases, you will find these folders quite intuitive to you:

Directory	Description
configuration	This directory contains the configuration files for the standalone server that runs from this installation. All configuration information for the running server is located here and is the single place for configuration modifications for the standalone server.
data	This directory contains the persistent information written by the server to survive a restart of the server.
deployments	The end user deployment content can be placed in this directory for automatic detection and deployment of that content into the server's runtime.
lib/ext	This directory is the location for the installed library Jar files, referenced by the applications using the Extension-List mechanism.
log	This directory contains the standalone server logfiles.
tmp	This directory contains the location of the temporary files written by the server.

The domain directory structure is quite similar to the standalone equivalent, with one important difference. As you can see from the following table, the deployments folder is not present since the domain mode does not support deploying content based on scanning a filesystem. We need to use the WildFly managed instruments (CLI and web admin console) in order to deploy applications to a domain.

Directory	Description
configuration	This directory contains the configuration files for the domain Host Controller and any servers running on this installation. All the configuration information for the servers managed within the domain is located here and is the single place for configuration information.
data/content	This directory is an internal working area for the Host Controller, which controls this installation. This is where it internally stores the deployment content. This directory is not meant to be manipulated by the end users. It is created after the first server startup.
log	This directory is the location where the Host Controller process writes its logs. The Process Controller, a small, lightweight process that actually spawns other Host Controller processes and any application server processes, also writes logs here. It is created after the first server startup.

Directory	Description
servers	This directory is a writable area used by each application server instance that runs from this installation. Each application server instance will have its own subdirectory, created when the server is first started. In each server's subdirectory, the following subdirectories will be present: • data: This is the information written by the server that needs to survive a restart of the server • log: This is the server's logfiles • tmp: This is the location of the temporary files written by the server. This folder is created after the first server startup.
tmp	This directory contains the location of the temporary files written by the server.

Managing the application server

WildFly provides three different means to configure and manage servers: a web interface, a command-line client, and a set of XML configuration files. No matter what approach you choose, the configuration is always synchronized across the different views and finally persisted to the XML files. After saving the changes using the web interface, you will instantly see an updated XML file in your server's configuration directory.

Managing WildFly 8 with the web interface

The web interface is a **Google Web Toolkit** (**GWT**) application, which can be used to manage a standalone or domain WildFly distribution. The GWT application known in JBoss AS 7 has been updated to match the new visual theme. It was also extended with new features, such as role-based security and patching support. By default, it is deployed on a localhost on the 9990 port; the property that controls the port socket binding is jboss.management.http.port, as specified in the server configuration (standalone.xml/domain.xml). The server configuration is given in the following code snippet:

```
<socket-binding-group name="standard-sockets" default-
interface="public">
      <socket-binding name="management-http" interface="management"
port="${jboss.management.http.port:9990}"/>
      . . . . . . . . .
</socket-binding-group>
```

Wildfly 8 is secured out of the box and the default security
mechanism is based on a username or password, making use of
HTTP Digest. The reason for securing the server by default is that if
the management interfaces are accidentally exposed on a public IP
address, authentication is required to connect. For this reason, there
is no default user in the distribution.

The users are stored in a properties file called `mgmt-users.properties` under
standalone/configuration or domain/configuration depending on the running mode
of the server. This file contains the username information along with a precalculated
hash of the username, plus the name of the realm and user's password.

To manipulate the files and add users, the server has provided utilities
such as `add-user.sh` and `add-user.bat` to add the users and generate hashes.
So just execute the script and follow the guided process. This is shown in the
following screenshot:

```
What type of user do you wish to add?
 a) Management User (mgmt-users.properties)
 b) Application User (application-users.properties)
(a): a

Enter the details of the new user to add.
Using realm 'ManagementRealm' as discovered from the existing property files.
Username : admin
The username 'admin' is easy to guess
Are you sure you want to add user 'admin' yes/no? yes
Password recommendations are listed below. To modify these restrictions edit the add-user.properties
 configuration file.
 - The password should not be one of the following restricted values {root, admin, administrator}
 - The password should contain at least 8 characters, 1 alphabetic character(s), 1 digit(s), 1 non-a
lphanumeric symbol(s)
 - The password should be different from the username
Password :
Re-enter Password :
What groups do you want this user to belong to? (Please enter a comma separated list, or leave blank
 for none)[  ]:
About to add user 'admin' for realm 'ManagementRealm'
Is this correct yes/no? yes
Added user 'admin' to file 'C:\DevTools\wildfly-8.1.0.Final\standalone\configuration\mgmt-users.prop
erties'
Added user 'admin' to file 'C:\DevTools\wildfly-8.1.0.Final\domain\configuration\mgmt-users.properti
es'
Added user 'admin' with groups  to file 'C:\DevTools\wildfly-8.1.0.Final\standalone\configuration\mg
mt-groups.properties'
Added user 'admin' with groups  to file 'C:\DevTools\wildfly-8.1.0.Final\domain\configuration\mgmt-g
roups.properties'
Is this new user going to be used for one AS process to connect to another AS process?
e.g. for a slave host controller connecting to the master or for a Remoting connection for server to
 server EJB calls.
yes/no? yes
To represent the user add the following to the server-identities definition <secret value="MTIzIUAjc
Xd1" />
```

In order to create a new user, you need to provide the following information:

- **Type of user**: The type of user will be Management User, since it will manage the application server.

- **Realm**: This must match the realm name used in the configuration, so unless you have changed the configuration to use a different realm name, leave this set to ManagementRealm.

- **Username**: This is the username of the user you are adding.

- **Password**: This is the user's password.

- **User groups**: This is a list of comma-separated groups that should be assigned to the newly created user; they are used for the role-based access control and auditing system, which was introduced in WildFly. The information about user groups is stored in the mgmt-groups.properties file.

If the validation is successful, you will be asked to confirm whether you want to add the user; only then the properties files will be updated.

The final question (Is this new user going to be used to connect one AS process to another?) can be used to **add the slave Host Controllers** that authenticate against a master domain controller. This, in turn, requires adding the secret key to your slave host's configuration in order to authenticate with the master domain controller. (For more information about domain configuration, please visit https://docs.jboss.org/author/display/WFLY8/Admin+Guide#AdminGuide-ManagedDomain.)

Launching the web console

Now that we have added at least one user, we can launch the web console at the default address, http://<host>:9990/console (keep in mind that you have to start the server first, for example, with standalone.bat or standalone.sh).

The login screen will be prompted. Enter data into the **User Name** and **Password** fields, which we had formerly created. This is shown in the following screenshot:

Once logged in, you will be redirected to the web administration main screen. The web console, when running in the standalone mode, will be divided into three main tabs: **Configuration**, **Runtime**, and **Administration**. This is shown in the following screenshot:

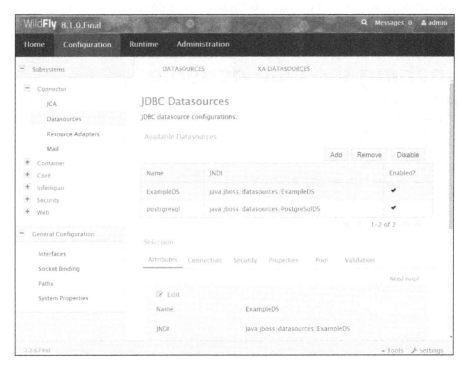

The **Configuration** tab contains all the single subsystems that are part of a server profile. So, once you select the **Configuration** tab on the left frame, you can access all the subsystems and edit their configurations (in the previous screenshot, we saw the Data Sources subsystem).

The other tab named **Runtime** can be used for two main purposes: to manage the deployment of applications and check the server metrics. This is shown in the following screenshot:

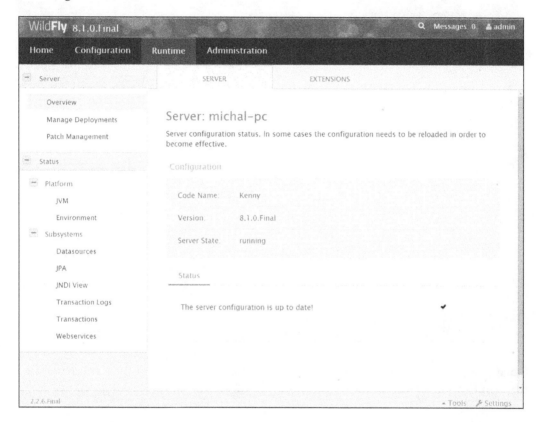

The **Administration** tab has been introduced with WildFly and Red Hat JBoss EAP 6.2 and currently contains only the options associated with role based access control. You can now limit permissions of management users, for example, so that not every administrator can undeploy an application using the web console. By default, this feature is disabled. You have to enable it manually using the CLI mechanism. This is shown in the following screenshot:

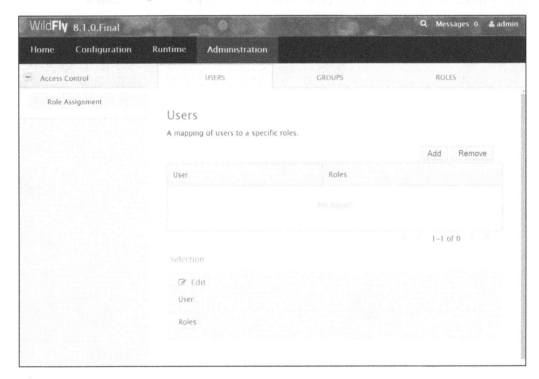

Once you have learned how to access the web console, it is about time you try your first application example.

Deploying your first application to WildFly 8

In order to test launch our first application, we will create a `HelloWorld` web project using Eclipse. The main part will be a `servlet` class, used to generate HTML markup. So, launch Eclipse and choose to create a new web project by navigating to **File | New | Dynamic Web Project**. This is shown in the following screenshot:

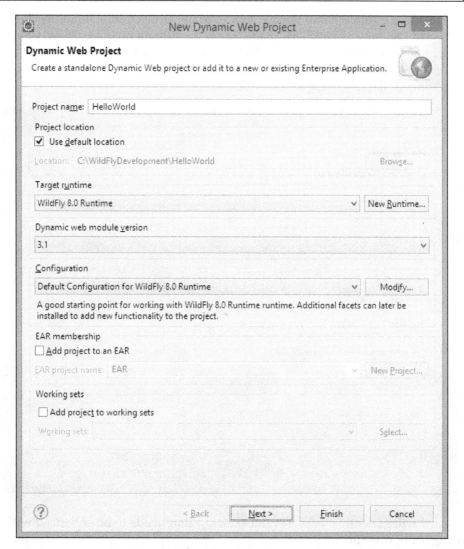

Choose a name for your application and check the **Use default location** box if you want to create your project within the same location of your Eclipse workspace. If you have correctly configured a new WildFly server in Eclipse, you should see the **WildFly 8.0 Runtime** option selected by default, and **Target Runtime** and **Default Configuration** for **WildFly 8.0 Runtime** preselected in the **Configuration** box.

Select **3.1** as the Dynamic web module version, which makes development easy by using the Servlet 3.1 specifications, and also leave the **EAR membership** and **Add project to working sets** checkboxes unselected.

Click on **Finish** to continue.

Now, let's add a quintessential simple servlet to our project, which merely dumps a **Hello World** message as an HTML page. From the **File** menu, go to **New | Servlet** and enter a meaningful name and package for your servlet, such as `TestServlet` as the name and `com.packtpub.wflydevelopment.chapter2` as the package name. This is shown in the following screenshot:

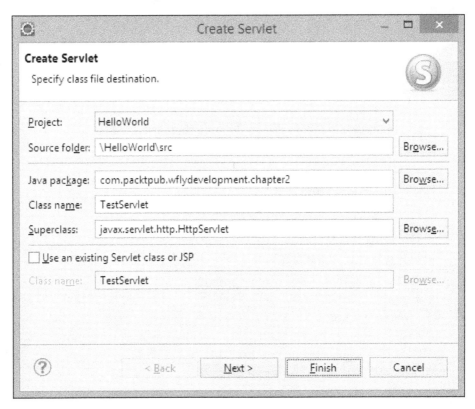

The wizard will generate a basic servlet skeleton that needs to be enhanced with the following set of code lines:

```
@WebServlet("/test")
public class TestServlet extends HttpServlet {
    private static final long serialVersionUID = 1L;

    private static final String CONTENT_TYPE =
      "text/html;charset=UTF-8";
    private static final String MESSAGE = "<!DOCTYPE html><html>" +
            "<head><title>Hello!</title></head>" +
```

```
        "<body>Hello World WildFly</body>" +
        "</html>";

    @Override
    protected void doGet(HttpServletRequest request,
                    HttpServletResponse response)
        throws ServletException, IOException {
      response.setContentType(CONTENT_TYPE);
      try (PrintWriter out = response.getWriter()) {
          out.println(MESSAGE);
      }
    }
}
```

The servlet will respond with a static HTML page (we defined the content type as Text/HTML with an UTF-8 charset) for every GET HTTP request that will be issued against its URL address.

Notice that TextServlet bears the @WebServlet annotation, which has been introduced by the Servlet 3.0 API, and it allows registering a servlet without using the web.xml configuration file. In our example, we used it to customize the servlet URL binding to employ /test, which would otherwise be defaulted by Eclipse to the class name.

We will complete the application with the creation of a JBoss file descriptor named jboss-web.xml in /WebContent/WEB-INF/ directory; although this is not mandatory, it can be used to redefine the context root, as shown in the following code snippet:

```
<jboss-web>
    <context-root>/hello</context-root>
</jboss-web>
```

The schema definition file for jboss-web.xml is named jboss-web_8_0.xsd and can be located in the JBOSS_HOME/docs/schema folder.

Keep in mind that creating jboss-web.xml makes the application non-portable to other Java EE Application Servers. The default application path when such a file is not defined is a concatenation of the application name and its version, for example, for application TestServlet with Version 1.0, it would be TestServlet-1.0.

Now, we will add the web application to the list of deployed resources by right-clicking on the Eclipse **Server** tab and selecting **Add and Remove**. This is shown in the following screenshot:

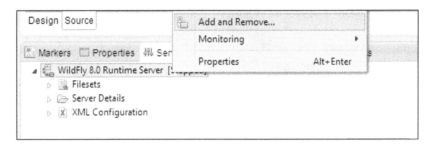

Next, click on **Add** to add the project to the list of configured resources on the server as shown in the following screenshot:

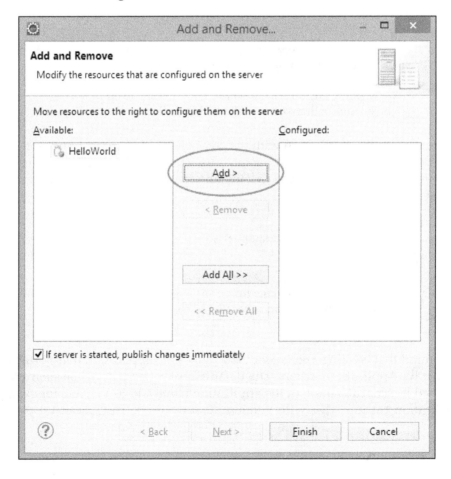

If you have started WildFly from inside Eclipse, the resource will be automatically deployed by checking the flag to see whether the server has started, and publish changes immediately.

If, on the other hand, you have started the application server externally, then you can fully publish your resource by right-clicking on the application and selecting **Full Publish** as shown in the following screenshot:

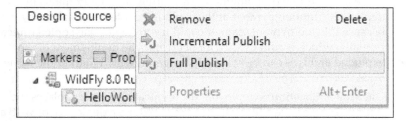

Now, move to the browser and check that the application responds at the configured URL, as shown in the following screenshot:

This example is also available in the form of a Maven (will be introduced in the next chapter) project in your Packt Publishing account.

Advanced Eclipse deployment options

As it is, Eclipse has published a `HelloWorld.war` folder in `JBOSS_HOME/standalone/deployments`.

> You might have noticed that Eclipse has also added a marker file named `HelloWorld.war.dodeploy`. This step is necessary because, by default, exploded deployments in WildFly aren't automatically deployed. Autodeployment of the exploded content is disabled by default because the deployment scanner could try to deploy the copied directory partially, which would cause a lot of errors. The deployment of the exploded archives can be manually triggered with a marker file named `application.[jar/war/ear].dodeploy`.
>
> Once the application is deployed, the application server replaces the `.dodeploy` marker file with `HelloWorld.war` deployed, or with a `HelloWorld.war.failed` file, should the deployment fail.

You can change the default deployment options by double-clicking on WildFly 8.0 (in the **Server** tab), and selecting the **Deployment** tab as shown in the following screenshot:

In the **Deployment** tab, you can choose to deploy your application on a custom deploy folder by checking the **Use a custom deploy folder** option and entering an appropriate value into the corresponding textbox.

Please note that the custom deployment folder also needs to be defined in WildFly; check the next section for more information about it.

Also, take note of the **Deploy projects as compressed archives** option, which can be useful in some circumstances, for example, if you are distributing the application via other instruments such as the CLI, which can deploy only compressed archives.

Managing deployments with the web console

Deploying the application using Eclipse is a straightforward task and is likely to be your option when you are developing apps. We will see here how to use the web console to deploy the application, which can be one more arrow in your quiver.

 A typical scenario for this example could be if you are running the AS in the domain mode, or simply deploying your application on a remote WildFly instance.

Start the web console and click on the **Runtime** tab. From the panel on the left, go to **Server** | **Manage Deployments** as shown in the following screenshot:

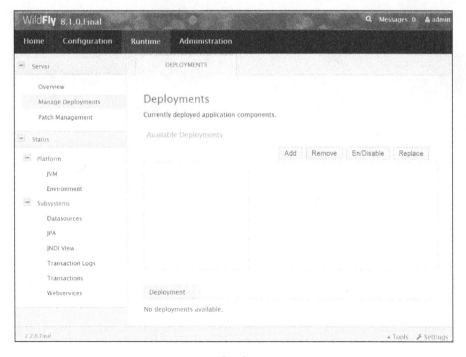

In the central panel, we can manage deployments using the **Add**, **Remove**, **En/Disable**, and **Update** buttons. Select the **Add** button to add a new deployment unit. In the next screen, pick up the file you want to deploy (for example, the HelloWorld.war artifact, which can be created from our test project in Eclipse by navigating to **File | Export | Web | WAR File**) from your local filesystem, as shown in the following screenshot:

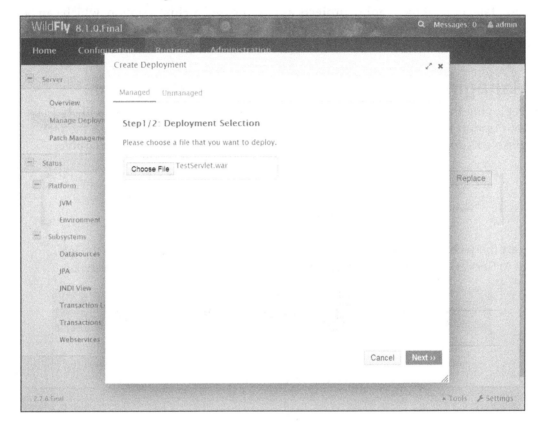

Complete the wizard by verifying the deployment's name and clicking on **Save**, as shown in the following screenshot:

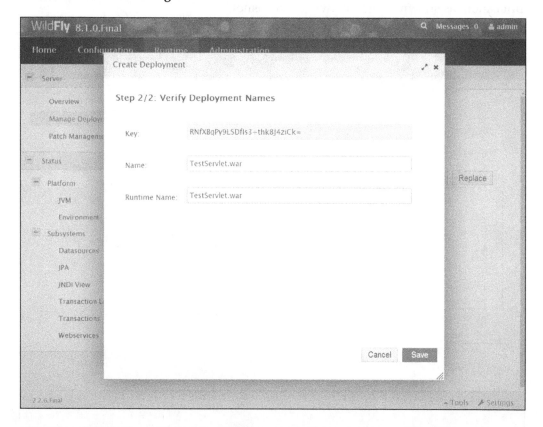

Now, the deployment is listed in the Deployments table. It is, however, not enabled by default. Click on the **En/Disable** button to enable the deployment of the application, as shown in the following screenshot:

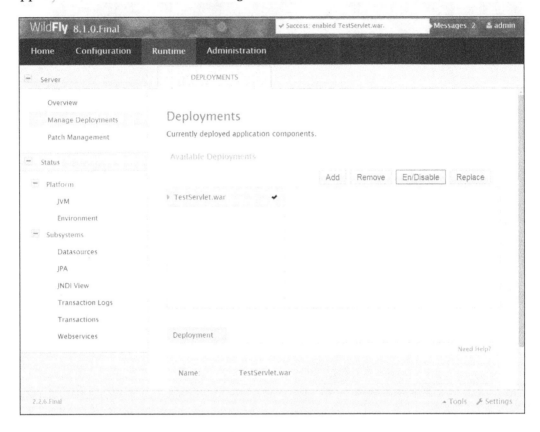

Changing the deployment scanner properties

As we have seen before, applications running in the standalone mode are scanned in the `deployments` folder by default. You can change this behavior (and also the deployment scanner's properties) by clicking on the **Configuration** tab and navigating to **Subsystems | Core | Deployment Scanners** from the left menu. This is shown in the following screenshot:

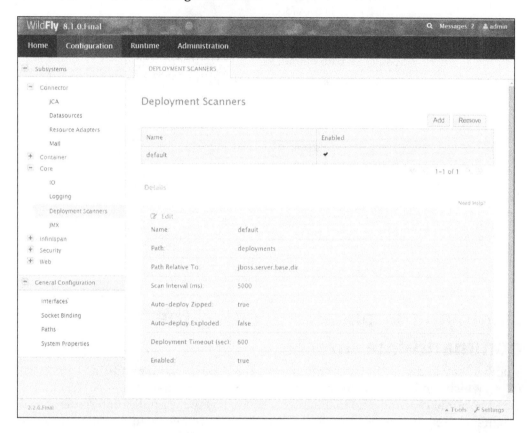

In **Deployment Scanners**, you can set the core deployment's attributes. You can click on the **Edit** button to define new values for these properties. Most of them are self-explanatory; however, the following table summarizes them:

Attribute	Description
name	This is the deployment scanner's name (by default, the name default is provided).
path	This is the absolute path where deployments are scanned. If the attribute Path Relative to is set, then it's appended to the relative path definition.
Enabled	This attribute determines whether the deployment scanner is enabled or not.
Path Relative to	If included, this attribute must point to a system path that will be used to build the relative path expression.
Scan Interval	This is the time frequency (in milliseconds) for which deployments will be scanned.
Auto-deploy Zipped	Setting this to true will enable automatic deployments for zipped applications. Its default value is true.
Auto-deploy Exploded	Setting this to true will enable automatic deployments for exploded applications. Its default value is true.
Deployment timeout	This refers to the time-out after which a deployment action will be marked as failed.

Deploying applications using the command-line interface

Another way to deploy an application is via the WildFly **Command-line Interface** (**CLI**), which can be started from jboss-cli.bat (or jboss-cli.sh for Linux users). Don't be afraid of using a textual interface to manage your application server; as a matter of fact, the console provides built-in autocomplete features and you can display the available commands at any time by simply hitting the *Tab* key, as shown in the following screenshot:

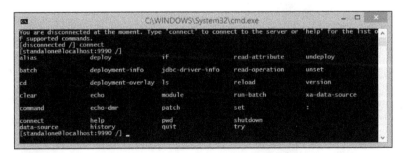

As you might have guessed, in order to deploy an application, you need to issue the `deploy` shell command. When used without arguments, the `deploy` shell command provides a list of applications that are currently deployed. Refer to the following code:

```
[standalone@localhost:9990 /] deploy
ExampleApp.war
```

If you feed a resource archive such as `.war` to shell, it will deploy it on the standalone server right away, as shown in the following command line:

```
[standalone@localhost:9990 /] deploy ../HelloWorld.war
```

As you can see from the preceding command line, the CLI uses the folder where your deployments were actually launched at its initial location, which is `JBOSS_HOME/bin` by default. You can, however, use absolute paths when specifying the location of your archives; the CLI expansion facility (using the *Tab* key) makes this option fairly simple. This is demonstrated in the following command line:

```
[standalone@localhost:9990 /] deploy c:\deployments\HelloWorld.war
```

There is no error message after issuing the command; therefore, the application is deployed and activated so that the user can access it. If you want to just perform the deployment of the application and defer the activation to a later time, you have to add the `--disabled` switch, as shown in the following command line:

```
[standalone@localhost:9990 /] deploy ../HelloWorld.war --disabled
```

In order to activate the application, simply issue another `deploy` shell command without the `--disabled` switch, as shown in the following command line:

```
[standalone@localhost:9990 /] deploy --name=HelloWorld.war
```

Redeploying the application requires an additional flag for the `deploy` shell command. Use the `-f` argument to force the application's redeployment, as shown in the following command line:

```
[localhost:9990 /] deploy -f ../HelloWorld.war
```

Undeploying the application can be done with the `undeploy` command, which takes the application that is deployed as an argument. This is shown in the following command line:

```
[localhost:9990 /] undeploy HelloWorld.war
```

Deploying applications to a domain

Deploying applications when running in the domain mode is slightly different from doing this in the standalone mode. The difference boils down to the fact that an application can be deployed just to one server group or to all the server groups. As a matter of fact, one reason why you might split your domain into different server groups might be that you are planning to offer different types of services (and hence applications) to each server group.

So, in order to deploy your `HelloWorld.war` application to all server groups, issue the following command:

```
[domain@localhost:9990 /] deploy HelloWorld.war --all-server-groups
```

If, on the other hand, you want to undeploy an application from all server groups belonging to a domain, you have to issue the `undeploy` command, as shown in the following command line:

```
[domain@localhost:9990 /] undeploy HelloWorld.war --all-relevant-server-groups
```

You can also deploy your application just to one server group of your domain by specifying one or more server groups (separated by a comma) with the `--server-groups` parameter, as shown in the following command line:

```
[domain@localhost:9990 /] deploy HelloWorld.war --server-groups=main-server-group
```

You can use the tab completion facility in order to complete the value for the list of `--server` groups elected for deployment.

Now, suppose we wish to undeploy the application from just one server group. There can be two possible scenarios. If the application is available just on that server group, you will just need to feed the server group to the `--server-groups` flag, as shown in the following command line:

```
[domain@localhost:9990 /] undeploy HelloWorld.war --server-groups=main-server-group
```

On the other hand, if your application is available on other server groups as well, you need to provide the additional `--keep-content` flag; otherwise, the CLI will complain that it cannot delete an application that is referenced by other server groups, as shown in the following command line:

```
[domain@localhost:9990 /] undeploy HelloWorld.war --server-groups=main-server-group --keep-content
```

Summary

In this chapter, we went through a crash course on the application server, focusing on the available management instruments: the web interface and Command-line interface. We then saw how to use these tools to deploy a sample application to a standalone environment and domain environment.

In the next chapter, we will dive deep into Java EE 7 components, starting from Enterprise JavaBeans, which still plays an important role in the evolving scenario of Java Enterprise applications.

3
Introducing
Java EE 7 – EJBs

In the previous chapter, you learned some basics about how to set up and deploy a Hello World application on WildFly. In this chapter, we will go a little deeper and learn how to create, deploy, and assemble Enterprise JavaBeans, which are at the heart of most Enterprise applications. Additionally, you will learn how to use Maven, a popular build tool, which can ease the packaging process of our beans.

In more detail, here is what you will learn in this chapter:

- What changes are introduced by the new EJB 3.2 specification
- How to create a Java EE 7 Maven project
- How to develop a singleton EJB
- How to create stateless and stateful Enterprise JavaBeans
- How to add and manage schedulers and timers to your application
- How to make use of asynchronous APIs in an EJB project

EJB 3.2 – an overview

Based on the **Enterprise JavaBeans (EJB)** specification, Enterprise JavaBeans are components that typically implement the business logic of Java Enterprise Edition applications (for Java EE, note that Oracle advises against using JEE as the acronym for Java Enterprise Edition; for more information about acronyms for Java-related technologies, visit https://java.net/projects/javaee-spec/pages/ JEE). Because of their transactional nature, EJBs are also commonly used for the construction of the data access layer in many applications. However, in the newest version of the specification, container-managed transactions are no longer exclusive for Enterprise JavaBeans and can be reused in other parts of the Java EE platform.

There are basically three types of Enterprise JavaBeans:

- **Session beans**: This is the most commonly used EJB type. The container manages multiple instances of every class that is defined as a session bean (with an exception for singletons, which have only one instance). When an operation implemented by EJB must be executed (for example, because a user has requested an update of an entity in the database), the container assigns a session bean instance for the specific user. This code is then executed on behalf of the calling client. The container is responsible for providing session beans with multiple system-level services, for example, security, transactions, or distribution of beans.

- **Message-driven beans** (**MDB**): MDBs are Enterprise beans that can asynchronously process messages sent by any JMS producer. (We will discuss MDBs in *Chapter 6, Developing Applications with JBoss JMS Provider.*)

- **Entity objects**: An EJB is used to represent entities in a database. The newest version of the specification made this type of Enterprise JavaBeans optional, so they may not be supported in all containers (their support has also been dropped in WildFly). Entity objects will be removed from the specification in Java EE 8. Currently, in Java EE 7, the main persistence technology is Java Persistence API. We will discuss JPA in *Chapter 5, Combining Persistence with CDI.*

Additionally, session beans can be divided into three subtypes based on their characteristics and usage scenarios.

- **Stateless session beans** (**SLSB**): These are objects whose instances have no conversational state with the client that has invoked an operation on them. This means that all these bean instances are equal when they are not servicing a client, and the container can prepare a pool for them to handle multiple requests in parallel. Because they do not store any state, their performance overhead is quite low. A common usage scenario for an SLSB would be a stateless service responsible for retrieving objects from a database.

- **Stateful session beans** (**SFSB**): SFSB supports conversational services with tightly coupled clients. A stateful session bean accomplishes a task for a particular client and it cannot be shared between multiple callers. It maintains the state for the duration of a client session. After session completion, the state is not retained. The container may decide to passivate (serialize and store for future usage) a stale SFSB. This is done to save resources of the application server or in some cases, to support SFSB failover mechanism in a domain of application servers (this is the case in JBoss AS 7 and WildFly). Starting from EJB 3.2, it is possible to disable passivation for a specific SFSB, although it may affect the server's stability and failover capability. A shopping cart could serve as a simple use case for an SFSB.

- **Singleton EJB**: This is essentially similar to a stateless session bean; however, it uses a single instance to serve client requests. So, you can guarantee the use of the same instance across invocations. Singletons can use a richer life cycle for a set of events, along with the possibility to control when a bean is initialized. Also, a more strict locking policy to control concurrent access to the instance can be enforced, so that the shared state of the singleton bean can be used by multiple clients. If the application is distributed on multiple nodes of a domain, then every running JVM will have its own instance of the singleton bean. We will discuss this a little further in *Chapter 11, Clustering WildFly Applications*. Because of their special characteristics, singletons can be used to save the state of the application, cache, or initialize some resources during the application's startup.

As we mentioned earlier, the container manages the instances of the beans, but the clients should call them through business interfaces. There are three types of a session bean's views available:

- **Local business interface**: This session bean is used when the bean and its client are in the same container. It uses the pass-by-reference semantic, so the return values and method parameters are based on references and not copies of the objects.

- **Remote business interface**: In this session bean, the locations of the client and the bean are independent (the client may reside in another container or without a container at all, for example, as a standalone application). Every parameter and return value is serialized and copied.

- **No-interface view**: This session bean is a variant of the local business view that does not require a separate interface, that is, all `public` methods of the bean class are automatically exposed to the caller.

Since EJB 3.1, it is possible to use asynchronous methods. These are able to process client requests asynchronously, just like MDBs, except that they expose a typed interface and follow a more complex approach to process client requests. It is possible to use two approaches to achieve this kind of behavior:

- Fire-and-forget asynchronous void methods, which are invoked by the client
- Retrieve-result-later asynchronous methods, which have the `Future<?>` return type

What more should you know about EJBs before proceeding? When you develop an Enterprise JavaBean, you have to follow some general rules, which are as follows:

- Avoid using nonfinal static fields

- Don't manually create threads (we will cover this topic more deeply in *Chapter 12, Long-term Tasks' Execution*)

- Don't use synchronization primitives (except in singletons with bean-managed concurrency)

- Manual file operations on the filesystem and listening on sockets are forbidden

- Native libraries should not be loaded

Disobeying these rules could cause security and stability issues with the EJB container. A comprehensive list of disallowed activities can be found at `http://www.oracle.com/technetwork/java/restrictions-142267.html` along with some explanations for specific points.

Since it's easier to grasp the concepts with real examples, in the next section, we will provide a concrete application example that introduces some of the features that we described in this section.

Developing singleton EJBs

As the name implies, `javax.ejb.Singleton` is a session bean that guarantees that there is at most one instance in the application.

 Besides this, singleton EJBs fill a well-known gap in EJB applications, that is, the ability to have an EJB notified when the application starts and also when the application stops. So, you can do all sorts of things with an EJB that you previously (before EJB 3.1) could only do with a load-on-startup servlet. EJB also gives you a place to hold data that pertains to the entire application and all the users using it, without the need for static class fields.

In order to turn your EJB into a singleton, all that is needed is to apply the `@javax.ejb.Singleton` annotation on top of it.

A singleton bean is similar to a stateful bean, in that, state information is maintained across method invocations. However, there is just one singleton bean for each server JVM, and it is shared by all of the EJBs and clients of an application. This type of bean provides a convenient means to maintain the overall state of an application. However, if the application is distributed on multiple machines (and therefore multiple JVMs), the singleton is unique on every one of them. Any application state must be synchronized between the nodes.

Another annotation that is worth learning is `@javax.ejb.Startup`, which causes the bean to be instantiated by the container when the application starts. This invokes the method decorated with the `@javax.annotation.PostConstruct` annotation if you have defined one in your EJB.

We now have enough information to understand our first EJB example. There is more than one alternative to create a Java Enterprise project. In the earlier chapter, we illustrated how to start from a project based on Eclipse Java EE (a dynamic web project), binding it later to a WildFly runtime installation. This is obviously the simplest choice, and you can easily run the examples contained in this book using this pattern; however, when it comes to enterprise solutions, it's no surprise that almost every project now uses some kind of build automation tool. For this book, we will propose Apache Maven, as it is one of the most popular choices, but not the only one. Gradle is a similar project that uses the Groovy language to describe project structure, dependencies, and build workflow.

Some of the benefits that you will achieve when turning to Maven projects include a well-defined dependency structure, the conventions of a project build's best practices, and project modular design, just to mention a few. Additionally, when you have an automated build process, you can use continuous integration tools (such as Jenkins) to schedule automated tests and deployments of your applications.

All major IDEs have built-in Maven support. This includes the Eclipse Java EE Luna release.

So, let's create our first Maven project directly from Eclipse. Navigate to **File |
New | Other | Maven | Maven Project**. This is shown in the following screenshot:

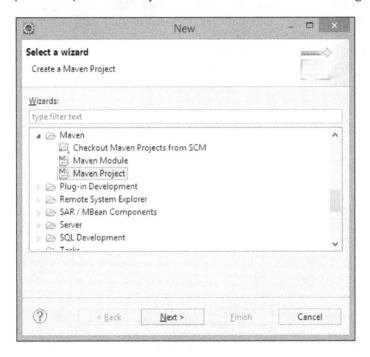

Click on **Next**; you will be taken to the following intermediary screen:

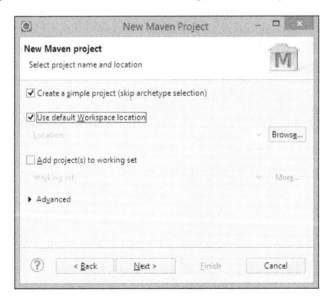

Maven allows the use of archetypes when creating a new project. They define a project's basic dependencies, resources, structure, and so on. For example, you can use a web application archetype in order to get an empty project skeleton, which you can just build and deploy. Unfortunately, archetypes are often outdated, and you still need to adjust them for your needs. In order to use some Java EE 7 archetypes, you have to first define a repository and archetypes you would like to use, and then you can create a project. In real life, you will probably create every new project by just looking at your previous ones, without using any archetypes. So, here we will show how to create a project from scratch. You might also be interested in some additional Java EE-related tools such as JBoss Forge, whose description you will find in the *Appendix, Rapid Development Using JBoss Forge*.

On the visible screen, check the **Create a simple project** checkbox. With this option, we will skip the archetype selection. You can click on **Next**. Now, you have to complete some basic project information. We are creating a server-side EJB application, which also has a standalone client. These two projects can share some common information, for example, about dependencies and their versions. Hence, we want to create a Maven multimodule project. In this first step, let's create a parent project that has a POM packaging. POM is a Maven convention used to describe the structure of a project and its modules. More information on this can be found in Sonatype free books that we mentioned in previous chapters.

You can complete the wizard by entering some package-specific information, as shown in the following screenshot:

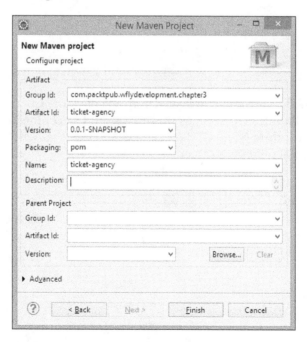

For **Group ID** (an abstract identifier with a similar role as in Java packages), you can use com.packtpub.wflydevelopment.chapter3. For **Artifact ID** (a simplified name of our project), just use ticket-agency. Set the **Packaging** field to **pom**, and you can leave the default selection for the project's **Version** field. Click on **Finish** in order to complete the wizard.

Take a look at our newly created project. At the moment, it contains only pom.xml, which will be the base for new modules. Navigate again to **File | New | Other | Maven** but now choose the **New Maven Module**. You can now see the following screenshot:

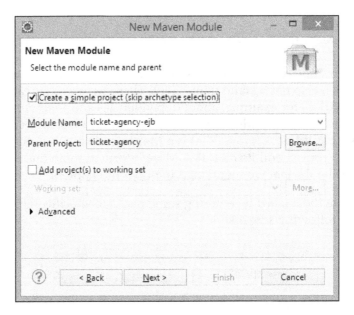

Again, we want to skip the archetype selection, so check the **Create a simple project** option. Under the **Parent Project**, click on **Browse** and select the parent we created a while ago. Under **Module Name**, enter ticket-agency-ejb. Click on **Next**. You will be presented with the following screen.

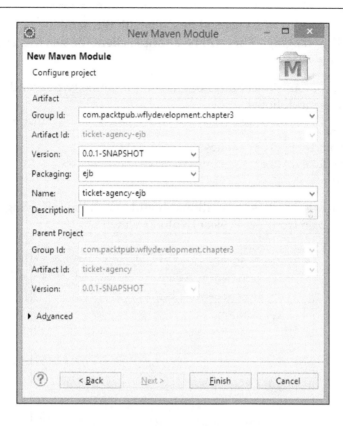

Now, let's discuss the packaging type. There are a few possible archive types for Java EE deployments:

- **The EJB module**: This module usually contains classes for EJBs, packed as a .jar file.

- **The web module**: This archive can additionally contain web elements such as servlets, static web files, REST endpoints, and so on. It is packed as a .war file (web archive) file.

- **The resource adapter module**: This archive contains files related to JCA connectors (described in *Chapter 6, Developing Applications with JBoss JMS Provider*). It is packed as a .rar file.

- **The Enterprise archive**: This archive aggregates multiple Java EE modules (EJB, Web) with related descriptors. It is packed as a .ear file.

Here, we want to deploy only EJBs without any web elements, so let's set the packaging to EJB (if it is not visible in the Eclipse drop-down menu, just manually type it) and click on **Finish**.

Follow the same steps to add a second module with the name `ticket-agency-ejb-client` and JAR packaging . This will be a simple client for services exposed in `ticket-agency-ejb`.

Now, look at our parent project `pom.xml`. It should define two recently created modules, which are as follows:

```
<modules>
    <module>ticket-agency-ejb</module>
    <module>ticket-agency-ejb-client</module>
</modules>
```

The expected outcome of these operations should match the following screenshot, which has been taken from the Project Explorer view:

As you can see, the **ticket-agency-ejb** and **ticket-agency-ejb-client** projects have been organized as a standard Maven project:

- `src/main/java` will contain our source code

- `src/main/resources` is meant for the configuration (containing a bare-bones `ejb-jar.xml` configuration file for the EJB project)
- `src/test/java` is used to store the test classes

At the moment, we will focus on the main file `pom.xml`, which needs to be aware of the Java EE dependencies.

Configuring the EJB project object module (pom.xml)

Before digging into the code, first you need to configure Maven's `pom.xml` configuration file further. This file is quite verbose, so we will illustrate just the core elements here that are required to understand our example, leaving the full listing to the code example package of this book.

The first thing we are going to add just after the properties section is a reference to Java EE 7 API, which is as follows:

```
<dependencies>
    <dependency>
        <groupId>javax</groupId>
        <artifactId>javaee-api</artifactId>
        <version>7.0</version>
        <scope>provided</scope>
    </dependency>
</dependencies>
```

This dependency will add all Java EE 7.0 APIs' definitions. Scope is set to be provided, which means the dependency is available on the target environment (in our case, the application server), and does not need to be included in the built archive. This dependency is universal, and should work with all Application Servers that are compatible with Java EE 7.0, not only with WildFly.

We also want to add a second dependency, which is the JBoss logging API. Place this definition in the same `<dependencies>` `</dependencies>` tags, for example, below `javaee-api`, as follows:

```
<dependency>
    <groupId>org.jboss.logging</groupId>
    <artifactId>jboss-logging</artifactId>
    <version>3.1.4.GA</version>
    <scope>provided</scope>
</dependency>
```

The scope provided includes the enterprise dependencies and corresponds to adding a library to the compilation path. Therefore, it expects the JDK or a container to provide the dependency at runtime. Besides dependencies, we would like to configure the build process. The created project specifies the EJB packaging, but the build is performed with the JDK 1.5 compliance level and an old EJB version. This is why we want to add an additional block to pom.xml, which is as follows:

```xml
<build>
    <plugins>
        <plugin>
            <groupId>org.apache.maven.plugins</groupId>
            <artifactId>maven-compiler-plugin</artifactId>
            <version>3.1</version>
            <configuration>
                <!-- enforce Java 8 -->
                <source>1.8</source>
                <target>1.8</target>
            </configuration>
        </plugin>
        <plugin>
            <groupId>org.apache.maven.plugins</groupId>
            <artifactId>maven-ejb-plugin</artifactId>
            <version>2.3</version>
            <configuration>
                <ejbVersion>3.2</ejbVersion>
                <!-- Generate ejb-client for client
project -->
                <generateClient>true</generateClient>
            </configuration>
        </plugin>
    </plugins>
</build>
```

This block does two things, which are as follows:

- The maven-compiler-plugin configuration enforces the usage of Java 8
- The maven-ejb-plugin configuration defines that EJB 3.2 version was used, and enables generation of the EJB client (disabled by default) package for EJB client applications

Also, check the `src/main/resources/META-INF/ejb-jar.xml` file. It might contain the configuration from EJB 2.1. Instead, use the following code:

```xml
<?xml version="1.0" encoding="UTF-8"?>
<ejb-jar xmlns="http://xmlns.jcp.org/xml/ns/javaee"
         xmlns:xsi="http://www.w3.org/2001/XMLSchema-instance"
         xsi:schemaLocation="http://xmlns.jcp.org/xml/ns/javaee"
         version="3.2">
    <display-name>ticket-agency-ejb</display-name>
    <ejb-client-jar>ticket-agency-ejbClient.jar</ejb-client-jar>
</ejb-jar>
```

At this point, you will be able to compile your project; so, we will start adding classes, but we will return to the `pom.xml` file when it's time to deploy your artifact.

Coding our EJB application

Creating EJB classes does not require getting mixed up with fancy wizards; all you need to do is add bare Java classes. Therefore, from the **File** menu, go to **New** | **Java Class**, and enter `TheatreBox` as the classname and `com.packtpub.wflydevelopment.chapter3.control` as the package name.

We will add the following implementation to the class:

```java
@Singleton
@Startup
@AccessTimeout(value = 5, unit = TimeUnit.MINUTES)
public class TheatreBox {

    private static final Logger logger = Logger.getLogger(TheatreBox.
class);

    private Map<Integer, Seat> seats;

    @PostConstruct
    public void setupTheatre() {
        seats = new HashMap<>();
        int id = 0;
        for (int i = 0; i < 5; i++) {
            addSeat(new Seat(++id, "Stalls", 40));
            addSeat(new Seat(++id, "Circle", 20));
            addSeat(new Seat(++id, "Balcony", 10));
        }
```

```
        logger.info("Seat Map constructed.");
    }

    private void addSeat(Seat seat) {
        seats.put(seat.getId(), seat);
    }

    @Lock(READ)
    public Collection<Seat> getSeats() {
        return Collections.unmodifiableCollection(seats.values());
    }

    @Lock(READ)
    public int getSeatPrice(int seatId) throws NoSuchSeatException {
        return getSeat(seatId).getPrice();
    }

    @Lock(WRITE)
    public void buyTicket(int seatId) throws SeatBookedException,
NoSuchSeatException {
        final Seat seat = getSeat(seatId);
        if (seat.isBooked()) {
            throw new SeatBookedException("Seat " + seatId + " already
booked!");
        }
        addSeat(seat.getBookedSeat());
    }

    @Lock(READ)
    private Seat getSeat(int seatId) throws NoSuchSeatException {
        final Seat seat = seats.get(seatId);
        if (seat == null) {
            throw new NoSuchSeatException("Seat " + seatId + " does
not exist!");
        }
        return seat;
    }
}
```

Let's see our application code in detail; the void method `setupTheatre` is invoked as soon as the application is deployed and takes care of assembling the theatre seats, creating a simple map of the `Seat` objects. Seat identifiers are key factors in this map. This happens right after deployment because our bean is annotated with `@Singleton` and `@Startup` that force the container to initialize the bean during startup. Each `Seat` object is constructed using a set of three field constructors, which includes the seat ID, its description, and the price (the booked field is initially set as false). This is given in the following code:

```
public class Seat {
    public Seat(int id, String name, int price) {
        this(id, name, price, false);
    }
    private Seat(int id, String name, int price, boolean booked) {
        this.id = id;
        this.name = name;
        this.price = price;
        this.booked = booked;
    }
    public Seat getBookedSeat() {
        return new Seat(getId(), getName(), getPrice(), true);
    }
    // Other Constructors, Fields and Getters omitted for brevity
}
```

Note that our `Seat` object is an immutable one. After we create an instance, we will not be able to change its state (the value of the fields, all of them are final, and no setters are exposed). This means that when we return a `Seat` object to the client (local or remote), it will be only available for reading.

Next, the singleton bean exposes four public methods; the `getSeats` method returns an unmodifiable collection of `Seat` objects, which will return the information regarding whether they have been reserved or not to the user. The collection must be unmodifiable because our Singleton exposes a no-interface view, which means that we are using the pass-by-reference semantic. If we will not protect the collection, then every change on an element of the returned collection will be done on our cache. What's more, the client can add or remove elements to our internal collection!

The `getSeatPrice` method is an utility method, which will pick up the seat price and return it as `int`, so it can be used to verify whether the user can afford to buy the ticket.

The getSeat method returns an immutable Seat object for a given ID. Once more, we return an immutable Seat because we don't want the client to change the object without using the TheatherBox bean.

Finally, the buyTicket method is the one that actually buys the ticket and, therefore, sets the ticket as booked. We cannot change the value of an immutable object, but we can replace it with a new one, which contains another value. The newly created object is placed in the hashmap instead of the old one.

Controlling bean concurrency

As you might have noticed, the bean includes a @Lock annotation on top of the methods managing our collection of Seat objects. This kind of annotation is used to control the concurrency of the singleton.

Concurrent access to a singleton EJB is, by default, controlled by the container. Read/write access to a singleton is limited to one client at a time. However, it is possible to provide a finer level of concurrency control through the use of annotations. This can be achieved using the @Lock annotation, whose arguments determine the type of concurrency access permitted.

By using a @Lock annotation of type javax.ejb.LockType.READ, multithreaded access will be allowed to the bean. This is shown in the following code:

```
@Lock(READ)
public Collection<Seat> getSeats() {
    return Collections.unmodifiableCollection(seats.values());
}
```

On the other hand, if we apply javax.ejb.LockType.WRITE, the single-threaded access policy is enforced, as shown in the following code:

```
@Lock(WRITE)
public void buyTicket(int seatId) throws SeatBookedException,
NoSuchSeatException {
    final Seat seat = getSeat(seatId);
    if (seat.isBooked()) {
        throw new SeatBookedException("Seat " + seatId + " already
booked!");
    }
    addSeat(seat.getBookedSeat());
}
```

The general idea is to use READ type locks on methods that just read values from the cache and WRITE type locks for methods that change the values of elements contained in the cache. Keep in mind that WRITE type locks block all methods with READ type locks. It is crucial that the singleton will have exclusive control of the modifications of its state. Lack of proper encapsulation mixed with the pass-by-reference semantic (used in local and no-interface views of EJBs) can lead to hard-to-find concurrency bugs. Using immutable objects as return values for singletons is a good strategy to solve these kind of problems. Another strategy would be to return only copies of our objects or switching to the pass-by-value semantic. The last strategy can be applied by switching to a remote business interface in the singleton.

In the `TheatreBox` code, you have probably noticed a `@AccessTimeout` annotation (with value 5 and unit `TimeUnit.MINUTES`). When you execute a query against a method with `@Lock (WRITE)`, and if some other thread is already accessing it, then after 5 seconds of waiting, you will get a timeout exception. In order to change this behavior (for example, by prolonging the allowed wait time), you can specify a `@javax.ejb.AccessTimout` annotation at the method or class level.

Using bean-managed concurrency

The other possible option is to use a bean-managed concurrency strategy that can be pursued by applying the `@javax.ejb.ConcurrencyManagement` annotation with an argument of `ConcurrencyManagementType.BEAN`. This annotation will disable the effect of the `@Lock` annotation we have used so far, putting the responsibility of ensuring that the singleton cache does not get corrupted on the developer.

So, in order to ensure that our bookings are preserved, we will need to use a well-known synchronized keyword on top of the `buyTicket` method, which is as follows:

```
@Singleton
@Startup
@ConcurrencyManagement(ConcurrencyManagementType.BEAN)
public class TheatreBox {
. . . .
  public synchronized void buyTicket(int seatId) {
    final Seat seat = getSeat(seatId);
    if (seat.isBooked()) {
        throw new SeatBookedException("Seat " + seatId + " already
booked!");
    }
    addSeat(seat.getBookedSeat());
  }
}
```

Since concurrent access is restricted when a thread enters the synchronized block, no other methods are allowed to access the object while the current thread is in the block. Using a synchronized block is equivalent to having a container-managed concurrency with default locks of type WRITE on all methods. This is one of the few places in Java EE when the developer may use synchronization primitives without affecting the stability of the container.

Cooking session beans

Our singleton EJB is equipped with the methods to handle our store of theatre seats. We will now add a couple of session beans to our project to manage the business logic, a stateless session bean that will provide a view of the theatre seats and stateful beans that will behave as a payment gateway to our system.

 The choice of splitting our information system into two different beans is not part of a design pattern in particular, but serves a different purpose. That is, we would like to show how to look up both types of beans from a remote client.

Adding a stateless bean

So, the first bean we will create is com.packtpub.wflydevelopment.chapter3. boundary.TheatreInfo, which barely contains the logic to look up the list of theatre seats. In practice, this bean acts as a facade for our singleton bean, as shown in the following code:

```java
@Stateless
@Remote(TheatreInfoRemote.class)
public class TheatreInfo implements TheatreInfoRemote {
    @EJB
    private TheatreBox box;

    @Override
    public String printSeatList() {
        final Collection<Seat> seats = box.getSeats();
        final StringBuilder sb = new StringBuilder();
        for (Seat seat : seats) {
            sb.append(seat.toString());
            sb.append(System.lineSeparator());
        }
        return sb.toString();
    }
}
```

Since we are planning to invoke this EJB from a remote client, we defined a remote interface for it with the `@Remote(TheatreInfoRemote.class)` annotation.

Next, take a look at the `@EJB TheatreBox` box, which can be used to safely inject an EJB into your class without the need of a manual JNDI lookup. This practice can be used to increase the portability of your application between different application servers, where different JNDI rules might exist.

The remote interface of your bean will be as simple as the following code:

```
public interface TheatreInfoRemote {
    String printSeatList();
}
```

If you are planning to expose your EJB to local clients only (for example, to a servlet), you can leave out the remote interface definition and simply annotate your bean with `@Stateless`. The application server will create a no-interface view of your session bean, which can safely be injected into your local clients such as servlets or other EJBs. Be mindful that this also changes the semantics of the methods parameters and return values. For remote views, they will be serialized and passed by value.

Adding a stateful bean

In order to keep track of how much money our customer has got in his pocket, we will need a session-aware component. Turning a Java class into a stateful session bean is just a matter of adding a `@Stateful` annotation on top of it, as in our example `com.packtpub.wflydevelopment.chapter3.boundary.TheatreBooker` class. This is shown in the following code:

```
@Stateful
@Remote(TheatreBookerRemote.class)
@AccessTimeout(value = 5, unit = TimeUnit.MINUTES)
public class TheatreBooker implements TheatreBookerRemote {
    private static final Logger logger = Logger.
getLogger(TheatreBooker.class);

    @EJB
    private TheatreBox theatreBox;
    private int money;

    @PostConstruct
    public void createCustomer() {
        this.money = 100;
```

```
        }

        @Override
        public int getAccountBalance() {
            return money;
        }

        @Override
        public String bookSeat(int seatId) throws SeatBookedException,
    NotEnoughMoneyException, NoSuchSeatException {
            final int seatPrice = theatreBox.getSeatPrice(seatId);
            if (seatPrice > money) {
                throw new NotEnoughMoneyException("You don't have enough
    money to buy this " + seatId + " seat!");
            }

            theatreBox.buyTicket(seatId);
            money = money - seatPrice;

            logger.infov("Seat {0} booked.", seatId);
            return "Seat booked.";
        }
    }
```

As you can see, the previous bean bears a `@PostConstruct` annotation to initialize a session variable (money) that will be used to check whether the customer has enough money to buy the ticket. When using EJBs, we don't use `constructors` and `destructors` to perform actions on an object to create or destroy. The reason is that the point object might not have injected all objects it depends on. The method annotated with `@PostConstruct` is executed when object creation is already finished, that is, all objects are injected to it. There is a second annotation related to the EJB life cycle, `@PreDestroy`, which is executed before the object is destroyed.

Besides this, the ultimate purpose of our SFSB is to invoke the `buyTicket` method of our singleton after having performed some business checks.

If the business checks do not pass, the application will issue some exceptions. This is the case, for example, if the seat has already been booked or if the customer hasn't got enough money to buy the ticket. In order to keep our conversation going, it's important that our exception will be an extension of the generic `Exception` class. Refer to the following code for more information:

```
public class SeatBookedException extends Exception {
    // some code
}
```

If we use a runtime exception (for example, `EJBException`), the bean instance will be discarded, and the communication between the remote client and server will be dropped. So, always take care to choose the appropriate type of exception when dealing with EJBs — choose to throw a runtime exception if you are dealing with an unrecoverable scenario (the connection with the enterprise information system is dropped). This kind of exception is called a System Exception. On the other hand, consider throwing a checked exception (or simply not throwing exceptions at all), if you are dealing with a business kind of exception; for example, if the booked seat is already engaged. Recoverable exceptions are called Application Exceptions.

There is also a possibility to mark a runtime exception (which would normally be a System Exception) as a recoverable exception, using the `@ApplicationException` annotation. You may even decide if the current transaction should be rolled back (which is the default behavior for system exceptions) using `@ApplicationException` (with rollback `true`) on an exception class or the `EJBContext.setRollbackOnly` statement inside a business method. The decision to roll back a transaction is up to the developer, and in most cases, it depends on the business scenario.

Deploying the EJB application

As it is, you should be able to package your EJB project by issuing the following Maven goal and starting a command-line prompt from your project root:

```
mvn package
```

The preceding command will compile and package the application that needs to be copied into the `deployments` folder of your application server. This is fine; however, we can expect lots more from Maven by installing just a couple of plugins. In our case, we will configure our project to use Maven's WildFly plugin by adding the following section:

```
<build>
    <finalName>${project.artifactId}</finalName>
    <plugins>
        <!-- WildFly plugin to deploy the application -->
        <plugin>
            <groupId>org.wildfly.plugins</groupId>
            <artifactId>wildfly-maven-plugin</artifactId>
            <version>1.0.2.Final</version>
            <configuration>
                <filename>${project.build.finalName}.jar</filename>
            </configuration>
        </plugin>
        <plugin>
```

```
            <groupId>org.apache.maven.plugins</groupId>
            <artifactId>maven-compiler-plugin</artifactId>
            <version>3.1</version>
            <configuration>
                <!-- enforce Java 8 -->
                <source>1.8</source>
                <target>1.8</target>
            </configuration>
        </plugin>
        <plugin>
            <groupId>org.apache.maven.plugins</groupId>
            <artifactId>maven-ejb-plugin</artifactId>
            <version>2.3</version>
            <configuration>
                <ejbVersion>3.2</ejbVersion>
                <!-- Generate ejb-client for client project -->
                <generateClient>true</generateClient>
            </configuration>
        </plugin>
    </plugins>
</build>
```

In the first part of the XML fragment, we specified the project's `finalName` attribute, which will dictate the name of the packaged artifact (in our example, the project's name corresponds to our project's artifact ID, so it will be named `ticket-agency-ejb.jar`).

The artifact ID named `wildfly-maven-plugin` will actually trigger the WildFly Maven plugin that will be used to deploy our project.

So, once you have configured the WildFly plugin, your application can be deployed automatically by entering from your project root. This can be done by typing the following command in the console:

`mvn wildfly:deploy`

Since deployment is a repetitive task for a developer, it would be convenient to execute this operation from within the Eclipse environment. All you need is to create a new **Run Configurations** setting from the upper menu by navigating to **Run | Run Configurations**.

Enter the project's base directory (hint: the **Browse Workspace...** utility will help you pick up the project from your project list) and type your Maven goal into the **Goals** textbox, as shown in the following screenshot:

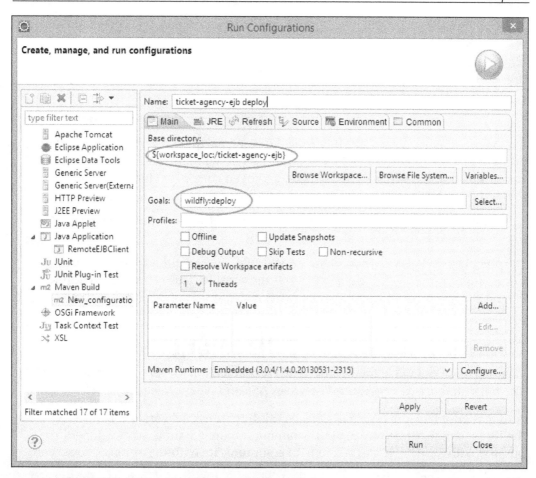

Once this is done, please ensure that your WildFly instance is running. Click on **Apply** to save your configuration and then click on **Run** to execute the deployment of the application. The Maven plugin will activate and once it is verified that all classes are up to date, start deploying the applications to WildFly using the remote API. Note that you do not need to pass any username or password for the deployment. This is possible because you are deploying your application from the same machine that WildFly is installed on. A local user authentication is done under the hood so that programmers will not need to cover this on their development machines.

After issuing the command, you should expect a success message on the Maven console, as shown in the following code:

```
INFO: JBoss Remoting version 4.0.3.Final
[INFO] ------------------------------------------------------------
[INFO] BUILD SUCCESS
[INFO] ------------------------------------------------------------
```

On the other hand, on the WildFly console, you have quite a verbose output that points out some important EJB JNDI bindings (we will return to it in a minute) and informs us that the application has been deployed correctly. This is depicted in the following code:

```
09:09:32,782 INFO  [org.jboss.as.server] (management-handler-thread -
1) JBAS018562: Deployed "ticket-agency-ejb.jar"
```

Despite the fact that we are working on WildFly, we can quite frequently see information from JBoss AS subsystems on the console. This is because WildFly is built straight on the JBoss AS 7 codebase, and should not be worried about.

Creating a remote EJB client

Creating a remote EJB client for the WildFly application server is very similar to AS7. The big difference can be noticed between AS6 and newer releases.

As a matter of fact, previous versions of WildFly (JBoss AS versions before 7.x) used the JBoss naming project as the JNDI naming implementation, so developers are familiar with `jnp://` PROVIDER_URL to communicate with the application server.

Starting with AS7, the JNP project is no longer used — neither on the server side nor on the client side. The client side of the JNP project has now been replaced by the jboss-remote-naming project. There were various reasons why the JNP client was replaced by the jboss-remote-naming project. One of them was that the JNP project did not allow fine-grained security configurations while communicating with the JNDI server. The jboss-remote-naming project is backed by the jboss-remoting project which allows much more and better control over security.

Besides the new naming implementation in AS7 and WildFly, there is no longer any support to bind custom JNDI names to EJBs. So the beans are always bound to the spec's mandated `java:global`, `java:app`, and `java:module` namespaces. Therefore, setting the JNDI name for the session bean element via an annotation or configuration file is no longer supported.

So, what will be the JNDI name used to invoke a stateless session bean? Here it is:

```
ejb:<app-name>/<module-name>/<distinct-name>/<bean-name>!<fully-
qualified-classname-of-the-remote-interface>
```

A bit verbose, isn't it? However, the following table will help you get through it:

Element	Description
app-name	This is the enterprise application name (without ear), if your EJB has been packed in an EAR
module-name	This is the module name (without .jar or .war), where your EJB has been packed
distinct-name	Using this, you can optionally set a distinct name for each deployment unit
bean-name	This is the bean's class name
fully-qualified-classname-of-the-remote-interface	This is the fully qualified class name of the remote interface

So the corresponding JNDI binding for your TheatreInfo EJB, packaged into a file named ticket-agency-ejb.jar, will be:

```
ejb:/ticket-agency-ejb//TheatreInfo! com.packtpub.wflydevelopment.
chapter3.boundary.TheatreInfoRemote
```

On the other hand, stateful EJBs will contain one more attribute, ?stateful, at the bottom of the JNDI string; this will result in the following JNDI naming structure:

```
ejb:<app-name>/<module-name>/<distinct-name>/<bean-name>!<fully-
qualified-classname-of-the-remote-interface>?stateful
```

Also, here's the corresponding binding for the TheatreBooker class:

```
ejb:/ticket-agency-ejb//TheatreBooker! com.packtpub.wflydevelopment.
chapter3.boundary.TheatreBookerRemote?stateful
```

If you pay attention to the server logs, you will see that once your application is deployed, a set of JNDI bindings will be displayed on the server console. For example:

```
java:global/ticket-agency-ejb/TheatreInfo!com.packtpub.
wflydevelopment.chapter3.boundary.TheatreInfoRemote

java:app/ticket-agency-ejb/TheatreInfo!com.packtpub.
wflydevelopment.chapter3.boundary.TheatreInfoRemote

java:module/TheatreInfo!com.packtpub.wflydevelopment.
chapter3.boundary.TheatreInfoRemote

java:jboss/exported/ticket-agency-ejb/TheatreInfo!com.
packtpub.wflydevelopment.chapter3.boundary.
TheatreInfoRemote
```

Some of these bindings reflect the standard bindings as per Java EE specifications plus JBoss custom bindings (java:/jboss). This information, as it is, is not relevant for us but can be use to build our EJB client lookup string by replacing the Java EE (or JBoss-specific prefix) with ejb:/. For example, replace java:/global with ejb:, and you will save yourself the headache of referring to the EJB lookup string.

Once we are done with decoding the JNDI binding string, we will code our EJB client. We have already created a separate subproject for it (ticket-agency-ejb-client) at the beginning of this chapter, but we must still complete its configuration before we dive into coding.

Configuring the client's project object module

Configuring the client dependencies (in pom.xml) will basically require all the libraries that connect and transport data to the server, along with the required EJB client dependencies. The first thing we will add, just as we did for the server project, is the BOM for the EJB client dependencies, which is demonstrated in the following code snippet:

```xml
<dependencyManagement>
    <dependencies>
        <dependency>
            <groupId>org.wildfly</groupId>
            <artifactId>wildfly-ejb-client-bom</artifactId>
            <version>8.1.0.Final</version>
            <type>pom</type>
            <scope>import</scope>
        </dependency>
    </dependencies>
</dependencyManagement>
```

Next, we will add a set of dependencies that are needed to resolve the EJB interfaces (`ticket-agency-ejb artifact`), the JBoss' transaction API (needed as EJBs are transaction-aware components), the `jboss-ejb-api` and `ejb-client` APIs, the `org.jboss.xnio` and `org.jboss.xnio` APIs (which provide a low-level input/output implementation), the `org.jboss.remoting3` API (the core transport protocol), which in turn requires `org.jboss.sasl` (to secure the transport), and finally, the `org.jboss.marshalling` API (to serialize the objects that are sent to and received from the server). This is shown in the following code snippet:

```xml
<dependencies>
    <dependency>
        <groupId>com.packtpub.wflydevelopment.chapter3</groupId>
        <artifactId>ticket-agency-ejb</artifactId>
        <type>ejb-client</type>
        <version>${project.version}</version>
    </dependency>

    <dependency>
        <groupId>org.jboss.spec.javax.transaction</groupId>
        <artifactId>jboss-transaction-api_1.2_spec</artifactId>
        <scope>runtime</scope>
    </dependency>

    <dependency>
        <groupId>org.jboss.spec.javax.ejb</groupId>
        <artifactId>jboss-ejb-api_3.2_spec</artifactId>
        <scope>runtime</scope>
    </dependency>

    <dependency>
        <groupId>org.jboss</groupId>
        <artifactId>jboss-ejb-client</artifactId>
        <scope>runtime</scope>
    </dependency>

    <dependency>
        <groupId>org.jboss.xnio</groupId>
        <artifactId>xnio-api</artifactId>
        <scope>runtime</scope>
    </dependency>
    <dependency>
        <groupId>org.jboss.xnio</groupId>
        <artifactId>xnio-nio</artifactId>
        <scope>runtime</scope>
```

```
        </dependency>

        <dependency>
            <groupId>org.jboss.remoting3</groupId>
            <artifactId>jboss-remoting</artifactId>
                <version>3.3.3.Final</version>
                <scope>runtime</scope>
        </dependency>

        <dependency>
            <groupId>org.jboss.sasl</groupId>
            <artifactId>jboss-sasl</artifactId>
            <scope>runtime</scope>
        </dependency>

        <dependency>
            <groupId>org.jboss.marshalling</groupId>
            <artifactId>jboss-marshalling-river</artifactId>
            <scope>runtime</scope>
        </dependency>
    </dependencies>
```

Many of these dependencies use the runtime scope. This means that classes that are provided by them are not used directly by our code; they are not needed to be bundled within our application package, but they are required at runtime.

Coding the EJB client

We are done with the configuration. We will finally proceed with adding a new Java class com.packtpub.wflydevelopment.chapter3.client.TicketAgencyClient, which will communicate with the ticket booking machine's EJB application. This is shown in the following code snippet:

```
public class TicketAgencyClient {

    private static final Logger logger =
        Logger.getLogger(TicketAgencyClient.class.getName());

    public static void main(String[] args) throws Exception {
        Logger.getLogger("org.jboss").setLevel(Level.SEVERE);    [1]
        Logger.getLogger("org.xnio").setLevel(Level.SEVERE);

        new TicketAgencyClient().run();
    }
```

```
    private final Context context;
    private TheatreInfoRemote theatreInfo;
    private TheatreBookerRemote theatreBooker;

    public TicketAgencyClient() throws NamingException {
        final Properties jndiProperties = new Properties(); [2]
        jndiProperties.setProperty(Context.URL_PKG_PREFIXES, "org.
jboss.ejb.client.naming");
        this.context = new InitialContext(jndiProperties);
    }

    private enum Command { [3]
        BOOK, LIST, MONEY, QUIT, INVALID;

        public static Command parseCommand(String stringCommand) {
            try {
                return valueOf(stringCommand.trim().toUpperCase());
            } catch (IllegalArgumentException iae) {
                return INVALID;
            }
        }
    }

    private void run() throws NamingException {
        this.theatreInfo = lookupTheatreInfoEJB();   [4]
        this.theatreBooker = lookupTheatreBookerEJB();   [5]

        showWelcomeMessage(); [6]

        while (true) {
            final String stringCommand = IOUtils.readLine("> ");
            final Command command =
              Command.parseCommand(stringCommand); [7]
            switch (command) {
                case BOOK:
                    handleBook();
                    break;
                case LIST:
                    handleList();
                    break;
                case MONEY:
                    handleMoney();
                    break;
                case QUIT:
```

```
                            handleQuit();
                            break;

                    default:
                            logger.warning("Unknown command " +
stringCommand);
                }
            }
        }

    private void handleBook() {
        int seatId;

        try {
            seatId = IOUtils.readInt("Enter SeatId: ");
        } catch (NumberFormatException e1) {
            logger.warning("Wrong SeatId format!");
            return;
        }

        try {
            final String retVal = theatreBooker.bookSeat(seatId);
            System.out.println(retVal);
        } catch (SeatBookedException | NotEnoughMoneyException |
NoSuchSeatException e) {
            logger.warning(e.getMessage());
            return;
        }
    }

    private void handleList() {
        logger.info(theatreInfo.printSeatList());
    }

    private void handleMoney() {
        final int accountBalance = theatreBooker.getAccountBalance();
        logger.info("You have: " + accountBalance + " money left.");
    }

    private void handleQuit() {
        logger.info("Bye");
        System.exit(0);
    }
```

```
    private TheatreInfoRemote lookupTheatreInfoEJB() throws
NamingException {
        return (TheatreInfoRemote) context.lookup("ejb:/ticket-agency-
ejb//TheatreInfo!com.packtpub.wflydevelopment.chapter3.boundary.
TheatreInfoRemote");
    }

    private TheatreBookerRemote lookupTheatreBookerEJB() throws
NamingException {
        return (TheatreBookerRemote) context.lookup("ejb:/ticket-
agency-ejb//TheatreBooker!com.packtpub.wflydevelopment.chapter3.
boundary.TheatreBookerRemote?stateful");
    }

    private void showWelcomeMessage() {
        System.out.println("Theatre booking system");
        System.out.println("======================================");
        System.out.println("Commands: book, list,money, quit");
    }
}
```

Let's see the most interesting points. First, in the main function, we set some logging rules [1] in order to avoid mixing the JBoss remoting log messages with the console application information.

Next, we create the `TicketAgencyClient` object and execute its `run` method. During object creation, we prepare the `InitialContext` object (further used to lookup remote objects). To do this, we will need a set of [2] properties, which specify what type of `ejb-client` is used.

In [3], we define a `Command` enum, which represents console commands that users can send to this application. The `run()` method first performs the lookup of the SLSB and SFSB ([4] and [5]) remote EJBs, and then shows the welcome message ([6]). In the infinite loop, we wait for the user to enter a command and parse it ([7]). Depending on the user's choice we can book a seat, list seats' information, get available money, or quit the application.

Adding the EJB client configuration

As you can see from the preceding code snippet, there is no indication about the location of the server where the EJBs are running. It is possible to specify this by code, but in this sample, we will choose the simpler way and add `jboss-ejb-client.properties` file in the client's classpath.

In Maven, the appropriate location for most of the resource files (like mentioned properties) is the `src/main/resources` directory.

The contents of the `jboss-ejb-client.properties` file are as follows:

```
remote.connections=default
remote.connection.default.host=localhost
remote.connection.default.port=8080
```

There is also a `remote.connectionprovider.create.options.org .xnio. Options.SSL_ENABLED` property, which enables the encryption of the XNIO connection; otherwise, plaintext will be used. (In *Chapter 10, Securing WildFly Applications*, we will discuss using SSL to secure the connection between the client and server.)

The `remote.connections` property can be set to define a list of logical names that will be used for connection purposes by the `remote.connection.[name].host` and `remote.connection.[name].port` attributes. If you define more than one connection, as in the following example, the connections will be split across various destinations, as shown in the following code snippet:

```
remote.connections=host1,host2
remote.connection.host1.host=192.168.0.1
remote.connection.host2.host=192.168.0.2
remote.connection.host1.port=8080
remote.connection.host2.port=8080
```

The default port used by the remoting framework is `8080`.

You may wonder how EJB remoting can work on the same port as the HTTP protocol. Starting from WildFly, remoting uses the HTTP protocol upgrade mechanism. The first connection is done on the `8080` port (via HTTP), then it is upgraded to EJB remoting, and switched to another port (chosen by WildFly).

Running the client application

In order to run your client application, the last requirement will be to add the required Maven plugins, which are needed to run the remote EJB client. This is given in the following code snippet:

```
<build>
    <finalName>${project.artifactId}</finalName>
    <plugins>
```

```xml
<!-- maven-compiler-plugin here -->

<plugin>
    <groupId>org.codehaus.mojo</groupId>
    <artifactId>exec-maven-plugin</artifactId>
    <version>1.2.1</version>
    <executions>
        <execution>
            <goals>
                <goal>exec</goal>
            </goals>
        </execution>
    </executions>
    <configuration>
        <executable>java</executable>
        <workingDirectory>${project.build.directory}/
          exec-working-directory</workingDirectory>
        <arguments>
            <argument>-classpath</argument>
            <classpath />
        <argument>com.packtpub.wflydevelopment.chapter3.client.
          TicketAgencyClient</argument>
        </arguments>
    </configuration>
</plugin>
</plugins>
</build>
```

As you can see in the preceding code snippet, besides the `maven-compiler-plugin` configuration that we omitted for the sake of brevity (we discussed it in the server project), we have included `exec-maven-plugin`, which adds the ability to execute Java programs using the `exec` goal.

Once all the plugins are in place, you can compile and execute your project by issuing the following Maven goal:

```
mvn package exec:exec
```

The preceding command can be executed either from a shell (positioned in the project's `root` folder) or from your Eclipse runtime configuration, as shown in the following screenshot:

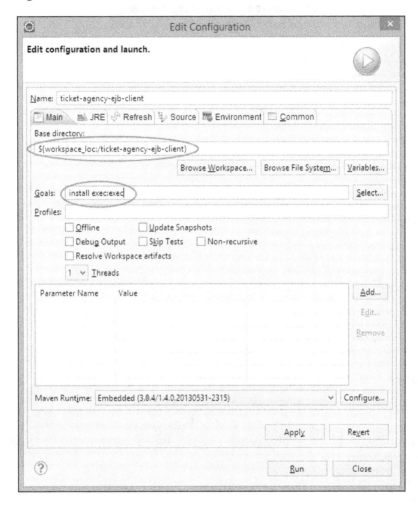

If executed from the Eclipse environment, you should be able to see the following GUI screenshot:

At the moment, our application provides three functions: a book to book a seat, a list to list all the theatre seats, and money to retrieve the account balance. In the next sections, we will enrich our application by adding some more commands.

Adding user authentication

If you are running this example from a client that is located on the same machine as the application server, the remoting framework will silently allow communication between the client and your EJB's classes. On the other hand, for a client located on a remote system, you will be required to provide authentication for your requests. In order to add an application user, launch the add-user.sh (or add-user.bat) script, which is located at JBOSS_HOME/bin.

Here's a transcript of a user creation example:

```
What type of user do you wish to add?
 a) Management User (mgmt-users.properties)
 b) Application User (application-users.properties)
(a): b

Enter the details of the new user to add.
Using realm 'ApplicationRealm' as discovered from the existing
property files.
Username : ejbuser
Password requirements are listed below. To modify these restrictions
edit the add-user.properties configuration file.
 - The password must not be one of the following restricted values
{root, admin, administrator}
 - The password must contain at least 8 characters, 1 alphanumeric
character(s), 1 digit(s), 1 non-alphanumeric symbol(s)
 - The password must be different from the username
```

```
Password :
Re-enter Password :
What groups do you want this user to belong to? (Please enter a comma
separated list, or leave blank for none) [   ]:
About to add user 'ejbuser' for realm 'ApplicationRealm'
Is this correct yes/no? yes
Added user 'ejbuser' to file 'C:\Programs\Dev\Servers\wildfly-
8.0.0.Final\standalone\configuration\application-users.properties'
Added user 'ejbuser' to file 'C:\Programs\Dev\Servers\wildfly-
8.0.0.Final\domain\configuration\application-users.properties'
Added user 'ejbuser' with groups  to file 'C:\Programs\Dev\Servers\
wildfly-8.0.0.Final\standalone\configuration\application-roles.
properties'
Added user 'ejbuser' with groups  to file 'C:\Programs\Dev\Servers\
wildfly-8.0.0.Final\domain\configuration\application-roles.properties'
Is this new user going to be used for one AS process to connect to
another AS process?
e.g. for a slave host controller connecting to the master or for a
Remoting connection for server to server EJB calls.
yes/no? no
Press any key to continue . . .
```

The defined user will be added for you in the `application-user.properties` file located in your `configuration` folder.

This file contains the default security realm named `ApplicationRealm`. This security realm uses the following format to store passwords:

```
username=HEX( MD5( username ':' realm ':' password))
```

With the passwords you've just entered, the file will contain the following entry:

```
ejbuser=dc86450aab573bd2a8308ea69bcb8ba9
```

Now, insert the username and password information into `jboss-ejb-client.properties`:

```
remote.connection.default.username=ejbuser
remote.connection.default.password=ejbuser123
```

Now, with all the previous information in the right place, you will be able to connect to your EJB application from a client that does not reside on the same machine as the server.

You can also force the normal authentication process on your local machine, by adding the following line to the `jboss-ejb-client` properties:

```
remote.connection.default.connect.options.org.xnio.Options.SASL_
DISALLOWED_MECHANISMS=JBOSS-LOCAL-USER
```

Using the EJB timer service

Applications that model business workflows often rely on timed notifications. The timer service of the enterprise bean container enables you to schedule timed notifications for all types of enterprise beans, except for stateful session beans. You can schedule a timed notification to occur according to a calendar schedule either at a specific time, after the duration of a time period, or at timed intervals.

There can be two main types of EJB timers: programmatic timers and automatic timers. Programmatic timers are set by explicitly calling one of the timer creation methods of the `TimerService` interface. Automatic timers are created upon the successful deployment of an enterprise bean, which contains a method annotated with the `java.ejb.Schedule` or `java.ejb.Schedules` annotations. Let's see both approaches in the following sections.

Programmatic timer creation

To create a timer, the bean invokes one of the `create` methods of the `TimerService` interface. These methods allow for either single-action, interval, or calendar-based timers to be created.

The simplest way to get a `TimerService` instance is to use resource injection. For example, in the `TheatreBox` singleton EJB, we will use the `@Resource` annotation to inject a `TimerService` object, as shown in the following code snippet:

```
@Resource
TimerService timerService;

private static final long DURATION = TimeUnit.SECONDS.toMillis(6);
```

The duration specifies the time (in milliseconds) when the single timer is fired. The method that will fire the timer will use the `TimerService` instance to invoke `createSingleActionTimer`, passing the duration and an instance of the `TimerConfig` class as an argument, which may optionally contain some basic information (such as the description of the timer). This is shown in the following code snippet:

```
public void createTimer(){
    timerService.createSingleActionTimer(DURATION, new TimerConfig());
}
```

Next, we will create a callback method named `timeout` and use the `@Timeout` annotation on top of the method. In the `timeout` method, we could, for example, reinitialize our singleton by invoking the `setupTheatre` method. Nothing fancy; however, this should give you an idea of how to get working with a single action timer. Refer to the following code for more information:

```
@Timeout
public void timeout(Timer timer){
    logger.info("Re-building Theatre Map.");
    setupTheatre();
}
```

Scheduling timer events

If you want to schedule timed notifications at fixed intervals, the simplest way is to use the `@Schedule` annotation. The `@Schedule` annotation takes a series of comma-delimited settings to express a time period or set of time periods, much as the Unix `cron` utility does. Each setting corresponds to a unit of time such as an hour or minute. A simple repeating event occurring every minute can be expressed using the `@Schedule` annotation as follows:

```
@Schedule(second="0", minute= "*", hour= "*")
```

You can find some more details about building the time string at.

For the purpose of our example, we will create a stateless session bean, which will act as an automatic buying system and therefore, buy tickets at our ticketing store. So, we will add one competitor in our quest for the best seat in the theatre! The following code snippet explains this:

```
@Stateless
public class AutomaticSellerService {

    private static final Logger logger = Logger.getLogger(AutomaticSel
lerService.class);

    @EJB
    private TheatreBox theatreBox;

    @Resource
    private TimerService timerService;    [1]

    @Schedule(hour = "*", minute = "*/1", persistent = false)    [2]
    public void automaticCustomer() throws NoSuchSeatException {
        final Optional<Seat> seatOptional = findFreeSeat();
```

```
        if (!seatOptional.isPresent()) {
            cancelTimers();
            logger.info("Scheduler gone!");
            return; // No more seats
        }

        final Seat seat = seatOptional.get();

        try {
            theatreBox.buyTicket(seat.getId());    [3]
        } catch (SeatBookedException e) {
            // do nothing, user booked this seat in the meantime
        }

        logger.info("Somebody just booked seat number " + seat.
getId());
    }

    private Optional<Seat> findFreeSeat() {
        final Collection<Seat> list = theatreBox.getSeats();
        return list.stream()
            .filter(seat -> !seat.isBooked())
            .findFirst();
    }
    private void cancelTimers() {   [4]
        for (Timer timer : timerService.getTimers()) {
            timer.cancel();
        }
    }
}
}
```

The first thing we should account for is the resource injection of the `Timer` object [1], which will be used in the `cancelTimers` method [4] to cancel all the scheduling when the theatre is fully booked. Please note that the `timerService.getTimers()` method retrieves all active timers associated only with the current bean. In order to get all timers from your application module, you have to use the `timerService.getAllTimers()` method, which was added recently in EJB 3.2.

Next, pay attention to the `Schedule` annotation [2] we are using, which will fire a non-persistent timer each minute.

Persistent timers (the default option) can survive application and server crashes. When the system recovers, any persistent timers will be recreated and missed callback events will be executed.

When a replay of missed timer events is not desired, a non-persistent timer should be used, as shown in the preceding example.

When an action is fired, the automaticCustomer method starts scanning the theatre seats for an available seat. (Nothing too complex; findSeat starts looking from the first available seat.)

Finally, if there are seats still available, the buyTicket method [3] of the TheatreBox singleton will be used to short circuit the purchase of the seat (obviously, we won't need to check the money for our automatic customer).

Adding asynchronous methods to our EJBs

Before the EJB 3.1 specification, the only way to provide asynchronous capabilities to enterprise applications was using message-driven bean recipes. This remains substantially a best practice, and we are going to discuss this in depth in *Chapter 6, Developing Applications with JBoss JMS Provider*; however, in some cases, it might be desirable (and easier) to use these asynchronous features from a component that follows the classical request-reply pattern.

You can make the EJB's method asynchronous by simply tagging it with the @Asynchronous annotation. Each time this method is invoked, it will immediately return, regardless of how long the method actually takes to complete.

This can be used in one of two ways:

- The first technique is a fire-and-forget manner, where the request is made up of the EJB and the client is not concerned about the success or failure of the request.

- The second modus operandi invokes the method but does not wait for the method to be completed. The method returns a Future object. This object is used later to determine the result of the request.

Using fire-and-forget asynchronous calls

If you don't care about the async result, you can just have your `async` method return void. For this purpose, we will add a new method named `bookSeatAsync` to `TheatreBooker` and simply tag it as `@Asynchronous`. This is shown in the following screenshot:

```
@Asynchronous
 public void bookSeatAsync(int seatId) throws NotEnoughMoneyException,
NoSuchSeatException, SeatBookedException {
       bookSeat(seatId);
}
```

As you can see, this method does not return anything; it just executes our synchronous `bookSeet` method. We will need to use some other instruments to check whether the transaction was completed successfully. For example, we can check from the theatre list whether the seat has been booked successfully.

Returning a Future object to the client

The other available option consists of returning a `java.util.concurrent.Future` object, which can later be inspected by our clients so that they know the outcome of our transaction. This is shown in the following code snippet:

```
@Asynchronous
@Override
public Future<String> bookSeatAsync(int seatId) {
        try {
               Thread.sleep(10000);
               bookSeat(seatId);
               return new AsyncResult<>("Booked seat: " + seatId + ".
Money left: " + money);
        } catch (NoSuchSeatException | SeatBookedException |
NotEnoughMoneyException | InterruptedException e) {
               return new AsyncResult<>(e.getMessage());
        }
    }
```

In this case, calls to the asynchronous `bookSeatAsync` method simply results, behind the scenes, in a `Runnable` or `Callable` Java object being created, which wraps the method and parameters you provide. This `Runnable` (or callable) object is given to an `Executor` object, which is simply a work queue attached to a thread pool.

After adding the work to the queue, the proxy version of the method returns a Future implementation that is linked to `Runnable`, which is now waiting in the queue.

When `Runnable` finally executes the `bookSeatAsync` method, it takes the return value and sets it to `Future`, making it available to the caller.

When dealing with `Future` objects, the client code needs to be adapted. As a matter of fact, in standard synchronous calls, we used exceptions to intercept some events such as when the customer does not have enough money to complete the transaction. When using `Future` calls, there's a change in this paradigm. The call to the asynchronous method is detached from the client; however, we have the option to check if the `Future` work has been completed with the `isDone` method issued on the Future return value.

For this purpose, let's add a `bookasync` command to `TicketAgencyClient`, which will issue asynchronous booking and a mail command that will simulate the reading of the outcome by e-mail, as shown in the following code snippet:

```java
private final List<Future<String>> lastBookings = new ArrayList<>();
[1]
 // Some code
    case BOOKASYNC:
        handleBookAsync();
        break;
    case MAIL:
        handleMail();
        break;
// Some code
private void handleBookAsync() {
    String text = IOUtils.readLine("Enter SeatId: ");
    int seatId;

    try {
        seatId = Integer.parseInt(text);
    } catch (NumberFormatException e1) {
        logger.warning("Wrong seatId format!");
        return;
    }

    lastBookings.add(theatreBooker.bookSeatAsync(seatId));   [2]
    logger.info("Booking issued. Verify your mail!");
}

private void handleMail() {
```

```
    boolean displayed = false;
    final List<Future<String>> notFinished = new ArrayList<>();
    for (Future<String> booking : lastBookings) {
        if (booking.isDone()) {    [3]
            try {
                final String result = booking.get();
                logger.info("Mail received: " + result);
                displayed = true;
            } catch (InterruptedException | ExecutionException e) {
                logger.warning(e.getMessage());
            }
        } else {
            notFinished.add(booking);
        }
    }

    lastBookings.retainAll(notFinished);
    if (!displayed) {
        logger.info("No mail received!");
    }
}
```

As you can see from the previous code snippet, we issue an asynchronous booking [2] and add Future<?> to lastBookings list [1]. On the EJB side, we introduced a pause of 10 seconds to complete the booking so that later on, we can check if the work has been completed by checking the isDone method [3] of the lastBookings list elements object.

Here is a screenshot of our richer client application:

Summary

In this chapter, we went through the EJB basics and changes in EJB 3.2 by following a simple lab example, which was enriched progressively. This example showed how the Maven project can be used from within the Eclipse environment to assist you in assembling the project with all the necessary dependencies.

Up to now, we have just coded a remote standalone client for our application. In the next chapter, we will see how to add a web frontend to our example using the context and dependency injections, to bridge the gap between the web tier and enterprise tier.

4
Learning Context and Dependency Injection

We saw that *Chapter 3, Introducing Java EE 7 – EJBs,* was challenging since we had to cover lots of ground, including Java Enterprise enhancements and a Maven-specific configuration. In this chapter, we'll discuss **Contexts and Dependency Injection (CDI)**, which was added to the Java EE specification in Java EE 6 (starting from JSR 299). It provides several benefits to Java EE developers that were missing, such as allowing any JavaBean to be used as a JSF managed bean, including stateless and stateful session beans. You can find more information on CDI and the newest version of the specification itself (JSR 346) at `http://www.cdi-spec.org/`.

Some of the topics that will be covered in this chapter are as follows:

- What Contexts and Dependency Injection is and how it relates to EJB
- How to rewrite our ticket-booking example to use the CDI and JavaServer Faces technology
- How to run the project using Maven

This chapter assumes familiarity with **JavaServer Faces (JSF)**, which will be used to provide a graphical interface for our applications. If you are looking for a start up guide for JSF, there are several excellent resources available online, including the relevant sections in the official Java EE 7 tutorial at `http://docs.oracle.com/javaee/7/tutorial/doc/jsf-develop.htm#BNATX`.

Introducing Contexts and Dependency Injection

CDI for the Java EE platform introduces a standard set of component management services to the Java EE platform. As a component of Java EE 7, CDI is in many ways a standardization of concepts that have been brewing in Spring for a long time, such as dependency injection and interceptors. In fact, CDI and Spring 3 share many similar features. There are also other dependency injection frameworks available for developers that are more lightweight and easier to use in a Java SE environment. **Google Guice** (`https://github.com/google/guice`) is a notable example. Providing full-blown support for the CDI container in a standalone Java SE application and separation from the application server are one of the goals of the upcoming CDI 2.0 specification. This will allow developers to use a common programming model on both client and server sides.

CDI lets you decouple concerns by what it refers to as loose coupling and strong typing. In doing so, it provides an almost liberating escape from the banalities of everyday Java programming, allowing injections of its objects and controlling their lifetimes.

Why is CDI required for Java EE?

If you have been programming with Java EE 5, you might argue that it already features resources injection of resources. However, this kind of injection can be used only for resources known to the container (for example, @EJB, @PersistenceContext, @PersistenceUnit, and @Resource). CDI, on the other hand, provides a general-purpose dependency injection scheme, which can be used for any component.

The CDI elementary unit is still the bean. Compared to EJBs, CDI features a different, more flexible kind of bean, which would often be a good place to put your business logic in. One of the most important differences between the two approaches is that CDI Beans are **contextual**; that is, they live in a well-defined scope.

Consider the following code snippet:

```
public class HelloServlet extends HttpServlet {

    @EJB
    private EJBSample ejb;

    public void doGet (HttpServletRequestreq,
                       HttpServletResponse res)
```

```
                throws ServletException, IOException {
        try(PrintWriter out = res.getWriter()) {
            out.println(ejb.greet());
        }
    }
}
```

Here, the injected EJB proxy (let's just assume that it is a POJO class annotated with a `@Stateless` annotation) just points to a pool of stateless instances (or a single bean instance for stateful beans). There is no automatic association between the HTTP request or HTTP session and a given EJB instance.

The opposite is true for CDI Beans, which live in well-defined scopes. For example, the following CDI Bean lives in `RequestScoped`; that is, it will be destroyed at the end of the request:

```
@RequestScoped
public class Customer {

    private String name;
    private String surname;

    public String getName(){
        return name;
    }

    public String getSurname(){
        return surname;
    }
}
```

The preceding CDI Bean can be safely injected into our former servlet; at the end of an HTTP session or HTTP request, all the instances associated with this scope are automatically destroyed, and thus, garbage collected:

```
public class HelloServlet extends HttpServlet {

    @Inject
    private Customer customer;

    public void doGet (HttpServletRequest req,
                        HttpServletResponse res)
            throws ServletException, IOException {
        // some code
    }
}
```

Named beans

In the earlier section, we came across the @Named annotation. Named beans allow us to easily inject our beans into other classes that depend on them and refer to them from JSF pages via the **Unified Expression Language** (UEL). Recall the earlier example:

```
@RequestScoped
@Named
public class Customer {

    private String name;
    private String surname;

    public String getName(){
        return name;
    }

    public String getSurname(){
        return surname;
    }
}
```

This class, decorated with the @Named annotation, can then be referenced from a JSF page:

```
<?xml version="1.0" encoding="UTF-8"?>
<!DOCTYPE html PUBLIC "-//W3C//DTD XHTML 1.0 Transitional//EN"
        "http://www.w3.org/TR/xhtml1/DTD/xhtml1-transitional.dtd">
<html xmlns="http://www.w3.org/1999/xhtml"
        xmlns:h="http://xmlns.jcp.org/jsf/html ">
    <h:body>
        <h:form>
            <h:panelGrid columns="2">
                <h:outputLabel for="name" value="Name" />
                <h:inputText id="name" value="#{customer.name}" />
                <h:outputLabel for="lastName" value="Surname" />
                <h:inputText id="surname" value="#{customer.surname}" />
                <h:panelGroup />
            </h:panelGrid>
        </h:form>
    </h:body>
</html>
```

By default, the name of the bean will be the class name with its first letter switched to lowercase; thus, the `Customer` bean can be referred to as `customer`.

If you want to use a different naming policy for your bean, you could use the `@Named` annotation as follows:

```
@Named(value="customNamed")
```

This way, we will be able to reference our CDI Beans using the identified `customNamed` value.

Instead of two `@RequestScoped` and `@Named` annotations, we can just use the `@Model` annotation that aggregates them.

CDI scopes

CDI Beans come with a set of predefined scopes and annotations, and each CDI Bean has a distinct life cycle determined by the scope it belongs to. The following table describes the built-in CDI scopes and annotations required to set these scopes:

Scope	Description
`@RequestScoped`	The `@RequestScoped` beans are shared during the length of a single request. This could be an HTTP request, a remote EJB invocation, a web services invocation, or message delivered to a Message Driven Bean (MDB). These beans are destroyed at the end of the request.
`@ConversationScoped`	The `@ConversationScoped` beans are shared across multiple requests in the same HTTP session but only if there is an active conversation maintained. Conversations are supported for JSF requests through the `javax.enterprise.context.Conversation` bean.
`@SessionScoped`	The `@SessionScoped` beans are shared between all the requests that occur in the same HTTP session and destroyed when the session is destroyed.
`@ApplicationScoped`	An `@ApplicationScoped` bean will live for as long as the application is running and be destroyed when the application is shut down.
`@Dependent`	The `@Dependent` beans are never shared between injection points. Any injection of a dependent bean is a new instance whose life cycle is bound to the life cycle of the object it is being injected into.

Other parts of Java EE can extend the list of available scopes. In Java EE 7 (in the Java Transaction API specification), a new scope has been introduced: `@TransactionScoped`. It bounds the life cycle of a bean with the current transaction. It is of course possible to introduce your own custom scopes.

In this chapter example, we will use the `RequestScoped` and `SessionScoped` beans to drive our simple ticket-booking system. In the next chapter, we will further enhance our example using `ConversationScoped` beans, which are a peculiar scope of CDI Beans. Providing a detailed explanation of all the named beans scopes is beyond the scope of this book. However, you can quench your thirst for knowledge by having a look at CDI Reference Implementation (JBoss Weld) docs at `http://docs.jboss.org/weld/reference/latest/en-US/html/scopescontexts.html`.

WildFly CDI implementation

Weld is the CDI Reference Implementation that originated as part of the Seam 3 project (`http://www.seamframework.org/`). Weld provides a complete CDI implementation, which can be a part of a Java EE 7 container such as WildFly.

Therefore, in order to run CDI-based applications on WildFly, you don't need to download any extra libraries as Weld is part of the server modules, and it is included in all server configurations as stated by the following extension:

```
<extension module="org.jboss.as.weld"/>
```

Having your module installed, however, does not mean that you can blindly use it in your applications. The general rule is that on WildFly, every application module is isolated from other modules; this means, by default, it does not have visibility on the AS modules, nor do the AS modules have visibility on the application.

To be accurate, we could state that all WildFly modules fall into the following three categories:

- **Modules that are implicitly added to your applications**: This category includes the most common APIs such as `javax.activation`, `javax.annotation`, `javax.security`, `javax.transaction`, `javax.jms`, and `javax.xml`. Using these modules does not require any extra effort as WildFly will add them for you if you are referencing them in your application.

- **Modules that are added on conditions**: This category includes `javax.ejb`, `org.jboss.resteasy` and `org.hibernate`, `org.jboss.as.web`, and finally `org.jboss.as.weld`. All these modules will be added on the condition that you supply its core annotations (such as `@Stateless` for EJB) or its core configuration files, for example, `web.xml` for a web application.

- **Modules that need to be explicitly enabled by the application deployer**:
  This includes all other modules, such as your custom modules, that you
  can add to the application server. The simplest way to allow you to have
  visibility to these modules is adding an explicit dependency to your
  `META-INF/MANIFEST.MF` file. For example, if you want to trigger the
  log4j dependency, you have to code your manifest file as follows:

```
Dependencies: org.apache.log4j
```

There is also a custom descriptor file available, which is used by WildFly to resolve
dependencies – `jboss-deployment-structure.xml`. It allows the developer to
configure the required dependencies in a fine-grained matter. The file is placed in the
top-level deployment file, in the `META-INF` directory (or `WEB-INF` for a web archive).
A sample content of the XML file (along with the XSD schema) is available at
`https://docs.jboss.org/author/display/WFLY8/Class+Loading+in+WildFly`.

So, if you have followed our checklist carefully, you will be aware that in order to
let Weld libraries kick in and automatically discover your CDI beans, you should
add its core configuration file, which is `beans.xml`. This file can be placed in your
application at the following locations:

- In your `WEB-INF` folder if you are developing a web application
- In your `META-INF` folder if you are deploying a JAR archive

The `beans.xml` file is based on the following schema reference:

```
<beans xmlns="http://xmlns.jcp.org/xml/ns/javaee"
       xmlns:xsi="http://www.w3.org/2001/XMLSchema-instance"
       xsi:schemaLocation="http://xmlns.jcp.org/xml/ns/javaee
       http://xmlns.jcp.org/xml/ns/javaee/beans_1_1.xsd"
       version="1.1" bean-discovery-mode="all">
</beans>
```

However, it is perfectly legal to place an empty `beans.xml` file in the correct location;
if you do so, CDI will be enabled in your application. If you, however, do not place a
`beans.xml` file, then only an annotated subset of classes will be considered as beans.
In such a case, the container will create beans only for classes that are annotated
with CDI-related annotations and ignore the rest. Most of the times, this is not the
behavior we expect, and it differs from the default mode in Java EE 6 (when the
`beans.xml` file was required).

You might have noticed that the `bean-discovery-mode` attribute is set to `all` in our `beans.xml` file. This allows us to configure the CDI discovery mode we discussed in the previous paragraph. It states that every legible class in our archive will be treated as a managed bean. You can place a `@Vetoed` annotation on a class to filter it out from the bean discovery process. It is also possible to set the discovery mode to `annotated` so that you can place a scope annotation for every class that you would like to use as a bean. This is the default value of the newest CDI version (also when there is no `beans.xml`), so be sure to set it on for all our samples.

Rethinking your ticketing system

Once you have learned the basics of CDI, we will start re-engineering the ticket-booking system using CDI Beans wherever necessary. We will turn it into a leaner application by dropping a few items such as remote interfaces or asynchronous methods, which are not needed in this example. By doing this, you will be able to focus just on the components that are actually used in the web application.

Let's create a new Maven project, just as we did in the previous chapter:

1. From the **File** menu, go to **New | Maven Project**; follow the wizard as we did previously (remember to check the **Create a simple project** option).

2. On the next screen, enter `com.packtpub.wflydevelopment.chapter4` as **Group Id**, `ticket-agency-cdi` as **Artifact Id**, and set packaging to **war**:

3. Click on **Finish**. The Maven plugin for Eclipse will generate a project structure for you that you know from the previous chapter.

4. The only difference is that besides the standard `java` (for Java classes) and `resources` (for configuration files) folders, a new directory named `webapp` that will host the web application views.

Adding the required dependencies

In order to compile and run the project, our Maven's `pom.xml` file will require the following set of dependencies known from the previous chapter:

```
<dependencies>
    <dependency>
        <groupId>javax</groupId>
        <artifactId>javaee-api</artifactId>
        <version>7.0</version>
        <scope>provided</scope>
    </dependency>
    <dependency>
        <groupId>org.jboss.logging</groupId>
        <artifactId>jboss-logging</artifactId>
        <version>3.1.4.GA</version>
        <scope>provided</scope>
    </dependency>
</dependencies>
```

We will also require two plugins from the previous chapter (note that we changed the extension of the filename from `jar` to `war`):

```
<build>
    <finalName>${project.artifactId}</finalName>
    <plugins>
        <!-- WildFly plugin to deploy the application -->
        <plugin>
            <groupId>org.wildfly.plugins</groupId>
            <artifactId>wildfly-maven-plugin</artifactId>
            <version>1.0.2.Final</version>
            <configuration>
                <filename>${project.build.finalName}.war</filename>
            </configuration>
        </plugin>
        <plugin>
            <groupId>org.apache.maven.plugins</groupId>
            <artifactId>maven-compiler-plugin</artifactId>
            <version>3.1</version>
```

```
            <configuration>
                <!-- enforce Java 8 -->
                <source>1.8</source>
                <target>1.8</target>
            </configuration>
        </plugin>
    </plugins>
</build>
```

In case you have any problems with the POM configuration file, be sure that you check the source code attached to this book and the material from the previous chapter.

Creating the beans

Once your project is properly configured, we can start modeling our beans. The first bean we will upgrade is TheatreBooker, which will drive the user session, accessing the ticket list from our TheatreBox bean:

```
package com.packtpub.wflydevelopment.chapter4.controller;

import com.packtpub.wflydevelopment.chapter4.boundary.TheatreBox;
import org.jboss.logging.Logger;

import javax.annotation.PostConstruct;
import javax.enterprise.context.SessionScoped;
import javax.faces.application.FacesMessage;
import javax.faces.context.FacesContext;
import javax.inject.Inject;
import javax.inject.Named;
import java.io.Serializable;

@Named [1]
@SessionScoped [2]
public class TheatreBooker implements Serializable {

    @Inject
    private Logger logger; [3]

    @Inject
    private TheatreBox theatreBox; [4]

    @Inject
    private FacesContext facesContext; [5]
```

```
    private int money;

    @PostConstruct
    public void createCustomer() {
        this.money = 100;
    }

    public void bookSeat(int seatId) {
        logger.info("Booking seat " + seatId);
        int seatPrice = theatreBox.getSeatPrice(seatId);

        if (seatPrice > money) {
            FacesMessage m = new FacesMessage(FacesMessage.SEVERITY_
ERROR, "Not enough Money!", "Registration unsuccessful"); [6]
            facesContext.addMessage(null, m);
            return;
        }

        theatreBox.buyTicket(seatId);

        FacesMessage m = new FacesMessage(FacesMessage.SEVERITY_INFO,
"Booked!", "Booking successful");
        facesContext.addMessage(null, m);
        logger.info("Seat booked.");

        money = money - seatPrice;
    }

    public int getMoney() {
        return money;
    }
}
```

As you can see, the bean has been tagged as `Named` [1], which means that it can be directly referenced in our JSF pages. The bean is `SessionScoped` [2] since it stores the amount of money available to the customer during its session.

We would also like to inject `logger` [3] and `FacesContextFacexContexts` [5] instead of manually defining it. To do this, we will need to register a bean that produces loggers, which are parameterized with the name of the class. We will cover this process of producing beans in a moment.

Finally, notice that we can safely inject EJBs into our CDI Beans using the `Inject` [4] annotation. Also, the reverse is perfectly legal, that is, injecting CDI Beans into EJBs.

Compared to our earlier project, here we don't raise Java exceptions when the customer is not able to afford a ticket. Since the application is web based, we simply display a warning message to the client using `JSF Faces Messages [6]`.

The other bean that we still use in our application is `TheatreInfo`, which has been moved to the `controller` package as it will actually provide the application with the list of available seats:

```java
package com.packtpub.wflydevelopment.chapter4.controller;

import com.google.common.collect.Lists;
import com.packtpub.wflydevelopment.chapter4.boundary.TheatreBox;
import com.packtpub.wflydevelopment.chapter4.entity.Seat;

import javax.annotation.PostConstruct;
import javax.enterprise.event.Observes;
import javax.enterprise.event.Reception;
import javax.enterprise.inject.Model;
import javax.enterprise.inject.Produces;
import javax.inject.Inject;
import javax.inject.Named;
import java.util.Collection;

@Model [1]
public class TheatreInfo {

    @Inject
    private TheatreBox box;

    private Collection<Seat> seats;

    @PostConstruct
    public void retrieveAllSeatsOrderedByName() {
        seats = box.getSeats();
    }

    @Produces [2]
    @Named
    public Collection<Seat> getSeats() {
        return Lists.newArrayList(seats);
    }
```

```
    public void onMemberListChanged(@Observes(notifyObserver =
Reception.IF_EXISTS) final Seat member) {
        retrieveAllSeatsOrderedByName(); [3]
    }
}
```

At first, have a look at the `@Model` annotation [1], which is an alias (we call this kind of annotations **stereotypes**) for two commonly used annotations: `@Named` and `@RequestScoped`. Therefore, this bean will be named into our JSF page and will carry a request scope.

Next, pay attention to the `getSeats` method. This method returns a list of seats, exposing it as a `producer` method [2].

> The `producer` method allows you to have control over the production of the dependency objects. As a Java factory pattern, they can be used as a source of objects whose implementation may vary at runtime or if the object requires some custom initialization that is not to be performed in the constructor.
>
> It can be used to provide any kind of concrete class implementation; however, it is especially useful to inject Java EE resources into your application.

One advantage of using a `@Producer` annotation for the `getSeats` method is that its objects can be exposed directly via JSF's **Expression Language** (EL), as we will see in a minute.

Finally, another feature of CDI that was unleashed in this example is the **observer**. An observer, as the name suggests, can be used to observe events. An observer method is notified whenever an object is created, removed, or updated. In our example, it allows the list of seats to be refreshed whenever they are needed.

> To be precise, in our example, we are using a conditional observer that is denoted by the expression `notifyObserver = Reception.IF_EXISTS`. This means that in practice, the `observer` method is only called if an instance of the component already exists. If not specified, the default option (`ALWAYS`) will be that the observer method is always called. (If an instance doesn't exist, it will be created.)

In the newest CDI version, it is possible to get additional information about the fired event in the observer by adding an `EventMetadata` parameter to the observer's method.

Whenever a change in our list of seats occurs, we will use the `javax.enterprise.event.Event` object to notify the observer about the changes. This will be done in our singleton bean, which gets injected with the seat's event [1], and notifies the observer by firing the event when a seat is booked [2]:

```
package com.packtpub.wflydevelopment.chapter4.boundary;
import javax.enterprise.event.Event;

@Singleton
@Startup
@AccessTimeout(value = 5, unit = TimeUnit.MINUTES)
public class TheatreBox {

    @Inject [1]
    private Event<Seat> seatEvent;

    @Lock(WRITE)
    public void buyTicket(int seatId) {
        final Seat seat = getSeat(seatId);
        final Seat bookedSeat = seat.getBookedSeat();
        addSeat(bookedSeat);

        seatEvent.fire(bookedSeat); [2]
    }
    // Rest of the code stays the same, as in the previous chapter
}
```

Earlier, we mentioned that a preconfigured logger should be injected to a bean if it requests it. We will create a simple logger producer that will use the information about the injection point (the bean that requests a logger) to configure an instance:

```
package com.packtpub.wflydevelopment.chapter4.util;

import javax.enterprise.inject.Produces;
import javax.enterprise.inject.spi.InjectionPoint;
import org.jboss.logging.Logger;

public class LoggerProducer {
```

```
    @Produces
    public Logger produceLogger(InjectionPoint injectionPoint) {
        return Logger.getLogger(injectionPoint.getMember().
getDeclaringClass().getName());
    }
}
```

We also allowed the injection of `FacesContext` instead of using the standard `FacesContext.getCurrentInstance()` static method. This context is used, for example, to display the stated error messages:

```
package com.packtpub.wflydevelopment.chapter4.util;

import javax.enterprise.context.RequestScoped;
import javax.enterprise.inject.Produces;
import javax.faces.context.FacesContext;

public class FacesContextProducer {

    @Produces
    @RequestScoped
    public FacesContext produceFacesContext() {
        return FacesContext.getCurrentInstance();
    }
}
```

The last class we will include in our project is the `Seat` bean, known from the previous chapter, which will be used as our model without any change (remember to include it in your project with a proper package).

Building the view

Once we have coded the server side of our example, creating the front end will be quite easy, as we have made all our resources available through CDI Beans.

One notable difference between some of the earlier editions of this book is that **Facelets** are now the preferred view technology for JSF. Earlier versions of JSF used **JavaServer Pages (JSP)** as their default view technology. As JSP technology predates JSF, using JSP with JSF sometimes felt unnatural or created problems. For example, the life cycle of JSPs is different from the life cycle of JSF.

Compared to the simpler request-response paradigm on which the JSP life cycle is based, the JSF life cycle is much more complex since the core of JSF is the MVC pattern, which has several implications. User actions in JSF-generated views take place in a client that does not have a permanent connection to the server. The delivery of user actions or page events is delayed until a new connection is established. The JSF life cycle must handle this delay between event and event processing. Also, the JSF life cycle must ensure that the view is correct before rendering it, and also that the JSF system includes a phase to validate inputs and another to update the model only after all the inputs pass validation.

Most of the time Facelets are used to build JavaServer Faces views using HTML-style templates and component trees. Templating is a useful feature available with Facelets that allows you to create a page that will act as the template for the other pages in an application (something like Struts Tiles). The idea is to obtain portions of reusable code without repeating the same code on different pages.

So here's the main application structure that contains a template page named `default.xhtml` that is referenced by views in the template attribute of the page's composition element. The template contains two main HTML `div` elements that will be used to contain the main application panel (`content`) and a footer div (`footer`), which will barely output the application title.

In order to add the template at first, add a new JSF page to the `WEB-INF/templates` folder of your application and name it `default.xhtml`:

```
<?xml version='1.0' encoding='UTF-8' ?>
<!DOCTYPE html PUBLIC "-//W3C//DTD XHTML 1.0 Transitional//EN"
        "http://www.w3.org/TR/xhtml1/DTD/xhtml1-transitional.dtd">
<html xmlns="http://www.w3.org/1999/xhtml"
      xmlns:h="http://xmlns.jcp.org/jsf/html"
      xmlns:ui="http://xmlns.jcp.org/jsf/facelets">
<h:head>
    <meta http-equiv="Content-Type" content="text/html;
charset=utf-8"/>
    <h:outputStylesheet name="style.css"/>
</h:head>
<h:body>
    <div id="container">
        <div id="content">
            <ui:insert name="content">
                [Template content will be inserted here]
            </ui:insert>
        </div>
```

```
            <div id="footer">
                <p>
                    <em>WildFly Development Ticket Booking example.</
em><br/>
                </p>
            </div>
        </div>
    </h:body>
</html>
```

Next, we will add the main page view, which will be embedded into your template.
For this purpose, add a JSF page named index.xhtml to the webapp folder of your
Maven project:

```
<?xml version="1.0" encoding="UTF-8"?>
<ui:composition xmlns="http://www.w3.org/1999/xhtml"
                xmlns:ui="http://xmlns.jcp.org/jsf/facelets"
                xmlns:f="http://xmlns.jcp.org/jsf/core"
                xmlns:h="http://xmlns.jcp.org/jsf/html"
                template="/WEB-INF/templates/default.xhtml"> [1]
    <ui:define name="content">
        <h1>TicketBooker Machine</h1>
        <h:form id="reg">
            <h3>Money: $ #{theatreBooker.money}</h3> [2]
            <h:messages errorClass="error" infoClass="info"
                        globalOnly="true"/>
            <h:panelGrid columns="1" border="1" styleClass="smoke">
                <h:dataTable var="_seat" value="#{seats}" [3]
                             rendered="#{not empty seats}"
styleClass="simpletablestyle">

                    <h:column>
                        <f:facet name="header">Id</f:facet>
                        #{_seat.id}
                    </h:column>

                    <h:column>
                        <f:facet name="header">Name</f:facet>
                        #{_seat.name}
                    </h:column>
                    <h:column>
                        <f:facet name="header">Price</f:facet>
                        #{_seat.price}$
                    </h:column>
                    <h:column>
```

```
                    <f:facet name="header">Booked</f:facet>
                    #{_seat.booked}
                </h:column>
                <h:column>
                    <f:facet name="header">Action</f:facet>
                    <h:commandButton id="book"
            action="#{theatreBooker.bookSeat(_seat.id)}"  [4]
                    disabled="#{_seat.booked}"
                    value="#{_seat.booked ? 'Reserved' : 'Book'}" />
                </h:column>

            </h:dataTable>
        </h:panelGrid>
    </h:form>
    </ui:define>
</ui:composition>
```

The ui:composition element is a templating tag that wraps content
to be included in another Facelet. Specifically, it will be included in the
default.xhtml[1] template.

The creation of the view is done in three steps. First, we will display the customer's
money [2], which is bound to the session variable called money.

> Notice how we directly reference CDI Beans (for example,
> TheatreBooker) from JSF expressions, just as we used to do
> with JSF Managed Beans.

The next thing on the checklist is printing all JSF messages [3] that are meant to be
produced by the application via the messages element.

The main task of this view is to produce a view of all tickets and let the users
purchase them. This is achieved by means of a dataTable object [3] that can
be used to produce a tabular list of objects, which are generally stored as
java.util.List in your beans.

Pay attention to the value attribute of the dataTable object:

```
<h:dataTable var="_seat" value="#{seats}"
rendered="#{not empty seats}" styleClass="simpletablestyle">
```

In this case, we don't directly reference a CDI Bean, but we reference an object that has been produced by a CDI Bean. To be precise, it has been produced by `TheatreInfo` that, as we have seen, has a `@Produces` and `@Named` annotation on our list of seats:

```
private List<Seat> seats;

@Produces
@Named
public List<Seat>getSeats() {
    return seats;
}
```

This `dataTable` object will be displayed only if it contains some data in it (as dictated by the `not empty seats` EL expression). In one of the `dataTable` columns, we have added `commandButton [4]` that will be used to book the seat displayed on that row. Notice one of the JSF 2 goodies here, as we call the `bookSeat` method of `TheatreBooker` passing an argument as one parameter, which is the `seatId` field.

JSF 2 facet suggestions

By enabling JSF 2 facets on your project configuration, you can enjoy some additional benefits while designing your views.

Enabling JSF 2 project facets takes half a minute. Right-click on your project and navigate to **Properties | Project Facets**. Then, select the **JSF 2.2 Project facets** checkbox and click on the **OK** button:

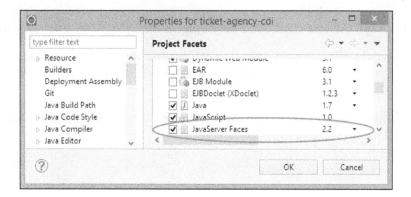

 Once the JSF facet is enabled, Eclipse will notify you that the JSF library configuration is missing; just disable the JSF library configuration that is a part of Maven's duty.

Once JSF 2 facets are configured, if you press *Ctrl* + Space bar before referencing a field or method, a suggestion pop-up window will let you choose the method or attribute of the Bean you want to reference.

Getting ready to run the application

OK, now your application is almost ready. We just need to configure a JSF mapping in a `web.xml` file as follows:

```
<web-app xmlns="http://xmlns.jcp.org/xml/ns/javaee"
         xmlns:xsi="http://www.w3.org/2001/XMLSchema-instance"
         xsi:schemaLocation="http://xmlns.jcp.org/xml/ns/javaee
http://xmlns.jcp.org/xml/ns/javaee/web-app_3_1.xsd"
         version="3.1">

    <servlet>
        <servlet-name>Faces Servlet</servlet-name>
        <servlet-class>javax.faces.webapp.FacesServlet</servlet-class>
        <load-on-startup>1</load-on-startup>
    </servlet>
    <servlet-mapping>
        <servlet-name>Faces Servlet</servlet-name>
        <url-pattern>/faces/*</url-pattern>
    </servlet-mapping>
    <welcome-file-list>
        <welcome-file>faces/index.xhtml</welcome-file>
    </welcome-file-list>
</web-app>
```

This will then run the `FacesServlet` servlet for all the pages at `/faces/*` url.

Finally, as stated previously, in order to activate our `war` file as an explicit bean archive, we need to add an empty `beans.xml` file to the `WEB-INF` folder of your application.

So, if you follow the same naming convention used in this chapter, you will end up with the following project structure:

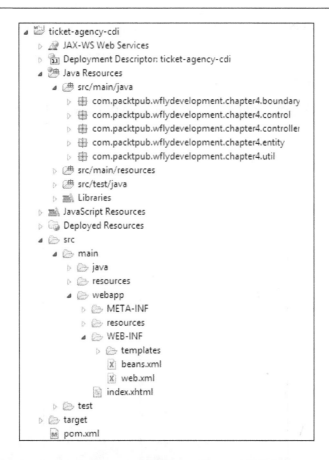

At this point, you must be familiar with building and deploying your Maven applications using Eclipse or a shell. Assuming that you are managing your application from a shell, start by building up the project using the following:

```
mvn package
```

Then, publish it using the WildFly Maven plugin, as we did in the previous chapter.

If the WildFly server is started, you can execute the following command:

```
mvn wildfly:deploy
```

If the WildFly server is not started, you can execute the following command and then the WildFly Maven plugin will automatically start an instance:

```
mvn wildfly:run
```

The application will be available at `http://localhost:8080/ticket-agency-cdi`.

Then, to do this with a unique command, you can execute the following:

```
mvn clean package wildfly:deploy
```

After so much work, you will be pleased to have your application running on your browser:

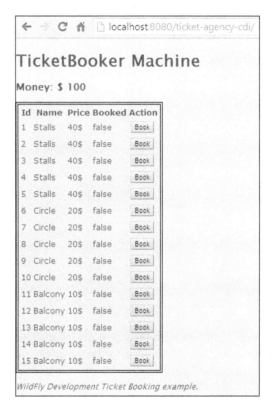

Right now, you will be able to book tickets up to the budget ($ 100) defined in your `SessionScoped` bean. So enjoy this first taste of JSF and CDI.

Of course, in this chapter, we only scratched the surface of JSF features. There is also a new higher-level approach introduced in JSF 2.2 that can be used for flow-based scenarios such as a shopping cart. The new feature is called **FacesFlow** and comes with a `@FlowScoped` annotation. However, we will now focus on adding some other features to our current application.

Combining the scheduler into our application

Up to now, we have not included the scheduler, which was in charge of simulating other customer-requesting tickets, into our application. This was not an oversight; as a matter of fact, introducing an external system in a web application poses some challenges. For example, what if the scheduler updates some data used by the application? How will the user know it?

There are several strategies to address this requirement; however, they all boil down to using some intelligence in your client application. For example, if you are familiar with web scripting languages, you can use the popular jQuery API to poll the server for some updates. The newest version of JSF 2.2 comes with great support for HTML5 and JavaScript frameworks, thanks to the custom data attributes and pass-through elements. These are simple mechanisms that allow the JSF's render kit to render parts of the page without any further changes so that custom tags may be interpreted by the browser (or a JavaScript framework).

Since not all Java EE developers might be skilled in JavaScript, we would rather show a simple and effective way to fulfill our requirement using **RichFaces** libraries (http://www.jboss.org/richfaces), which provide advanced Ajax support along with a rich set of ready-to-use components.

Installing RichFaces

Installing RichFaces requires a set of core libraries that are generally available at the RichFaces download page.

Additionally, you need to provide a set of third-party dependencies that are used by the RichFaces API. Never mind, that's what Maven is for! Start by adding the latest **Bill of Materials (BOM)** for the `RichFaces` API in the upper dependency-management section:

```
<dependencyManagement>
  ...
    <dependency>
        <groupId>org.richfaces</groupId>
        <artifactId>richfaces-bom</artifactId>
        <version>4.3.5.Final</version>
        <scope>import</scope>
        <type>pom</type>
    </dependencies>
</dependencyManagement>
```

Then, it's just a matter of adding the rich UI libraries and the core API:

```
<dependency>
    <groupId>org.richfaces.ui</groupId>
    <artifactId>richfaces-components-ui</artifactId>
</dependency>
<dependency>
    <groupId>org.richfaces.core</groupId>
    <artifactId>richfaces-core-impl</artifactId>
</dependency>
```

Making your application rich

Once we have installed RichFaces libraries, we will just need to reference them on each XHTML page in your project. Here's the new `index.xhtml` page using the RichFaces namespaces:

```
<ui:composition xmlns="http://www.w3.org/1999/xhtml"
                xmlns:h="http://xmlns.jcp.org/jsf/html"
                xmlns:f="http://xmlns.jcp.org/jsf/core"
                xmlns:ui="http://xmlns.jcp.org/jsf/facelets"
                xmlns:a4j="http://richfaces.org/a4j"
                xmlns:rich="http://richfaces.org/rich"
                template="/WEB-INF/templates/default.xhtml">
    <ui:define name="content">
        <f:view>

            <h:form>
                <a4j:poll id="poll" interval="2000"
                 enabled="#{pollerBean.pollingActive}"
                 render="poll,grid,bookedCounter"/>
                <rich:panel header="TicketBooker Machine"
                            style="width:350px">

                    <h2>Book your Ticket</h2>

                    <h3>Money: $ #{theatreBooker.money}</h3>
                    <h:messages errorClass="error" infoClass="info"
globalOnly="true"/>


                    <rich:dataTable id="grid" var="_seat"
                                    value="#{seats}"
                                    rendered="#{not empty seats}"
                                    styleClass="simpletablestyle">
```

```
                    <h:column>
                        <f:facet name="header">Id</f:facet>
                        #{_seat.id}
                    </h:column>

                    <h:column>
                        <f:facet name="header">Name</f:facet>
                        #{_seat.name}
                    </h:column>
                    <h:column>
                        <f:facet name="header">Price</f:facet>
                        #{_seat.price}
                    </h:column>
                    <h:column>
                        <f:facet name="header">Booked</f:facet>
                        #{_seat.booked}
                    </h:column>
                    <h:column>
                        <f:facet name="header">Action</f:facet>
                        <h:commandButton id="book"
action="#{theatreBooker.bookSeat(_seat.id)}"
disabled="#{_seat.booked}"
value="#{_seat.booked ? 'Not Available' :
'Book'}"/>
                    </h:column>
                </rich:dataTable>
        <h:outputText value="Booked seats on this page:
#{bookingRecord.bookedCount}"  id="bookedCounter" />
                </rich:panel>
            </h:form>
        </f:view>
    </ui:define>
</ui:composition>
```

We have highlighted the core enhancements added to this page. At first, as we said, we need to reference the RichFaces libraries at the top of the XHTML page.

Next, we added a rich Ajax component, **a4j:poll**, which does a simple but an effective job of polling the server for updates, allowing the re-rendering of our components—grid (which contains the main datatable), `poller` (to check whether it should still be running), and `bookedCounter`.

Additionally, this component references a CDI bean named `Poller`, which acts just as an on/off flag for our poller. We expect to turn off polling as soon as all the seats are sold out:

```
package com.packtpub.wflydevelopment.chapter4.controller;

import java.util.Optional;

import javax.enterprise.inject.Model;
import javax.inject.Inject;

import com.packtpub.wflydevelopment.chapter4.boundary.TheatreBox;
import com.packtpub.wflydevelopment.chapter4.entity.Seat;

@Model
public class Poller {

    @Inject
    private TheatreBox theatreBox;

    public boolean isPollingActive() {
        return areFreeSeatsAvailable();
    }

    private boolean areFreeSeatsAvailable() {
        final Optional<Seat> firstSeat = theatreBox.getSeats().
stream().filter(seat -> !seat.isBooked()).findFirst();
        return firstSeat.isPresent();
    }
}
```

Our seller service stays nearly the same as in the previous chapter (the only difference is the `logger` injection):

```
package com.packtpub.wflydevelopment.chapter4.control;

import com.packtpub.wflydevelopment.chapter4.boundary.TheatreBox;
import com.packtpub.wflydevelopment.chapter4.entity.Seat;
import org.jboss.logging.Logger;

import javax.annotation.Resource;
import javax.ejb.EJB;
import javax.ejb.Schedule;
import javax.ejb.Stateless;
import javax.ejb.Timer;
import javax.ejb.TimerService;
import javax.inject.Inject;
import java.util.Collection;
import java.util.Optional;

@Stateless
public class AutomaticSellerService {
```

```
    @Inject
    private Logger logger;

    @Inject
    private TheatreBox theatreBox;

    @Resource
    private TimerService timerService;

    @Schedule(hour = "*", minute = "*", second = "*/30", persistent =
false)
    public void automaticCustomer() {
        final Optional<Seat> seatOptional = findFreeSeat();

        if (!seatOptional.isPresent()) {
            cancelTimers();
            logger.info("Scheduler gone!");
            return; // No more seats
        }

        final Seat seat = seatOptional.get();

        theatreBox.buyTicket(seat.getId());

        logger.info("Somebody just booked seat number " + seat.
getId());
    }

    private Optional<Seat> findFreeSeat() {
        final Collection<Seat> list = theatreBox.getSeats();
        return list.stream().filter(seat -> !seat.isBooked()).
findFirst();
    }

    private void cancelTimers() {
        for (Timer timer : timerService.getTimers()) {
            timer.cancel();
        }
    }
}
```

Finally, we'll add a booking record, which will be bounded with the current view using the view scope. Its role will be to count the number of bookings done by the user in the current view (a single browser tab is considered a single view):

```
package com.packtpub.wflydevelopment.chapter4.controller;

import com.packtpub.wflydevelopment.chapter4.entity.Seat;

import java.io.Serializable;
```

```
import javax.enterprise.event.Observes;
import javax.faces.view.ViewScoped;
import javax.inject.Named;

@Named
@ViewScoped
public class BookingRecord implements Serializable {

    private int bookedCount = 0;

    public int getBookedCount() {
        return bookedCount;
    }

    public void bookEvent(@Observes Seat bookedSeat) {
        bookedCount++;
    }
}
```

You can experiment with the booked counter by trying to book tickets via two separate tabs in your browser.

You might have noticed that we placed two annotations on the bean: `@Named` and `@ViewScoped`. If you would like to define multiple beans with a specific set of CDI annotations, it would be a good idea to create your own custom annotation that already contains the desired ones. This kind of construction is called a stereotype. It is possible to incorporate the following elements:

- A default scope
- Optionally, interceptor bindings
- Optionally, a `@Named` annotation
- Optionally, an `@Alternative` annotation

To create a stereotype, you need to add the wanted annotations along with the `@Stereotype` annotation:

```
@ViewScoped
@Named
@Stereotype
@Target(ElementType.TYPE)
@Retention(RetentionPolicy.RUNTIME)
public @interface NamedView {

}
```

Now you can define the `BookinRecord` bean as follows:

```
@NamedView
public class BookingRecord implements Serializable {
    //Some code here
}
```

The `@Model` stereotype is available in CDI by default. It defines a request scoped named bean, and you can use it on your beans right out of the box.

Running the application

With all the libraries in place, you can now test run your new rich application. As you can see, every 30 seconds a ticket is sold out and buttons are turned, in real time, into **Not available**:

TicketBooker Machine

Book your Ticket

Money: $ 100

Id	Name	Price	Booked	Action
1	Stalls	40	true	Not Available
2	Stalls	40	true	Not Available
3	Stalls	40	false	Book
4	Stalls	40	false	Book
5	Stalls	40	false	Book
6	Circle	20	false	Book
7	Circle	20	false	Book
8	Circle	20	false	Book
9	Circle	20	false	Book
10	Circle	20	false	Book
11	Balcony	10	false	Book
12	Balcony	10	false	Book
13	Balcony	10	false	Book
14	Balcony	10	false	Book
15	Balcony	10	false	Book

Booked seats on this page: 0

WildFly Development Ticket Booking example.

Creating interceptors

There is one more CDI feature worth mentioning here, the interceptors. Sometimes, applications contain logic and cross-cutting multiple layers; the most simple example is logging. Under the Java EE platform, it can be achieved using interceptors. First, we need to create a new annotation:

```
@Inherited
@InterceptorBinding [1]
@Retention(RetentionPolicy.RUNTIME)
@Target({ ElementType.METHOD, ElementType.TYPE })
public @interface Logged {
    // empty
}
```

This annotation defines an interceptor binding. It can be used to specify methods that you would like to intercept. The bindings can be used on types as well; in that case, every method call on that type is intercepted. The most important part of this definition is the @InterceptorBinding [1] annotation. Be sure to add it!

Then, we have to create the interceptor definition itself:

```
@Interceptor
@Logged [1]
public class LoggingInterceptor implements Serializable {

    @AroundInvoke [2]
    public Object log(InvocationContext context) throws Exception {
        final Logger logger = Logger.getLogger(context.getTarget().
getClass());
        logger.infov("Executing method {0}", context.getMethod().
toString());
        return context.proceed() [3];
    }
}
```

We start by stating that our class is @Interceptor and it will be using the interceptor binding that we've defined earlier (@Logged [1]). Next, we create a method log that will be executed around every method execution (@AroundInvoke [2]) on annotated classes. Inside of it, we will call the context.proceed() method that will basically forward the call to the original receiver. Note that the interceptor can decide (based on some security logic, for instance) whether the call should be dropped. It could even analyze or change the returned value.

Finally, we have to enable it in the `beans.xml` file by adding the following code:

```
<interceptors>
  <class>com.packtpub.wflydevelopment.chapter4.util.LoggingInterceptor
    </class>
</interceptors>
```

Now, let's move on to just the annotated classes or methods that you want to log using the `@Logged` annotation. For instance, refer to the following:

```
@Named
@SessionScoped
@Logged
public class TheatreBooker implements Serializable {
    // Some code
}
```

All calls to the `TheatreBooker` public methods will now be logged in to the console:

```
21:02:11 INFO  [com.packtpub.wflydevelopment.chapter4 .controller.
TheatreBooker$Proxy$_$$_WeldSubclass] (default task-8) Executing
method public int com.packtpub.wflydevelopment.chapter4.controller.
TheatreBooker.getMoney()
```

In the case of multiple interceptors, the order in which they are executed is determined by the `@Interceptor.Priority` annotation. Interceptors with lowest priorities will be called first. Be sure to check the constants defined in the `Priority` annotation. Your own interceptor's priorities should be between the `APPLICATION` and `LIBRARY_AFTER` scope.

There are also other interesting CDI mechanisms that we will not cover in this book, but are definitely worth exploring: decorators and alternatives. Decorators are basically strongly typed interceptors that are focused on the business logic of your application. Alternatives can be used to provide alternative implementations for specific beans.

Are EJBs and JSF Managed Beans obsolete?

At the end of this chapter, we would like to give our honest opinion about a common question posed by developers, that is, how EJB, JSF Managed Beans, and CDI interact and where the boundary between them lies. Are there redundancies between them? It is indeed a bit confusing since there are now multiple component models available in Java EE.

JSF Managed Beans have been, for a long time, the actual glue between the application view and the business methods. Since Release 2.0 of JSF, you can declare JSF Managed Beans via an annotation, and the scopes are expanded with a **view scope** and the ability to create custom scopes. However, there is very little still going on for JSF Managed Beans. Most of its features can be replaced by CDI Beans that are much more flexible and allow you to have a better integration with other Java EE components. Even the view scope, in the newest version of JSF, has been implemented as a CDI custom scope (`javax.faces.view.ViewScoped`), which replaces the old `javax.faces.bean.ViewScoped` (notice the name of the package; it's a common mistake to mix them up).

On the other hand, EJBs, even though they use a less flexible injection mechanism, still maintain some unique features such as schedulable timers, asynchronous operations, and pooling that are essential for throttling and assuring that the application provides a good quality of service. Beginning from Java EE 7, EJBs no longer are the only components that have a transactional nature. The new `@Transactional` annotation allows you to use declarative transactions in CDI beans by simply placing it on selected methods.

Despite this, it's likely that EJBs are not disappearing from our code, rather it is likely (and desirable too) that they will continue to be used for some of their unique features. For the remaining part though, its functionality will be exposed via CDI instead of EJBs' own annotations such as `@Stateless` and `@EJB`.

Summary

In this chapter, we provided an introduction to CDI. We covered how JSF pages can access CDI-named beans as if they were JSF Managed Beans. We also covered how CDI makes it easy to inject dependencies into our code via the `@Inject` annotation. Additionally, we explained how we can add another library of the JBoss ecosystem (RichFaces) uncovering just one aspect of its potentiality.

Until now, we have worked with in-memory data, so it's time to introduce storage for our CDI applications using the Java Persistence API, which is the theme of the next chapter.

5
Combining Persistence with CDI

In the earlier chapters, we discussed Java EE, combining several technologies such as CDI. The examples so far, however, are based on a false assumption that all the information can be stored in memory. In this chapter, we will show how to use a persistent data store for our application in the form of a standard relational database.

The **Enterprise JavaBeans** (**EJB**) 3.2 specification includes a reference to a persistence specification called the **Java Persistence API** (**JPA**). It is an API to create, remove, and query Java objects called **entities** that can be used within both a compliant EJB 3.x container and a standard Java SE environment. In Java EE 7, it has been updated to Version 2.1. You can check out the current version of the specification I the JSR 338 at https://jcp.org/en/jsr/detail?id=338.

We need to warn you that in this chapter, you have a lot of things to learn and hence concepts will be coming at you from every direction. However, at the end of it, you will be able to appreciate exactly how to create and deploy a complete Java EE 7 application.

Specifically, we will cover the following topics:

- The key features of JPA
- How to create your entities and database schema
- How to manipulate the entities using CDI Beans and EJBs
- Delivering a frontend tier for our application using JSF and Facelets technology

Data persistence meets the standard

The arrival of an Enterprise Java Persistence standard based on the **Plain Old Java Object (POJO)** development model fills a substantial gap in the Java EE platform. The previous attempt (the EJB 2.x specification) missed the mark and created a stereotype of EJB entity beans that was awkward to develop and too heavy for many applications. Therefore, it never achieved widespread adoption or general approval in many sectors of the industry.

Software developers knew what they wanted, but many could not find it in the existing standards, so they decided to look elsewhere. What they found was lightweight persistence frameworks, both in the commercial and open source domains.

In contrast to EJB 2.x entity beans, the EJB 3.0 **Java Persistence API (JPA)** is a metadata driven POJO technology, that is, to save the data held in Java objects in a database, our objects are not required to implement an interface, extend a class, or fit into a framework pattern.

Another key feature of JPA is the query language called the **Java Persistence Query Language (JPQL)**, which gives you a way to define the queries in a portable way, independent of the particular database you use in an enterprise environment. JPA queries resemble SQL queries by syntax but operate against entity objects rather than directly with database tables.

Working with JPA

Inspired by ORM frameworks such as Hibernate, JPA uses annotations to map objects to a relational database. JPA entities are POJOs that do not extend any class nor implement any interface. You don't even need XML descriptors for your mapping. Actually, the JPA API is made up of annotations and only a few classes and interfaces. For example, we will mark the Company class as @Entity, shown as follows:

```
import javax.persistence.Entity;
import javax.persistence.Id;

@Entity
public class Company {

    // Some code

    @Id
    private String companyName;
```

```
public Company () {   }

// Some code
```

}

The preceding piece of code shows the minimal requirements for a class to be persistent, which are as follows:

- It must be identified as an entity using the @javax.persistence.Entity annotation
- It must have an identifier attribute annotated with @javax.persistence.Id
- It must have a no-argument constructor in at least the protected scope

Since you will learn better with an example, we will show how to create and deploy a sample JPA application in WildFly in the next section.

Adding persistence to our application

In order to persist data, JPA needs a relational database; we will use the PostgreSQL database, which is pretty popular among developers and can be downloaded for free from http://www.postgresql.org/download/. It is recommended to download the latest stable release of PostgreSQL 9.x and install it using the simple installation wizard. If you don't need a full-blown database, then keep in mind that later we will also show you how to use an in-memory database provided by WildFly, which can be a really useful alternative during development.

Setting up the database

We will create a database named ticketsystem; we will then add a user named jboss and assign him/her all privileges on the schemas.

Open a shell under the bin folder of your PostgreSQL installation and launch the executable psql -U postgres. Once logged in with the password from your installation, execute the following commands:

```
CREATE DATABASE ticketsystem;
CREATE USER jboss WITH PASSWORD 'jboss';
GRANT ALL PRIVILEGES ON DATABASE ticketsystem TO jboss;
```

Our simple schema will be made up of two tables: the SEAT table, which contains the list of all the available seats in the theatre, and the SEAT_TYPE table, which is used to categorize the seat types. The two tables are in a *1-n* relationship and the SEAT table hosts a foreign key that relates to the ID of the SEAT_TYPE table. We will, however, let JPA generate the schema for us, based on our class hierarchy, which we will model in a moment.

Installing the JDBC driver in WildFly

Database connectivity is carried out in Java using JDBC drivers, which are used either directly in your applications or behind the scenes in JPA. The PostgreSQL JDBC driver can be downloaded for free from `http://jdbc.postgresql.org/download.html`.

Once the download is complete, place the `postgresql-9.X-X.jdbc41.jar` file at a convenient location on your filesystem. We will now see how to install the JDBC driver in WildFly.

In JBoss AS 5 and 6, you used to install the JDBC driver in the `common/lib` folder of your server distribution. In the new modular server architecture (introduced in JBoss AS 7), you have more than one option to install your JDBC driver. The recommended approach consists of installing the driver as a module.

The procedure to install a new module requires creating a module path under `JBOSS_HOME/modules` and placing the `.jar` libraries and the `module.xml` file (that declares the module name and its dependencies) there.

In our example, we will add the following units to our filesystem:

- `JBOSS_HOME/modules/org/postgresql/main/postgresql-9.3-1101.jdbc41.jar`
- `JBOSS_HOME/modules/org/postgresql/main/module.xml`

Start by simply creating the required directories in your WildFly installation (to which the `JBOSS_HOME` variable points), and copying the downloaded JAR file to them.

Now, in the main folder, add a file named `module.xml`. This file contains the actual module definition; the most interesting part of it is the module name (`org.postgresql`), which corresponds to the module attribute defined in your data source.

Next, you need to state the path to the JDBC driver resource and the module dependencies, as follows:

```
<module xmlns="urn:jboss:module:1.1" name="org.postgresql">
  <resources>
    <resource-root path="postgresql-9.3-1101.jdbc41.jar"/>
  </resources>
  <dependencies>
    <module name="javax.api"/>
    <module name="javax.transaction.api"/>
  </dependencies>
</module>
```

We are done with the module installation. Now we need to define a data source in our configuration that will use this module and hold a pool of connections in our PostgreSQL database. In order to do this, you can edit `standalone.xml`/`domain.xml`, adding a driver element to the data source's subsystem (be sure to merge this configuration with any existing data sources in your configuration):

```
<subsystem xmlns="urn:jboss:domain:datasources:1.0">
  <datasources>
    <datasource jta="false"
        jndi-name="java:jboss/datasources/wflydevelopment"
        pool-name="wflydevelopment" enabled="true">
            <connection-url>
             jdbc:postgresql://localhost:5432/ticketsystem
            </connection-url>
            <driver-class>org.postgresql.Driver</driver-class>
            <driver>postgresql</driver>
            <security>
                <user-name>jboss</user-name>
                <password>jboss</password>
            </security>
    </datasource>
    <drivers>
            <driver name="postgresql" module="org.postgresql"/>
    </drivers>
  </datasources>
</subsystem>
```

As you can see, the new configuration file borrows the same XML schema definition from the earlier JBoss AS configurations, so it should not be difficult to migrate to the new schema. Basically, you will define the connection path to the database using the `connection-url` string and the JDBC driver class with the `driver` section.

Since JBoss AS 7.1.0, it's mandatory that the data source be bound to the `java:/` or `java:jboss/` JNDI namespace. This will standardize the resources definition among developers, avoiding bizarre JNDI bindings.

Using the command-line interface to create a new data source

The application server provides more than one option to add a data source to your configuration. We will just mention the command-line interface approach, which can be quite useful, especially if you plan to modify your configuration using script files.

Launch the `jboss-cli.sh` script (or `jboss-cli.bat`) and connect to the application server, as follows:

```
[disconnected /] connect
[standalone@localhost:9990 /]
```

Now issue the following command, which actually creates a new data source, accomplishing the same goal we obtained by editing the configuration file:

```
/subsystem=datasources/data-source=wflydevelopment:add(jndi-
name=java:jboss/datasources/wflydevelopment, driver-name=postgresql,
connection-url= jdbc:postgresql://localhost:5432/ticketsystem,user-
name="jboss",password="jboss")
```

The CLI should respond with a `success` message if everything goes well.

Creating the Maven project

The application that we're going to create in this chapter will require only standard Java EE 7 APIs from us. Having knowledge from previous chapters, you should be able to set up a project for this chapter by yourself! Just use your favorite IDE and create a Maven project with `war` type. Remember to include the configuration for Java SE 8, `beans.xml` and `faces-config.xml` files. If you face any problems, remember that code samples available with this book contain a full project based on this example.

Adding the Maven configuration

Now that your Maven skeleton is set up, we will include the required dependencies so that Eclipse will be able to compile your classes as you code them. The only dependency you will need for this type is `javaee-api`:

```
<dependency>
    <groupId>javax</groupId>
    <artifactId>javaee-api</artifactId>
    <version>7.0</version>
    <scope>provided</scope>
</dependency>
```

Cooking entities

Now that we're done with the configuration part, we will add our entities to the project. Some valuable options exist to autogenerate our entities, starting with the database schema. For example, the Eclipse's **File** menu includes an option **JPA Entities from Table** that (once a connection has been set up in the database) allows you to reverse your DB schema (or a part of it) into Java entities.

If you are willing to try this option, remember that you need to activate the **Eclipse JPA** facet in your project, from **Project Properties**, as shown in the following screenshot:

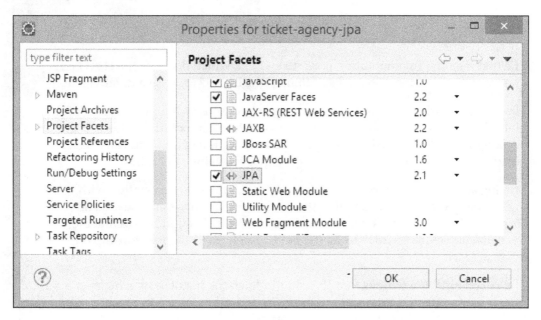

One more option is mentioned in *Appendix, Rapid Development Using JBoss Forge*, which discusses JBoss Forge, a powerful, rapid application development (aimed at Java EE) and project comprehension tool.

In this chapter, we will focus on generating SQL scripts from Java classes. Whatever your strategy is, the expected outcome needs to conform to the following entities. Here is the first one, SeatType, which maps the table SEAT_TYPE:

```
@Entity [1]
@Table(name="seat_type") [2]
public class SeatType implements Serializable {

    @Id    [3]
    @GeneratedValue(strategy=GenerationType.IDENTITY)
    private Long id;

    private String description;

    private int price;

    private int quantity;

    //bi-directional many-to-one association to Seat
    @OneToMany(mappedBy="seatType", fetch=FetchType.EAGER) [4]
    private List<Seat> seats;

    // Getters and Setters omitted for brevity
}
```

The first meaningful annotation is @Entity [1], which declares the class Entity. The @Table [2] annotation is used to map the bean class with a database table.

The @Id annotation, [3], is a mandatory one; it describes the primary key of the table. Along with @Id, there is the @GeneratedValue annotation. This is used to declare that the database is in charge of generating the value. You can check the Javadoc of this class to explore other strategies for value generation.

Moving along, the @OneToMany annotation [4] defines an association with one-to-many cardinality. Actually, the SeatType class has many seats. The corresponding Seat reference is contained in a list collection. We define the mappedBy attribute in order to set the field, which owns the relationship on the many side.

The fetch attribute defines that JPA should fetch the list of seats whenever a seat type is loaded from the database. A lazy configuration for a relationship would cause the list to be fetched on the first call to that field.

Finally, note that we have not included here, for the sake of brevity, the field getters and setters that have been generated.

Let's take a look at the `Seat` entity:

```
@Entity
public class Seat implements Serializable {

    private static final long serialVersionUID = 89897231L;

    @Id
    @GeneratedValue(strategy=GenerationType.IDENTITY)
    private Long id;

    private boolean booked;

    //bi-directional many-to-one association to SeatType
    @ManyToOne [1]
    @JoinColumn(name="seat_id") [2]
    private SeatType seatType;

    // Getters and Setters omitted for brevity

}
```

As you can see, the `Seat` entity has the corresponding `@ManyToOne` [1] annotation, which naturally complements the `@OneToMany` relationship. The `@JoinColumn` [2] notifies the JPA engine that the `seatType` field is mapped through the foreign key of the database's seat ID.

Adding Bean Validation

Bean Validation (JSR-303) is a validation model available as part of the Java EE 6 platform. The new 1.1 version (**JSR-349**) is a part of Java EE 7. The Bean Validation model is supported by constraints in the form of annotations placed on a field, method, or class of a JavaBeans component, such as a managed bean.

In our example, the `SeatType` entity will be created using an input form; therefore, we will need to validate the data that has been entered by the user.

In our example, we will place a `@javax.validation.constraints.NotNull` constraint in every field that is part of the `SeatType` entry form, and a more complex constraint in the `description` field, which will set the maximum size for the seat description to 25 (the `@javax.validation.constraints.Size` constraint) and allow just letters and spaces in it (the `@javax.validation.constraints.Pattern` constraint):

```
@Entity
@Table(name="seat_type)
public class SeatType implements Serializable {

    private static final long serialVersionUID = 3643635L;

    @Id
    @GeneratedValue(strategy=GenerationType.IDENTITY)
    private Long id;

    @NotNull
    @Size(min = 1, max = 25, message = "You need to enter a Seat
Description (max 25 char)")
    @Pattern(regexp = "[A-Za-z ]*", message = "Description must
contain only letters and spaces")
    private String description;

    @NotNull
    private Integer price;

    @NotNull
    private Integer quantity;

    private SeatPosition position;

    // Getters/Setters here
}
```

As you can see, we can also place a description on a constraint, which can be used to provide a customized error message to the JSF layer should the data fail to pass the constraint. You can check the Oracle documentation for a full list of constraints available at http://docs.oracle.com/javaee/7/tutorial/doc/bean-validation001.htm#GIRCZ.

We also have added a seat position information to our seat type. It is a simple enum:

```java
public enum SeatPosition {
    ORCHESTRA("Orchestra", "orchestra"), BOX("Box", "box"),
BALCONY("Balcony", "balcony");

    private final String label;
    private final String dbRepresentation;

    private SeatPosition(String label, String dbRepresentation) {
        this.label = label;
        this.dbRepresentation = dbRepresentation;

    }

    public String getDatabaseRepresentation() {
        return dbRepresentation;
    }

    public String getLabel() {
        return label;
    }
}
```

When we save our `SeatType` entity in the database, we will also store the enum value with it. Earlier versions of JPA gave us two options to address it automatically (besides manually managing their status), `@Enumarated(EnumType.STRING)` and `@Enumarated(EnumType.ORDINAL)`; both had their flaws. The first one is sensitive towards enum renaming; the entities in the database will have the full name of the enum stored (which sometimes is also a waste of the storage space). The second one could create problems when the order of enums would be changed (because it stored the index of the enum value). From JPA 2.1, we can create a converter, which will automatically convert our enum attributes to specific entries in the database. We only need to create an annotated class, which implements the `AttributeConverter` interface:

```java
import javax.persistence.AttributeConverter;
import javax.persistence.Converter;

@Converter(autoApply = true)
public class SeatPositionConverter implements AttributeConverter<SeatPosition, String> {
```

```
    @Override
    public String convertToDatabaseColumn(SeatPosition attribute) {
        return attribute.getDatabaseRepresentation();
    }

    @Override
    public SeatPosition convertToEntityAttribute(String dbData) {
        for (SeatPosition seatPosition : SeatPosition.values()) {
            if (dbData.equals(seatPosition.
getDatabaseRepresentation())) {
                return seatPosition;
            }
        }
        throw new IllegalArgumentException("Unknown attribute value "
+ dbData);
    }
}
```

That's all, no additional configuration is required. The `autoApply` attribute set to `true` signals JPA to take care of all of our `SeatPosition` enums in entities.

Configuring persistence

The Entity API looks great and is very intuitive, but how does the server know which database is supposed to store/query the entity objects? The `persistence.xml` file, which will be placed under `src/main/resources/META-INF` of your project, is the standard JPA configuration file. By configuring this file, you can easily switch from one persistence provider to another and thus, also from one application server to another (believe it or not, this is a huge leap towards application server compatibility).

In the `persistence.xml` file, we will basically need to specify the persistence provider and the underlying data source used. Simply create the following file under `src/main/resources/persistence.xml`:

```
<?xml version="1.0" encoding="UTF-8"?>
<persistence xmlns="http://xmlns.jcp.org/xml/ns/persistence"
             xmlns:xsi="http://www.w3.org/2001/XMLSchema-instance"
             xsi:schemaLocation="http://xmlns.jcp.org/xml/ns/
persistence http://xmlns.jcp.org/xml/ns/persistence/persistence_2_1.
xsd"
             version="2.1">
    <persistence-unit name="primary">
        <jta-data-source>java:jboss/datasources/ExampleDS</jta-data-
source>
```

```
        <class>com.packtpub.wflydevelopment.chapter5.entity.Seat</
class>
        <class>com.packtpub.wflydevelopment.chapter5.entity.SeatType</
class>
        <properties>
            <property name="javax.persistence.schema-generation.
database.action" value="drop-and-create"/>
        </properties>
    </persistence-unit>
</persistence>
```

We have highlighted the most important attributes in `persistence.xml`. The `name` attribute is a mandatory element, which will be used to reference the persistence unit from our Enterprise JavaBeans.

In the example code, we use the WildFly built-in memory H2 database (`http://www.h2database.com/`) available by default at `java:jboss/datasources/ExampleDS` (so that it is possible to run the example without any setup). However, you can use a configured PostgreSQL connection here, `java:jboss/datasources/wflydevelopment`, which we created earlier. In Java EE 7, you could even omit the whole `jta-data-source` tag. Every container is now obliged to provide a default data source for applications to use. For WildFly, it would be the aforementioned H2 database.

We also define the classes that should be considered as entities. This is an optional step; if the entities are in the same archive as the `persistence.xml` file, they will be autodiscovered.

In previous JPA versions, almost every configuration needed some provider-specific properties. In JPA 2.1, a number of standard properties were added, such as presented `javax.persistence.schema-generation.database.action`. The `drop-and-create` value can be used to create and drop your database tables each time you deploy your application. This can be an advantage if you want to start with a clean storage each time you deploy the application.

However, it is also possible to instruct JPA to generate SQL scripts for you, so you can manually apply them to the database. Simply add the following entries to your `persistence-unit` tag:

```
<property name="javax.persistence.schema-generation-target"
value="scripts"/>
<property name="javax.persistence.ddl-create-script-target"
value="createSeats.sql"/>
<property name="javax.persistence.ddl-drop-script-target"
value="dropSeats.sql"/>
```

If you don't specify the location by specifying an additional property, then the generated scripts will be placed in the JBOSS_HOME/bin directory, with the names that you provided in the configuration. The names can be absolute paths, so you can get the scripts to any place in your filesystem (if WildFly is permitted to write them there of course).

Adding producer classes

Producer classes have been introduced in the earlier chapter as a means of providing some resources through CDI to our application. In this example, we will use it to produce many resources, such as the JPA Entity Manager and the list of objects that are transferred to the JSF views. For this reason, we provided the LoggerProducer, FacesContextProducer, and EntityManagerProducer classes that contain some general-purpose resources and single instances of the SeatProducer and SeatTypeProducer classes, which will be used to produce collections of entities.

Here's the content of the three basic producer classes:

```
public class LoggerProducer {

    @Produces
    public Logger produceLoger(InjectionPoint injectionPoint) {
        return Logger.getLogger(injectionPoint.getMember().
getDeclaringClass().getName());
    }
}


public class FacesContextProducer {

    @Produces
    @RequestScoped
    public FacesContext produceFacesContext() {
        return FacesContext.getCurrentInstance();
    }
}

public class EntityManagerProducer {

    @Produces
    @PersistenceContext
    private EntityManager em;
}
```

As you can see, these classes will be the factory for the following three kinds of resources:

- `EntityManager`: This will resolve the primary persistence unit since there is just one persistence unit defined
- `java.util.Logger`: This will trace some information on the server console
- `FacesContext`: This will be used to output some JSF messages on the screen

Producers versus the Java EE 5 @Resource injection

If you have never used the dependency injections framework before, you might wonder what the benefit of adding an extra layer to produce some container resources is. The reason becomes evident once you need to change some configuration elements, such as the persistence unit. With the older Java EE 5 approach, you will be forced to change the @Resource injection's details wherever they are used; however, using a producer method for it will centralize resource creation, making changes trivial.

Next, we will add some entity producers; let's add the `SeatTypeProducer` and `SeatProducer` classes:

```
@javax.enterprise.context.RequestScoped
public class SeatTypeProducer {

    @Inject
    private SeatTypeDao seatTypeDao;

    private List<SeatType> seatTypes;

    @PostConstruct
    public void retrieveAllSeatTypes() {
        seatTypes = seatTypeDao.findAll();
    }

    @Produces
    @Named
    public List<SeatType> getSeatTypes() {
        return seatTypes;
    }

    public void onListChanged(@Observes(notifyObserver = Reception.
IF_EXISTS) final SeatType member) {
        retrieveAllSeatTypes();
    }
}
```

If you have gone through our example in *Chapter 4, Learning Context and Dependency Injection*, you will find nothing new here; as you can see, the class will merely produce a collection of seatTypes, which is tagged as @Named so that they can be accessed from JSF EL as well. Additionally, the class contains an observer handler method (onListChanged), which will be fired when data in the collection is changed.

The collection data is filled using the retrieveAllSeatTypes method (loaded the first and only time when the class is constructed) of the SeatTypeDao CDI Bean. We will define this bean in a moment; right now, we will add the last producer class used in this example, the SeatProducer bean:

```
@javax.enterprise.context.RequestScoped
public class SeatProducer implements Serializable {

    @Inject
    private SeatDao seatDao;

    private List<Seat> seats;

    @PostConstruct
    public void retrieveAllSeats() {
        seats = seatDao.findAllSeats();
    }

    @Produces
    @Named
    public List<Seat> getSeats() {
      return seats;
    }

    public void onMemberListChanged(@Observes(notifyObserver =
Reception.IF_EXISTS) final Seat member) {
        retrieveAllSeats();
    }
}
```

The preceding bean will be used to produce the list of Seat objects that will actually be available for booking.

Coding queries for your application

As you can see from the earlier code, the producer classes make use of beans named `SeatDao` and `SeatTypeDao` to fill their collections of data. These beans perform some simple finds on the `Seat` and `SeatType` objects, as shown in the following code:

```java
@Stateless
public class SeatDao extends AbstractDao<Seat> {

    public SeatDao() {
        super(Seat.class);
    }
}


@Stateless
public class SeatTypeDao extends AbstractDao<SeatType> {

    public SeatTypeDao() {
        super(SeatType.class);
    }
}

@TransactionAttribute(TransactionAttributeType.REQUIRED)
public abstract class AbstractDao<T extends Serializable> implements
Serializable {

    private final Class<T> clazz;

    @Inject
    private EntityManager em;

    public AbstractDao(Class<T> clazz) {
        this.clazz = clazz;
    }

    public T find(Object id) {
        return em.find(clazz, id);
    }

    public void persist(final T entity) {
        em.persist(entity);
    }
```

```
    public List<T> findAll() {
        final CriteriaQuery<T> criteriaQuery =
em.getCriteriaBuilder().createQuery(clazz);
        criteriaQuery.select(criteriaQuery.from(clazz));
        return em.createQuery(criteriaQuery).getResultList();
    }

    public void deleteAll() {
        final CriteriaDelete<T> criteriaDelete =
em.getCriteriaBuilder().createCriteriaDelete(clazz);
        criteriaDelete.from(clazz);
        em.createQuery(criteriaDelete).executeUpdate();
    }
}
```

As you can see, both `SeatDao` and `SeatTypeDao` beans extend the generic `AbstractDao` class. It wraps `EntityManager` and provides basic type-safe CRUD operations such as `findAll`, `persist`, and so on using the JPA Criteria API. JPA allows execution of the following three types of queries:

- **Native SQL**: These queries use the standard SQL language. When using this type of queries, you have to remember queries can be incompatible when migrating between different databases.

- **Java Persistence Query Language (JPQL)**: These queries can be formed using special language similar to SQL. In practice, this method is often hard to maintain without good IDE support, especially during refactoring. These queries can also be compiled at startup, which means that they are not resolved multiple times. Finally, they can be used by a caching mechanism to avoid unnecessary database operations for queries that are called frequently. You can define a query and its name in the entity in the `@NamedQuery(name="...", query="...")` annotation.

- **Criteria API**: These queries can be formed by simply executing Java methods and the usage of appropriate objects. Since JPA 2.1, it's possible to perform bulk updates and deletions through this API.

Let's make a simple comparison of these three methods using an example. We want to just get all the objects of a given type. Using native SQL, this query would look like this:

```
entityManager.createNativeQuery("SELECT * from seat_type").
getResultList()
```

As you can see, it uses standard SQL in the form of a string. Now let's look at JPQL:

```
entityManager.createQuery("select seatType from SeatType seatType").
getResultList();
```

It's easy to notice its similarity to SQL but a bit different. It uses, for example, class name instead of table name. However, again, it's a query in a string. The last example is the Criteria API:

```
final CriteriaQuery<SeatType> criteriaQuery =
                em.getCriteriaBuilder().createQuery(SeatType.class);
criteriaQuery.select(criteriaQuery.from(SeatType.class));
em.createQuery(criteriaQuery).getResultList();
```

At first glance, it looks like the most complicated one, but it has some advantage, that is, it does not use any strings (which are usually error-prone and hard to refactor). Both JPQL and Criteria API have many improvements in the newest JPA version, concerning join operations using the on condition, database functions support, and arithmetic subqueries.

You may ask yourself, "Which one should I use?" It's a hard question because all of them have their pros and cons so it depends on the specific case. Basically, Criteria query and named queries are normally a safe bet. Native SQL should have a really good justification, as it's usually not portable between different vendors and cannot be validated by JPA before the execution.

Adding services to your application

Until now, we coded all the information that will be visible to the user through the application screen. What is obviously missing here is all the business logic that translates ultimately into inserting data or updating the existing data. For this reason, we will now add two classes; first, under com.packtpub.wflydevelopment.chapter5.control package and second under com.packtpub.wflydevelopment.chapter5.controller. The first one is TicketService, which is a stateless EJB that will be used to perform the core business logic of this application, and the second one is our stateful EJB's counterpart, the BookerService class. Let's start with the stateless EJB:

```
@Stateless
public class TicketService {

    @Inject
    private Logger log;
```

```
    @Inject
    private Event<SeatType> seatTypeEventSrc;

    @Inject
    private Event<Seat> seatEventSrc;

    @Inject
    private SeatDao seatDao;

    @Inject
    private SeatTypeDao seatTypeDao;

    public void createSeatType(SeatType seatType) throws Exception {
        log.info("Registering " + seatType.getDescription());
        seatTypeDao.persist(seatType);
        seatTypeEventSrc.fire(seatType);
    }

    public void createTheatre(List<SeatType> seatTypes) {
        for (SeatType type : seatTypes) {
            for (int ii = 0; ii < type.getQuantity(); ii++) {
                final Seat seat = new Seat();
                seat.setBooked(false);
                seat.setSeatType(type);
                seatDao.persist(seat);
            }
        }
    }

    public void bookSeat(long seatId) {
        final Seat seat = seatDao.find(seatId);
        seat.setBooked(true);
        seatDao.persist(seat);
        seatEventSrc.fire(seat);
    }

    public void doCleanUp() {
        seatDao.deleteAll();
        seatTypeDao.deleteAll();
    }
}
```

Why has this component been coded as an EJB instead of a CDI Bean?

One of the main advantages of using EJBs is that they are inherently transactional components. However, in Java EE 7, we can use CDI Beans with an additional `@Transactional` annotation. The choice now is up to the developer, but EJBs can still prove useful in some cases, even for local calls; for example, we can easily demarcate security for them (which we will do in the future chapters).

This service is made up of four methods. The first is the `createSeatType` method, which will be used in the first application screen to add a new `SeatType` object to our theatre. The next method, `createTheatre`, will be invoked once we are done with setting up our theatre; so we create the list of seats that will be available for booking in the next screen.

Next in the list is the `bookSeat` method, which, as you might have guessed, will be used to book a seat. Finally, the `doCleanUp` method is actually used to perform a cleanup if you want to restart the application.

The last piece of our puzzle is the `BookerService` class, which adds a tiny session layer to your application:

```java
@Named
@javax.faces.view.ViewScoped
public class BookerService implements Serializable {

    private static final long serialVersionUID = -4121692677L;

    @Inject
    private Logger logger;

    @Inject
    private TicketService ticketService;

    @Inject
    private FacesContext facesContext;

    private int money;

    @PostConstruct
    public void createCustomer() {
        this.money = 100;
    }
```

```
    public void bookSeat(long seatId, int price) {
        logger.info("Booking seat " + seatId);

        if (price > money) {
            final FacesMessage m = new FacesMessage(FacesMessage.
SEVERITY_ERROR, "Not enough Money!",
                    "Registration successful");
            facesContext.addMessage(null, m);
            return;
        }

        ticketService.bookSeat(seatId);

        final FacesMessage m = new FacesMessage(FacesMessage.SEVERITY_
INFO, "Registered!", "Registration successful");
        facesContext.addMessage(null, m);
        logger.info("Seat booked.");

        money = money - price;
    }

    public int getMoney() {
        return money;
    }
}
```

The preceding class uses the view scope, which we already described in the previous chapters.

Adding a controller to drive user requests

The link between the persistence layer and the user's view falls on the TheatreSetupService bean, which will drive requests to the actual services exposed by our application. Since this bean will be bound to RequestScope and we need to expose it to our views as well (using @Named), we can use the convenient @Model annotation for it, which is a sum of the following two attributes:

```
@Model
public class TheatreSetupService {

    @Inject
    private FacesContext facesContext;

    @Inject
```

```
    private TicketService ticketService;

    @Inject
    private List<SeatType> seatTypes;

    @Produces [1]
    @Named
    private SeatType newSeatType;

    @PostConstruct
    public void initNewSeatType() {
        newSeatType = new SeatType();
    }

    public String createTheatre() {
        ticketService.createTheatre(seatTypes);
        return "book";
    }

    public String restart() {
        ticketService.doCleanUp();
        return "/index";   [4]
    }

    public void addNewSeats() throws Exception {
        try {
            ticketService.createSeatType(newSeatType);

            final FacesMessage m = new FacesMessage(FacesMessage.
SEVERITY_INFO, "Done!", "Seats Added");
            facesContext.addMessage(null, m);
            initNewSeatType();
        } catch (Exception e) {
            final String errorMessage = getRootErrorMessage(e);
            FacesMessage m = new FacesMessage(FacesMessage.SEVERITY_
ERROR, errorMessage, "Error while saving data");
            facesContext.addMessage(null, m);
        }
    }

    private String getRootErrorMessage(Exception e) {
        // Default to general error message that registration failed.
        String errorMessage = "Registration failed. See server log for
more information";
```

```
        if (e == null) {
            // This shouldn't happen, but return the default messages
            return errorMessage;
        }

        // Start with the exception and recurse to find the root cause
        Throwable t = e;
        while (t != null) {
            // Get the message from the Throwable class instance
            errorMessage = t.getLocalizedMessage();
            t = t.getCause();
        }
        // This is the root cause message
        return errorMessage;
    }

    public List<SeatPosition> getPositions() {
        return Arrays.asList(SeatPosition.values());
    }

}
```

The `TheatreSetupService` class is expected to complete the following tasks:

1. At first, the `TheatreSetupService` class produces a `SeatType` object [1] and exposes it to the JSF View layer using the `@Named` annotation.

> This technique is a great addition provided by CDI since it removes the need to create a boilerplate object, `SeatType`, to transport the information from the view to the services. The `SeatType` object is produced by the controller and will be populated by the JSF view and persisted by the `TheatreSetupService` class.

2. It then drives user navigation between the application screens by returning to the home page [4].

3. We are done with the Java classes. You should now check to make sure that your project structure matches the following screenshot:

```
┌─────────────────────────────────────────────────────────────────┐
│ 🖹 Project Explorer ⊠          ⇦ ⇨ ⊕ │ 🗖 🗐 │ 🖳 ▽ ⊟ 🗖 │
│ ────────────────────────────────────────────────────────────── │
│ ticket-agency-jpa                                               │
│   ▲ 🗁 src/main/java                                            │
│     ▲ ⊞ com.packtpub.wflydevelopment.chapter5.control           │
│       ▷ 🗎 AbstractDao.java                                     │
│       ▷ 🗎 SeatDao.java                                         │
│       ▷ 🗎 SeatProducer.java                                    │
│       ▷ 🗎 SeatTypeDao.java                                     │
│       ▷ 🗎 SeatTypeProducer.java                                │
│       ▷ 🗎 TicketService.java                                   │
│     ▲ ⊞ com.packtpub.wflydevelopment.chapter5.controller        │
│       ▷ 🗎 BookerService.java                                   │
│       ▷ 🗎 TheatreSetupService.java                             │
│     ▲ ⊞ com.packtpub.wflydevelopment.chapter5.entity            │
│       ▷ 🗎 Seat.java                                            │
│       ▷ 🗎 SeatPosition.java                                    │
│       ▷ 🗎 SeatPositionConverter.java                           │
│       ▷ 🗎 SeatType.java                                        │
│     ▲ ⊞ com.packtpub.wflydevelopment.chapter5.util              │
│       ▷ 🗎 EntityManagerProducer.java                           │
│       ▷ 🗎 FacesContextProducer.java                            │
│       ▷ 🗎 LoggerProducer.java                                  │
└─────────────────────────────────────────────────────────────────┘
```

Coding the JSF view

Now that our middle tier is completed, we just need to add a couple of JSF views to our application in the `views` folder of our web app. The first view, named `setup.xhtml`, will set up our theatre and the second one, named `book.xhtml`, will be used to book tickets, borrowing some of its code from the earlier chapter.

However, this time we would like to make our application a little bit more graphically appealing. To keep it simple, we will use **Bootstrap**, a very popular frontend framework that will nicely integrate with our JSF views. It heavily relies on JavaScript and CSS, but we will only need to use basic HTML to get it up and running in our application. Incorporating a strict frontend framework to our application will be an opportunity to show how to use Java EE 7 with the newest web technologies.

You can get the latest version of Bootstrap from `http://getbootstrap.com/` and just place all files in the resources directory; however, we won't do it here. We will use the WebJars, which are simply JARs that pack client-side web libraries. You can find dependencies at `http://www.webjars.org/`, which after adding to your `pom.xml` file will work just like manually adding static files to the project. However, thanks to WebJars, we get Maven to control our versions, and don't need to worry about polluting our codebase with external code.

Now, we need Bootstrap and jQuery, so we will add the following dependencies:

```xml
<dependency>
    <groupId>org.webjars</groupId>
    <artifactId>bootstrap</artifactId>
    <version>3.2.0</version>
</dependency>
<dependency>
    <groupId>org.webjars</groupId>
    <artifactId>jquery</artifactId>
    <version>1.11.0</version>
</dependency>
```

Now, when we have the Bootstrap's libraries in place, we have to link them to our code. We will add them to our `WEB-INF/templates/default.xhtml` file along with a simple navigation bar:

```html
<!DOCTYPE html PUBLIC "-//W3C//DTD XHTML 1.0 Strict//EN"
"http://www.w3.org/TR/xhtml1/DTD/xhtml1-strict.dtd">
<html xmlns="http://www.w3.org/1999/xhtml"
      xmlns:h="http://java.sun.com/jsf/html"
      xmlns:ui="http://java.sun.com/jsf/facelets">
<h:head>
    <meta http-equiv="Content-Type" content="text/html; charset=utf-8"
/>
    <title>#{app.applicationName}</title>
    <meta name="viewport" content="width=device-width, initial-
scale=1.0" />
    <meta name="description" content="" />
    <meta name="author" content="" />

    <h:outputStylesheet name="/webjars/bootstrap/3.2.0/css/bootstrap.
css " />
    <h:outputStylesheet name="/webjars/bootstrap/3.2.0/css/bootstrap-
theme.css " />

    <!-- Le HTML5 shim, for IE6-8 support of HTML5 elements -->
    <!--[if lt IE 9]>
      <script src="http://html5shim.googlecode.com/svn/trunk/html5.
js"></script>
    <![endif]-->

<style>
    body {
        padding-top: 60px;
    }
```

```
        </style>
    </h:head>
    <h:body>
        <div class="navbar navbar-inverse navbar-fixed-top"
    role="navigation">
        <div class="container">
        <div class="navbar-header">
            <h:link outcome="/index" class="navbar-brand" value="Ticket
    Agency" />
        </div>
        <div class="collapse navbar-collapse">
            <ul class="nav navbar-nav">
            <li class="#{view.viewId =='/views/setup.xhtml' ?
    'active':''}">
    <h:link outcome="/views/setup" value="Theatre setup" /></li>
            <li class="#{view.viewId =='/views/book.xhtml' ?
    'active':''}">
    <h:link  outcome="/views/book" value="Book tickets" /></li>
            </ul>
        </div>
        </div>
        </div>

        <div class="container">
            <ui:insert name="content">
                [Template content will be inserted here]
            </ui:insert>
            <hr />
            <footer>
            <p class="text-muted">&copy; Company 2014</p>
            </footer>
        </div>
        <h:outputScript name="/webjars/jquery/1.11.0/jquery.js" />
        <h:outputScript name="/webjars/bootstrap/3.2.0/js/bootstrap.js "
    />
    </h:body>
    </html>
```

Next, we will move to the content in `setup.xhtml`:

```
<ui:composition xmlns="http://www.w3.org/1999/xhtml"
                xmlns:h="http://xmlns.jcp.org/jsf/html"
                xmlns:f="http://xmlns.jcp.org/jsf/core"
                xmlns:ui="http://xmlns.jcp.org/jsf/facelets"
                template="/WEB-INF/templates/default.xhtml"
```

```
                        xmlns:p="http://xmlns.jcp.org/jsf/passthrough">
<div class="jumbotron">
    <h1>Theatre Setup</h1>
    <p>Enter the information about Seats</p>
</div>

<div class="row">
<div class="col-md-6">
    <div class="panel panel-default">
        <div class="panel-heading">
            <h3 class="panel-title">Add seats</h3>
        </div>
        <div class="panel-body">
            <h:form id="reg" role="form">
        <div class="form-group has-feedback #{!desc.valid? 'has-error'
: ''}">
            <h:outputLabel for="desc" value="Description"
                    styleClass="control-label" />
            <h:inputText id="desc" value="#{newSeatType.description}"
            p:placeholder="Enter a description here" class="form-
control"
                    binding="#{desc}" />
            <span class="#{!desc.valid ? 'glyphicon glyphicon-remove
form-control-feedback' : ''}" />
            <h:message for="desc" errorClass="control-label has-error"
/>
        </div>
        <div class="form-group  #{!price.valid and facesContext.
validationFailed? 'has-error' : ''}">
<h:outputLabel for="price" value="Price:"
                    styleClass="control-label" />
            <div class="input-group  has-feedback">
            <span class="input-group-addon">$</span>
            <h:inputText id="price" value="#{newSeatType.price}"
            class="form-control" p:placeholder="Enter a price"
                    binding="#{price}" />
            <span class="#{!price.valid ? 'glyphicon glyphicon-remove
input-group-feedback input-group-addon' : ''}" />
            </div>
            <h:message for="price" errorClass="control-label has-
error" />
        </div>
        <div class="form-group has-feedback #{!quantity.valid and
facesContext.validationFailed? 'has-error' : ''}">
```

```
            <h:outputLabel for="quantity" value="Number of Seats:"
                    styleClass="control-label" />
            <h:inputText id="quantity" value="#{newSeatType.quantity}"
                class="form-control" p:placeholder="Enter quantity"
                        binding="#{quantity}" />
            <span class="#{!quantity.valid ? 'glyphicon glyphicon-
remove form-control-feedback' : ''}" />
            <h:message for="quantity" errorClass="control-label has-
error" />
        </div>
        <div class="form-group">
            <h:outputLabel for="position" value="Position:"
                styleClass="control-label" />
            <h:selectOneMenu value="#{newSeatType.position}"
id="position"
                class="form-control">
            <f:selectItems value="#{theatreSetupService.positions}"
                    var="pos" itemValue="#{pos}" itemLabel="#{pos.label}"
/>
            </h:selectOneMenu>
        </div>

        <div class="form-group">
<h:commandButton id="Add" action = "#{theatreSetupService.
addNewSeats}" value="Add styleClass="btn btn-primary" />
        </div>
        <h:messages styleClass="messages" style="list-style: none;
padding:0; margin:0;" errorClass="alert alert-error" infoClass="alert
alert-success"
            warnClass="alert alert-warning" globalOnly="true" />
        </h:form>
        </div>
    </div>
</div>
// some code
</div>
</ui:define>
</ui:composition>
```

As you can see, the preceding view contains a form to enter a new seat type in the topmost section. The highlighted input text will actually pass data to the SeatType object, which will be transferred to the TheatreSetupService CDI Bean and ultimately persisted when the user clicks on the **Add** button.

You may also notice many `class` attributes on the tags. These attributes refer to the CSS classes defined by Bootstrap; we use them to visualize our validation. If a user places some invalid data in a form input, a proper CSS class is assigned to it (Bootstrap's `has-error` method in our case). This is, however, a strictly frontend-related addition. The JSF validation message will be shown with or without it thanks to the `h:messages` tag and the Bean Validation constraints defined in the earlier part of this chapter.

An interesting addition is the fact that we use one of the JSF 2.2 features, which eases integration with HTML5 frontend frameworks, the `pass-through` attributes. By using the `xmlns:p=http://xmlns.jcp.org/jsf/passthrough` namespacein `p:placeholder`, we instruct JSF to ignore an unknown attribute and pass it straight to the renderer. Then, Bootstrap's internal mechanisms can interpret the attribute, and provide our input controls with placeholder text, which disappears after a control gains focus.

The next part of the `setup.xhtml` file is available in the following code:

```
<div class="col-md-6">
    <div class="panel panel-default">
        <div class="panel-heading">
            <h2 class="panel-title">Seats List</h2>
        </div>
        <div class="panel-body">
            <h:form id="reg2">
                <h:commandButton id="Finish"
                    action="#{theatreSetupService.createTheatre}"
                    value="Finalize the theatre setup"
                    styleClass="btn btn-default  btn-block" />
            </h:form>
        </div>
        <h:panelGroup rendered="#{empty seatTypes}">
            <em>No Seats Added.</em>
        </h:panelGroup>
        <h:dataTable var="seatType" value="#{seatTypes}"
            rendered="#{not empty seatTypes}"
            styleClass="table table-hover table-striped ">
            <h:column>
                <f:facet name="header">Id</f:facet>
                #{seatType.id}
            </h:column>
            <h:column>
                <f:facet name="header">Name</f:facet>
                #{seatType.description}
            </h:column>
```

```
    <h:column>
        <f:facet name="header">Position</f:facet>
        #{seatType.position.label}
    </h:column>
    <h:column>
        <f:facet name="header">Price</f:facet>
        $ #{seatType.price}
    </h:column>
    <h:column>
        <f:facet name="header">Quantity</f:facet>
        #{seatType.quantity}
    </h:column>
</h:dataTable>

    </div>
  </div>
  </div>
  </ui:define>
```

Each time you add a new block of seats to your theatre, the dataTable method contained in the lower part of the screen will be updated. When you are done with your setup, click on the **Finish** button, which will recall the finish method of the TheatreSetupService CDI Bean, creating the list of seats.

This action will also redirect you to the next view, named book.xhtml, which is used to book seats:

```
<ui:define name="content">
<div class="page-header">
    <h2>TicketBooker Machine</h2>
</div>

<h3>Money: $ #{bookerService.money}</h3>

<h:form id="reg">
    <h:messages styleClass="messages"
        style="list-style: none; padding:0; margin:0;"
        errorClass="alert alert-error" infoClass="alert alert-
success"
        warnClass="alert alert-warning" globalOnly="true" />

    <h:commandButton id="restart" action="#{theatreSetupService.
restart}"
        value="Restart Application" class="btn btn-default" />
```

```
        <h:dataTable var="seat" value="#{seats}"
            rendered="#{not empty seats}"
            styleClass="table table-hover table-striped ">

            <h:column>
                <f:facet name="header">Id</f:facet>
                    #{seat.id}
            </h:column>

            <h:column>
                <f:facet name="header">Description</f:facet>
                    #{seat.seatType.description}
            </h:column>
            <h:column>
                <f:facet name="header">Price</f:facet>
                    #{seat.seatType.price}$
            </h:column>
            <h:column>
                <f:facet name="header">Position</f:facet>
                    #{seat.seatType.position.label}
            </h:column>
            <h:column>
                <f:facet name="header">Booked</f:facet>
                <span class="glyphicon glyphicon-#{seat.booked ? 'ok'
:'remove'}"></span>
            </h:column>
            <h:column>
                <f:facet name="header">Action</f:facet>
                <h:commandButton id="book"
                    action="#{bookerService.bookSeat(seat.id, seat.
seatType.price)}"
                    disabled="#{seat.booked}" class="btn btn-primary"
                    value="#{seat.booked ? 'Reserved' : 'Book'}" />
            </h:column>
        </h:dataTable>
    </h:form>
</ui:define>
```

Here's a snapshot of the project, expanded at the **webapp** level (as you can see, we have also included a basic index.html screen and an index.xhtml screen to redirect the user to the initial screen, setup.xhtml):

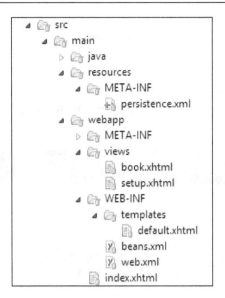

Running the example

Deploying the application requires, as usual, packaging it using the following Maven goal:

```
mvn package
[INFO] Scanning for projects...
[INFO]
[INFO] ------------------------------------------------------------
[INFO] Building ticket-agency-jpa 1.0
[INFO] ------------------------------------------------------------
[INFO] Building war: C:\chapter5\ticket-agency-jpa\target\ticket-
agency-jpa.war
. . . .
[INFO] ------------------------------------------------------------
[INFO] BUILD SUCCESS
[INFO] ------------------------------------------------------------
[INFO] Total time: 1.799s
```

Finally, provided that you have installed the WildFly Maven plugin, you can deploy your application using the following command:

```
mvn wildfly:deploy
```

Once the deployment has successfully completed, visit `http://localhost:8080/ticket-agency-jpa/` to view the application's welcome page, as shown in the following screenshot:

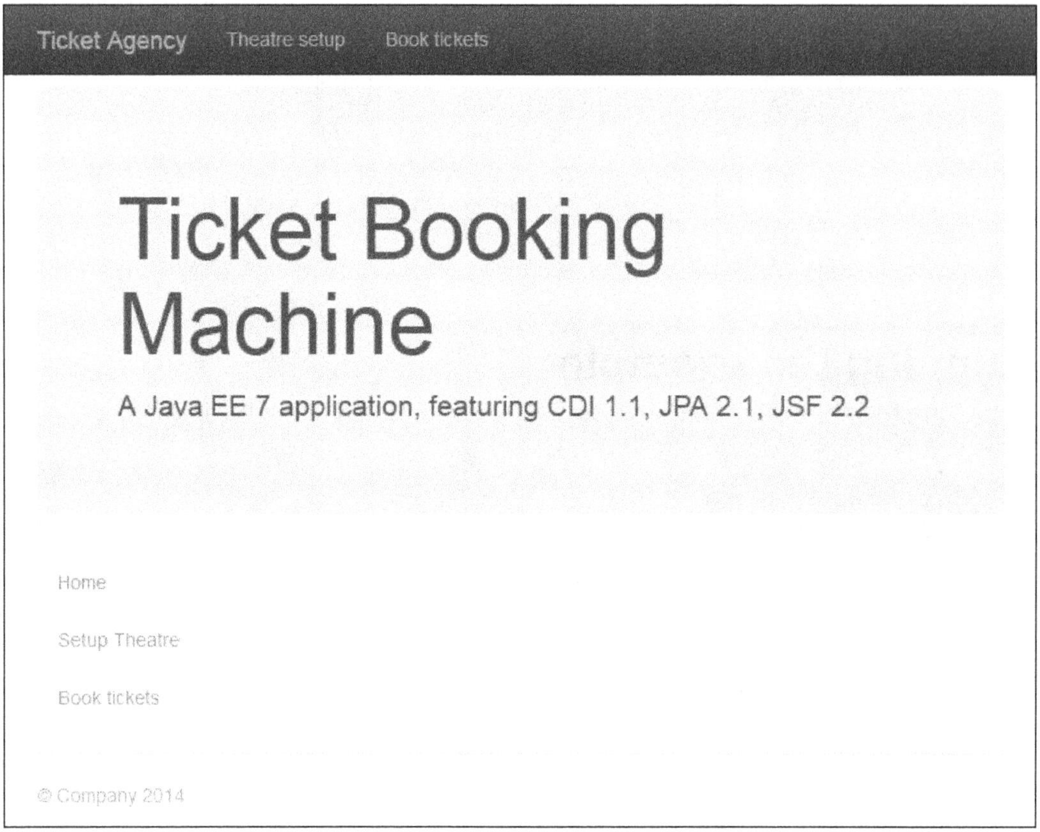

Ticket Agency   Theatre setup   Book tickets

Ticket Booking Machine

A Java EE 7 application, featuring CDI 1.1, JPA 2.1, JSF 2.2

Home

Setup Theatre

Book tickets

© Company 2014

Congratulations! You're done. By clicking on the **Setup Theatre** link, you can start creating places in the setup.xhtml page. Feel free to experiment with the inputs, and try to fill some letters in the price box or numbers in the description, as shown in the following screenshot:

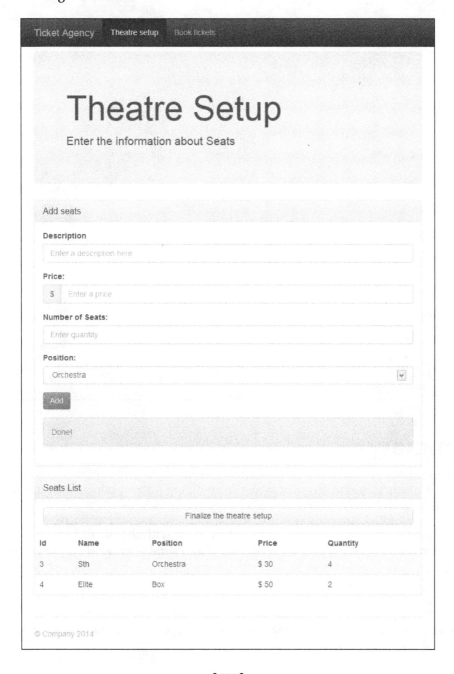

Once you click on the **Finalize the theatre setup** button, you will be redirected to the last screen, which performs seat booking in book.xhtml:

Ticket Agency	Theatre setup	Book tickets			

TicketBooker Machine

Money: $ 100

Restart Application

Id	Description	Price	Position	Booked	Action
8	Sth	30$	Orchestra	✖	Book
9	Sth	30$	Orchestra	✖	Book
10	Sth	30$	Orchestra	✖	Book
11	Sth	30$	Orchestra	✖	Book
12	Elite	50$	Box	✖	Book
13	Elite	50$	Box	✖	Book

© Company 2014

Summary

The aim of the new Java Persistence API is to simplify the development of persistent entities. It meets this objective through a simple POJO-based persistence model, which reduces the number of required classes and interfaces.

In this chapter, we covered a lot of ground, starting with the database schema that we reverse engineered using the JBoss tools plugins for Eclipse. Next, we coded the set of layers (producers, services, and controllers) that are part of the application, along with the JSF Facelets.

In the next chapter, we will discuss developing applications using **JBoss Messaging Provider (HornetQ)** by introducing examples with message-driven beans using the new simplified Java EE 7 API.

6
Developing Applications with JBoss JMS Provider

Messaging is a method of communication between software components and applications. **Java Message Service (JMS)** is a Java API—designed originally by Sun—that allows applications to create, send, receive, and read messages. The new 2.0 version of the API has been introduced with JSR 343 (`https://jcp.org/en/jsr/detail?id=343`).

Messaging differs from other standard protocols, such as **Remote Method Invocation (RMI)** or **Hypertext Transfer Protocol (HTTP)**, in two ways. First, the conversation is mediated by a messaging server so it's not a two-way conversation between peers. Second, the sender and the receiver need to know what message format and what destination to use. This is in contrast to tightly coupled technologies, such as Remote Method Invocation (RMI), that require an application to know about a remote application's methods.

In this chapter, we will cover the following:

- A brief introduction to message-oriented systems
- The building blocks of the JBoss messaging subsystem
- Setting up proof of concept programming examples
- How to use JMS and resource adapters to integrate with external systems

A short introduction to JMS

JMS defines a vendor-neutral (but Java-specific) set of programming interfaces to interact with asynchronous messaging systems. Messaging enables distributed communication that is loosely coupled. The whole messaging interchange is a two-step process where a component sends a message to a destination that is in turn retrieved by the recipient with the mediation of the JMS server. In JMS, there are two types of destinations: topics and queues. These have different semantics, which are explained next.

In a point-to-point model, messages are sent from producers to consumers via queues. A given queue might have multiple receivers, but only one receiver would be able to consume each of the messages. Only the first receiver who requests the message will get it, while the others will not, as shown in the following image:

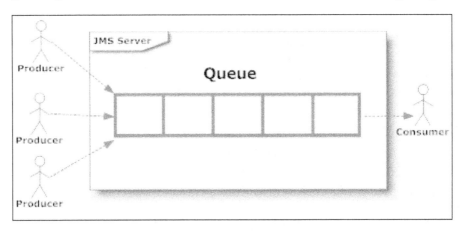

A message sent to a **topic**, on the other hand, might be received by multiple parties. Messages published on a specific topic are sent to all the message consumers who have registered (subscribed) themselves to receive messages on that topic. A subscription can be **durable** or **nondurable**. A nondurable subscriber can only receive messages that are published while it is **active**. A nondurable subscription does not guarantee the delivery of a message; it might deliver the same message more than once. A durable subscription, on the other hand, guarantees that the consumer receives the message exactly once, as depicted in the following image:

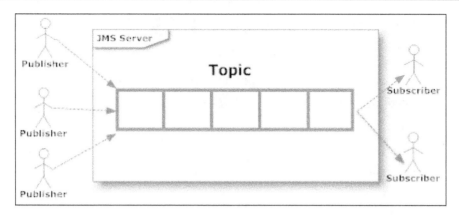

As far as message consumption is concerned, even though JMS is inherently asynchronous, the JMS specification allows messages to be consumed in either of the following two ways:

- **Synchronously**: A subscriber or a receiver explicitly fetches the message from the destination by calling the `receive()` method of any `MessageConsumer` instance. The `receive()` method can block until a message arrives or can take a time out if a message does not arrive within a specified time limit.
- **Asynchronously**: With the asynchronous mode, the client must implement the `javax.jms.MessageListener` interface and overwrite the `onMessage()` method. Whenever a message arrives at the destination, the JMS provider delivers the message by calling the listener's `onMessage` method, which acts on the contents of the message.

A JMS message consists of a header, properties, and a body. The message headers provide a fixed set of metadata fields that describe the message with information such as where the message is going and when it is received. The properties are a set of key-value pairs used for application-specific purposes, usually to help filter messages quickly when they are received. Finally, the body contains whatever data is being sent to the message.

The JMS API supports two delivery modes for messages to specify whether or not the messages are lost if the JMS provider fails, indicated by the following constants:

- The **persistent** delivery mode, which is the default, instructs the JMS provider to take extra care to ensure that a message is not lost in transit in the case of a JMS provider failure. A message sent with this delivery mode is logged to stable storage when it is sent.
- The **nonpersistent** delivery mode does not require the JMS provider to store the message or otherwise guarantee that it is not lost if the provider fails.

The building blocks of JMS

The basic building blocks of any JMS application consist of the following:

- Administered objects—connection factories and destinations
- Connections
- Sessions
- Message producers
- Message consumers
- Messages

Let's take a closer look at them:

- **Connection factory**: This object encapsulates a set of connection configuration parameters that have been defined by an administrator. A client uses it to create a connection with a JMS provider. A connection factory hides provider-specific details from JMS clients and abstracts administrative information into objects in the Java programming language.

- **Destination**: This is the component a client uses to specify the target of messages it produces and the source of messages it consumes. In the **point-to-point** (**PTP**) messaging domain, destinations are called queues; in the **publish/subscribe (pub/sub)** messaging domain, destinations are called topics.

- **Connection**: This encapsulates a virtual connection with a JMS provider. A connection could represent an open TCP/IP socket between a client and a provider service. You use a connection to create one or more sessions.

- **Session**: This is a single-threaded context for producing and consuming messages. You use sessions to create message producers, message consumers, and messages. Sessions serialize the execution of message listeners and provide a transactional context with which to group a set of sends and receives into an atomic unit of work.

- **Message producer**: This is an object created by a session and is used to send messages to a destination. The PTP form of a message producer implements the `QueueSender` interface. The pub/sub form implements the `TopicPublisher` interface. From JMS 2.0, it is possible to rely only on the `JMSProducer` interface.

- **Message consumer**: This is an object created by a session and is used to receive messages sent to a destination. A message consumer allows a JMS client to register interest in a destination with a JMS provider. The JMS provider manages the delivery of messages from a destination to the registered consumers of the destination. The PTP form of message consumer implements the `QueueReceiver` interface. The pub/sub form implements the `TopicSubscriber` interface. The latest JMS version supports a new `JMSConsumer` API.

The JBoss messaging subsystem

JBoss AS has used different JMS implementations across its releases, such as JBoss MQ and JBoss Messaging. Since JBoss AS 6.0, the default JMS provider is **HornetQ** (`http://www.jboss.org/hornetq`), which provides a multiprotocol, embeddable, high-performant, and clusterable messaging system.

At its core, HornetQ is designed simply as a set of **Plain Old Java Objects** (**POJOs**) with few dependencies on external JAR files. In fact, the only one JAR dependency is the Netty library, which leverages the Java **New Input-Output** (**NIO**) API to build high-performance network applications.

Because of its easily adaptable architecture, HornetQ can be embedded in your own project or instantiated in any dependency injection framework such as JBossMicrocontainer, Spring, or Google Guice.

In this book, we will cover a scenario where HornetQ is integrated into the WildFly subsystem as a module, as shown in the following diagram. This diagram depicts how the JCA Adapter and the HornetQ server fit in the overall picture:

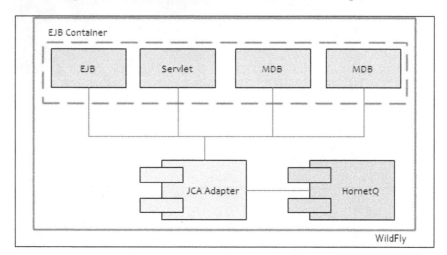

Creating and using connection factories

It is the job of the connection factory that encapsulates the connection's parameters to create new JMS connections. A connection factory is bound to the **Java Naming Directory Index (JNDI)** and can be looked up by both local and remote clients, provided they supply the correct environment parameters. Since a connection factory can be reused multiple times in your code, it's the kind of object that can be conveniently cached by a remote client or a message-driven bean.

The definition of connection-factory instances is included in the `full` and `full-ha` server configurations. You can choose either of the server configurations using the `-c` command argument, for instance, `standalone.bat -c standalone-full.xml`. We will cover the configuration profiles in depth in *Chapter 9, Managing the Application Server*. For now, just remember to start your server with the full configuration profile whenever you need JMS.

You can inspect the connection factories in the overall JMS configuration, which is available by surfing the admin console and navigating to **Configuration | Messaging Destinations | Connection Factories**, as shown in the following screenshot:

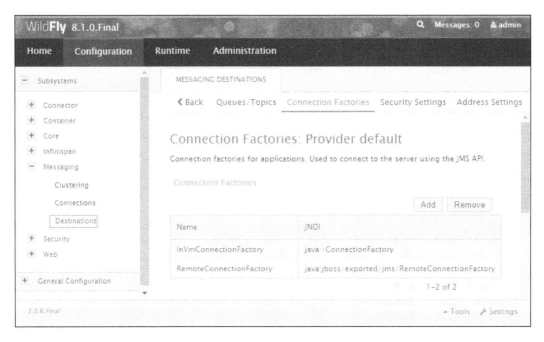

As you can see in the previous screenshot, there are the following two out-of-the-box connection-factory definitions:

- **InVmConnectionFactory**: This connection factory is bound under the java:/ConnectionFactory entry and is used when the server and client are part of the same process (that is, they are running on the same JVM).

- **RemoteConnectionFactory**: This connection factory is bounded under the java:jboss/exported/jms/RemoteConnectionFactory entry, and as the name implies, it can be used using Netty as the connector when JMS connections are provided by a remote server.

If you want to change the connection factory's JNDI binding, the simplest choice is to go through the server configuration file (for example, standalone-full.xml, for a standalone mode):

```
<connection-factory name="InVmConnectionFactory">
    <connectors>
        <connector-ref connector-name="in-vm"/>
    </connectors>
    <entries>
      <entry name="java:/ConnectionFactory"/>
    </entries>
</connection-factory>
<connection-factory name="RemoteConnectionFactory">
    <connectors>
      <connector-ref connector-name="http-connector"/>
    </connectors>
    <entries>
      <entry name="java:jboss/exported/jms/RemoteConnectionFactory"/>
    </entries>
</connection-factory>
<pooled-connection-factory name="hornetq-ra">
<transaction mode="xa"/>
    <connectors>
        <connector-ref connector-name="in-vm"/>
    </connectors>
    <entries>
        <entry name="java:/JmsXA"/>
        <entry name="java:jboss/DefaultJMSConnectionFactory"/>
    </entries>
</pooled-connection-factory>
```

The connection factory can be injected just like any other Java EE resource; the following code fragment shows how a stateless EJB gets the default connection factory injected:

```
@Stateless
public class SampleEJB {

    @Resource(mappedName = "java:/ConnectionFactory")
    private ConnectionFactory cf;
}
```

 In order to use the messaging subsystem, you have to start WildFly using a Java EE full profile, which includes the messaging subsystem. So, for example, if you want to start a standalone server instance that is JMS-aware, you can simply use the following code:

```
standalone.sh -c standalone-full.xml
```

Using JMS destinations

Along with the definition of connection factories, you will need to learn how to configure JMS destinations (queues and topics).

This can be achieved with a variety of instruments. Since we have started dealing with the web console, just navigate to the **Configuration** tab and pick the **Messaging** subsystem from the left panel. Select **Destinations** and click on the **View** central link.

From there, you can use the upper menu tab that contains a set of options, the first one of which—named **Queues/Topics**—can be used to configure your JMS destinations, as shown in the following screenshot:

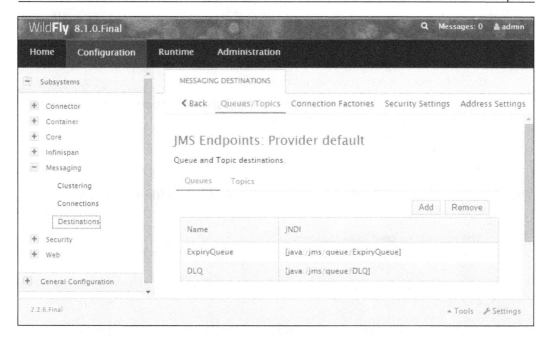

Now click on the **Add** button. You should see the following dialog:

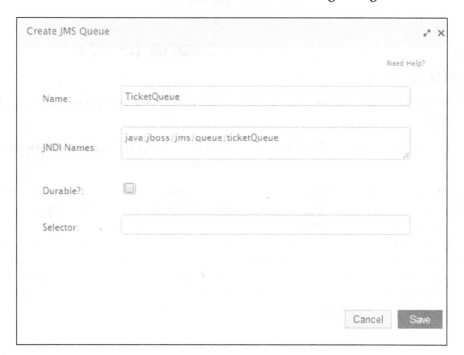

Enter the mandatory name for your destination and its JNDI. You can optionally choose to define your JMS destination as either of the following options:

- **Durable**: This option allows the JMS server to hold on to a message in case the subscriber is temporarily unavailable.

- **Selector**: This option allows a filter to the JMS destination (we will cover this in greater detail later in this chapter).

Click on the **Save** button and verify that the queue has been enlisted among the JMS destinations.

The preceding change will reflect in the server configuration file as follows:

```
<jms-destinations>
    <jms-queue name="TicketQueue">
        <entry name="java:jboss/jms/queue/ticketQueue"/>
            <durable>false</durable>
    </jms-queue>
</jms-destinations>
```

It's worth noting that the JMS configuration usually differs on every application server. In this chapter, we will cover only the approach used in WildFly, but the key concepts between different providers stay the same.

Adding message-driven beans to your application

Once we do the configuration, we can start coding a JMS message consumer, such as a message-driven bean.

Message-driven beans (**MDBs**) are stateless, server-side, and transaction-aware components that process asynchronous JMS messages.

One of the most important aspects of message-driven beans is that they can consume and process messages concurrently. This capability provides a significant advantage over traditional JMS clients, which must be custom built to manage resources, transactions, and security in a multithreaded environment. MDB containers manage concurrency automatically so the bean developer can focus on the business logic of processing the messages. An MDB can receive hundreds of JMS messages from various applications and process them all at the same time because numerous instances of it can be executed concurrently in the container.

From the semantic point of view, an MDB is classified as an enterprise bean, just like a session or entity bean, but there are some important differences. At first, the message-driven bean does not have component interfaces. These are absent because the message-driven bean is not accessible via the Java RMI API; it responds only to asynchronous messages.

Just as the entity and session beans have well-defined life cycles, so does the MDB bean. The MDB instance's life cycle has two states, **Does not Exist** and **Method ready Pool**, as shown in the following image:

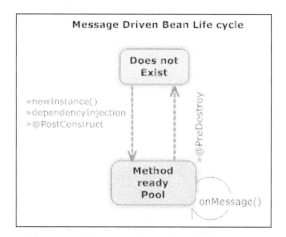

When a message is received, the EJB container checks to see whether any MDB instance is available in the pool. If a bean is available in the free pool, JBoss uses that instance. Once an MDB instance's onMessage() method is returned, the request is complete and the instance is placed back in the free pool. This results in the best response time, as the request is served without waiting for a new instance to be created.

On the other hand, if all the instances in the pool are busy, the new request will be serialized since it's guaranteed that the same instance will not be allowed to serve multiple clients at the same time. Also, if a client sends out multiple messages to the server containing an MDB, there is no guarantee that the same MDB instance will be used for each message or that the messages will be processed in the order in which the client sent them. This means that the application should be designed to handle messages that arrive out of order.

The number of MDBs in the pool is configured in the EJB pool, which can be reached from the console by navigating to **Configuration | Container | EJB 3 | Bean Pools** as depicted in the following screenshot:

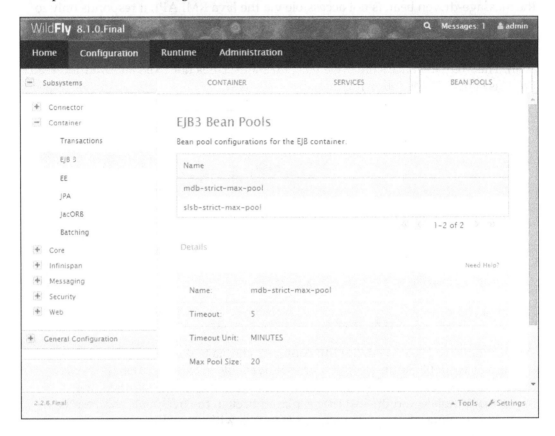

The bean pool's configuration is contained in the bean pool central tab, which holds both the stateless and MDB pool configurations. The default value for the MDB's max pool size is 20 units.

It is also possible to override pools for specific beans. You can use either the JBoss-specific `org.jboss.ejb3.annotation.Pool` annotation or the `jboss-ejb3.xml` deployment descriptor. For more information on overriding pools for the chosen beans, visit `https://docs.jboss.org/author/display/WFLY8/EJB3+subsystem+configuration+guide`.

If no bean instances are available, the request will be blocked until an active MDB completes a method call or the transaction times out.

Cooking message-driven beans

We will now add a message-driven bean to our application from the previous chapter, which will be used to intercept messages when a new ticket is booked. For the purpose of our example, we will just trace whether the JMS message has been received; however, you can also use it for more complex purposes such as notifying external systems.

Create a new Java class, say `BookingQueueReceiver`, and enter the package name as `com.packtpub.wflydevelopment.chapter6.jms`.

Once done, let's add the MDB configuration via an annotation, as shown here:

```
package com.packtpub.wflydevelopment.chapter6.jms;

import javax.ejb.ActivationConfigProperty;
import javax.ejb.MessageDriven;
import javax.inject.Inject;
import javax.jms.JMSException;
import javax.jms.Message;
import javax.jms.MessageListener;
import java.util.logging.Logger;

@MessageDriven(name = "BookingQueueReceiver", activationConfig = {
        @ActivationConfigProperty(propertyName = "destinationLookup",
            propertyValue = "java:jboss/jms/queue/ticketQueue"),   [1]
        @ActivationConfigProperty(propertyName = "destinationType",
            propertyValue = "javax.jms.Queue"),}
)
public class BookingQueueReceiver implements MessageListener {

    @Inject
    private Logger logger;

    @Override
    public void onMessage(Message message) {
        try {
            final String text = message.getBody(String.class);
            logger.info("Received message " + text);
        } catch (JMSException ex) {
            logger.severe(ex.toString());
        }
    }
}
```

Here we have connected the MDB to our `ticketQueue` destination [1] bound at `java:jboss/jms/queue/ticketQueue`. The purpose of this component will be to trace the message receipt via `java.util.Logger`.

Java EE 7 introduces an additional way of the queue definition. Now, you don't have to add a queue from the application server management tool. It is possible to define queues and their properties in the code using some basic annotations:

```
package com.packtpub.wflydevelopment.chapter6.jms;

import javax.jms.JMSDestinationDefinition;

@JMSDestinationDefinition(
        name = BookingQueueDefinition.BOOKING_QUEUE,
        interfaceName = "javax.jms.Queue"
)
public class BookingQueueDefinition {

    public static final String BOOKING_QUEUE =
        "java:global/jms/bookingQueue";
}
```

Then, in `BookingQueueReceiver`, you can just change `propertyValue = "java:jboss/jms/queue/ticketQueue"` to `propertyValue = BookingQueueDefinition.BOOKING_QUEUE`.

Adding the JMS producer

Once we're done with the JMS consumer, we need a component that will take care of sending JMS messages. For this purpose, we will add an Application Scoped CDI Bean, say `BookingQueueProducer`, which gets injected in the JMS resources:

```
package com.packtpub.wflydevelopment.chapter6.jms;

import javax.annotation.Resource;
import javax.enterprise.context.RequestScoped;
import javax.inject.Inject;
import javax.jms.JMSContext;
import javax.jms.Queue;

@ApplicationScoped
public class BookingQueueProducer {

    @Inject
    private JMSContext context;
```

```
    @Resource(mappedName = BookingQueueDefinition.BOOKING_QUEUE)
    private Queue syncQueue;

    public void sendMessage(String txt) {
        context.createProducer().send(syncQueue, txt);
    }
}
```

This might be a bit shocking for those who have used the previous versions of the JMS. For those who haven't, in the following code we present this code's equivalent in JMS 1.1:

```
package com.packtpub.wflydevelopment.chapter6.jms;

Import javax.annotation.Resource;
Import javax.enterprise.context.ApplicationScoped;
Import javax.jms.*;
Import java.util.logging.Logger;

@ApplicationScoped
public class BookingQueueProducer {

    @Inject
    private Logger logger;

    @Resource(mappedName = "java:/ConnectionFactory")
    private ConnectionFactorycf;

    @Resource(mappedName = BookingQueueDefinition.BOOKING_QUEUE)
    private Queue queueExample;

    public void sendMessage(String txt) {
        try {
            final Connection connection = cf.createConnection();
            Session session = connection
                .createSession(false, Session.AUTO_ACKNOWLEDGE);

            final MessageProducer publisher =
                session.createProducer(queueExample);

            connection.start();

            final TextMessage message =
                session.createTextMessage(txt);
            publisher.send(message);
```

```
            }
        catch (Exception exc) {
            logger.error("Error ! "+exc);
        }
        finally {
            if (connection != null) {
                try {
                    connection.close();
                } catch (JMSException e) {
                    logger.error(e);
                }
            }
        }
    }
}
```

Code amount change is impressive. API simplification was one of the major features of the new JMS version, and the specification authors did great work on it.

Now, you can use your service to notify some application-specific actions. For example, we will inject BookingQueueProducer into the BookerService bean and send a message whenever a user is registered:

```
public class BookerService implements Serializable {

    @Inject
    private BookingQueueProducer bookingQueueProducer;

    // Some code

    public void bookSeat(long seatId, int price) {
        logger.info("Booking seat " + seatId);

        if (price > money) {
            final FacesMessage m =
                    new FacesMessage(FacesMessage.SEVERITY_ERROR,
                        "Not enough Money!",
                        "Registration successful");
            facesContext.addMessage(null, m);
            return;
        }

        ticketService.bookSeat(seatId);
```

```
            final FacesMessage m =
                    new FacesMessage(FacesMessage.SEVERITY_INFO,
                        "Registered!",
                        "Registration successful");
            facesContext.addMessage(null, m);
            logger.info("Seat booked.");

            money = money - price;

            bookingQueueProducer.sendMessage("[JMS Message] User
    registered seat " + seatId);
        }
        // Some code


    }
```

From JMS 2.0, messages can be sent asynchronously, but then it is important to control whether the operations are successful or not. To do this, we have to create an object that implements the `CompletionListener` interface, as follows:

```
@ApplicationScoped
public class BookingCompletionListener implements CompletionListener {

    @Inject
    private Logger logger;

    @Override
    public void onCompletion(Message message) {
        try {
            final String text = message.getBody(String.class);
            logger.info("Send was successful: " + text));
        } catch (Throwable e) {
            logger.severe("Problem with message format");
        }
    }

    @Override
    public void onException(Message message, Exception exception) {
        try {
            final String text = message.getBody(String.class);
            logger.info("Send failed..." + text);
        } catch (Throwable e) {
            logger.severe("Problem with message format");
        }
    }
}
```

During the `send` operation, we have to specify the asynchronous and use this `listener` object. To do this, inject `BookingCompletionListener` to `BookingQueueProducer` and send messages with an updated call:

```
public void sendMessage(String txt) {
    context.createProducer()
        .setAsync(bookingCompletionListener).send(syncQueue, txt);
}
```

Now, appropriate listener methods will be executed when the message `send` is completed or failed:

```
[com.packtpub.wflydevelopment.chapter6.jms.BookingCompletionListener]
(Thread-3 (HornetQ-client-global-threads-269763340)) Send was
successful: [JMS Message] User registered seat 2
```

Compiling and deploying the application

We have based our code on the JPA application from the previous chapter. Thanks to `javaee-api`, you don't have to add any new project dependencies in order to use JMS! The only thing you have to do is to start WildFly in full profile using, for example, `standalone-full.xml standalone-full.xml` — the standard full profile configuration:

```
standalone.sh -c standalone-full.xml
```

> Remember, when switching to another server configuration, you will need to recreate all the example resources, such as data sources, that were set up initially for your standalone configuration.

Now deploy your application using either Eclipse's Server view or Maven and access the application at `http://localhost:8080/ticket-agency-jms/`.

Everything should work just like the earlier JPA project; however, in your application server console, you should notice the messages that confirm a seat has been booked.

Specifying which message to receive using selectors

Message selectors allow an MDB to be more selective about the messages it receives from a particular topic or queue. Message selectors use message properties as criteria in conditional expressions. Message properties, upon which message selectors are based, are additional headers that can be assigned to a message. They give the application developer the ability to attach more information to a message. This information can be stored using several primitive values (`boolean`, `byte`, `short`, `int`, `long`, `float`, and `double`) or as `String`.

For example, let's suppose that we want to process two kinds of messages with the same queue:

- A trace message indicating that a user has booked a seat
- A warning message indicating that an error has occurred

Hence, our `sendMessage` method can be changed slightly to include a `String` property that can be attached to the message:

```
@ApplicationScoped
public class BookingQueueProducer {

    @Inject
    private JMSContext context;

    @Inject
    private BookingCompletionListener bookingCompletionListener;

    @Resource(mappedName = BookingQueueDefinition.BOOKING_QUEUE)
    private Queue syncQueue;

    public void sendMessage(String txt, Priority priority) {
        context.createProducer()
                .setAsync(bookingCompletionListener)
                .setProperty("priority", priority.toString())
                .send(syncQueue, txt);
    }
}

public enum Priority {
    LOW, HIGH
}
```

Now, in our application context, we might use the `sendMessage` method, attaching a LOW value for priority when the user is registered:

```
bookingQueueProducer.sendMessage("[JMS Message] User registered seat "
+ seatId, Priority.LOW);
```

On the other hand, we could attach a HIGH priority when an error occurs:

```
bookingQueueProducer.sendMessage("Error during Transaction", Priority.
HIGH);
```

From the MDB perspective, all you need to do in order to filter through messages is include the message selector as part of your `ActivationConfigProperty` class as follows:

```
@MessageDriven(name = "BookingQueueReceiver", activationConfig = {
        @ActivationConfigProperty(propertyName = "destinationLookup",
                propertyValue = BookingQueueDefinition.BOOKING_QUEUE),
        @ActivationConfigProperty(propertyName = "destinationType",
                propertyValue = "javax.jms.Queue"),
        @ActivationConfigProperty(propertyName = "messageSelector",
                propertyValue = "priority = 'HIGH'"),}
)
public class BookingQueueReceiver implements MessageListener {

     // Some code
}
```

At the same time, you can deploy another MDB that is in charge of consuming messages that are sent with a LOW priority:

```
@MessageDriven(name = " LowPriorityBookingQueueReceiver",
activationConfig = {
        @ActivationConfigProperty(propertyName = "destinationLookup",
                propertyValue = BookingQueueDefinition.BOOKING_QUEUE),
        @ActivationConfigProperty(propertyName = "destinationType",
                propertyValue = "javax.jms.Queue"),
        @ActivationConfigProperty(propertyName = "messageSelector",
                propertyValue = "priority = 'LOW'"),}
)
public class LowPriorityBookingQueueReceiver implements
MessageListener {

     // Some code
}
```

When talking about filtering, we have to say a few words concerning performance. In HornetQ queues and topics, there are filtering messages on a different stage. In the case of queues, properties are filtered when they have already been received by the listener, while in topics, they are filtered before being added. Keep in mind this is not guaranteed by JMS specification (since a specification describes the API) and might act differently in other implementations. There are a lot of performance options that can be tuned in JMS providers; however, most of the configurations must be specifically chosen for every project. Be sure to check additional tuning tips in HornetQ's documentation at `http://docs.jboss.org/hornetq/2.4.0.Final/docs/user-manual/html_single/#perf-tuning`.

Transaction and acknowledgment modes

In order to control the overall performance and reliability of an asynchronous messaging system, we need to take two factors into account: persisting of messages and acknowledgment. Let's take a look at those characteristics.

Reliability of the system is focused on the ability to deliver messages exactly once. This means that no message is lost, and there are no duplicates. For most systems, it is a strong requirement that you don't miss or duplicate any orders (like in an e-commerce site). However, usually it is not a problem to miss an update from the stock market because a newer one would overwrite it in a moment. Of course, additional features such as reliability come at a price, and in the case of JMS, the price is paid in performance. The more reliable the system, the lower its message throughput is.

When a message is processed, it can be held only in the memory or persisted somewhere on the disk. Messages stored in the memory are lost in the case of a failure or when the messaging service is stopped. Persisted messages can be retrieved from the disk after the service is restarted and therefore delivered to the consumers at least once (but still without any guarantees about the acknowledgment). Without this mechanism, messages can potentially be lost in the system because a failure might occur before they are delivered. However, the overhead of storing them can have a serious impact on the system's performance characteristics.

Acknowledgment is important to inform the JMS service that the message was really received and processed by the consumer. Different levels of acknowledgments can be used to avoid duplicates or to trigger JMS to send the message once more, possibly to another consumer. A JMS provider will ensure that an acknowledged message is delivered only once. The application is responsible for properly handling rolled back messages that were redelivered (such messages are marked with the `JMSRedelivered` header).

If the consumer session is handled in a transaction, then the messages are acknowledged only when the transaction is committed. However, there is an option to disable transactional message-driven beans and manually handle the acknowledgment. In this case, there are the following three types of acknowledgement options:

- **AUTO_ACKNOWLEDGE**: With this, the consumed messages are being acknowledged automatically

- **DUPS_OK_ACKNOWLEDGE**: With this, the delivered messages are being lazily acknowledged; this means that the client might receive some duplicated messages

- **CLIENT_ACKNOWLEDGES**: With this, the client manually acknowledges received messages using the acknowledge method

The modes can be set when you retrieve JMSContext from a connection factory:

```
JMSContext context = connectionFactory.createContext(JMSContext.
CLIENT_ACKNOWLEDGE)
```

The first argument is an integer flag that accepts the values mentioned previously along with a SESSION_TRANSACTED entry (which is the standard mode for JTA-managed message-driven beans).

Using JMS to integrate with external systems

At the beginning of this chapter, we mentioned that the JCA adaptor handles the communication between the application server and the HornetQ server.

As a matter of fact, one possible way to perform **Enterprise Application Integration (EAI)** is via **Java Connector Architecture (JCA)**, which can be used to drive JMS's inbound and outbound connections.

Initially, Java connectors were intended to access legacy transaction servers on mainframes in a synchronous request/reply mode, and this is how the majority of the connectors worked in the beginning. The standard is currently evolving toward more asynchronous and two-way connectivity; this is exactly the case with JMS communication, which is inherently asynchronous (but also offers the capability of simulating a synchronous request/response mode). In the next section, we will show you how to use a Java Resource Adapter to enable communication between JBoss' HornetQ Messaging system and a standalone instance of the Apache ActiveMQ broker (which can be used, for instance, by a non-Java EE application).

JMS/JCA integration versus web services

If we are discussing EAI, we cannot help but talk about the difference between web services, which is the de facto standard for integrating heterogeneous systems.

One advantage of using the JMS/JCA integration is that it provides support for resource adaptation, which maps the Java EE security, transaction, and communication pooling to the corresponding EIS technology. This makes this technology fairly attractive, especially if you are trying to connect some existing, well-consolidated, and homogeneous systems (remember that if you are using JMS as the driver, you are bound to a Java-to-Java interaction).

On the other hand, if you are planning to connect different business partners (for example, Java and .NET applications) or simply build a new system from scratch with no clear interactions defined, it would be better to use web services for transport and connection.

We will learn more about web services in *Chapter 7, Adding Web Services to Your Applications*, which should provide you with quite a complete overview of your EAI alternatives.

A real-world example – HornetQ and ActiveMQ integration

In this section, we will provide an example scenario, which includes an external component such as the Apache ActiveMQ (Apache 2.0 open source licensed) message broker that fully implements **Java Message Service 1.1 (JMS)**. Another application could be communicating with our ticketing system using this broker, but in our sample, we will simulate the external system using the ActiveMQ administration console.

In order to run this example, we will need to pick up the ActiveMQ resource adapter, `activemq-rar-5.9.0.rar`, which can be downloaded from the Maven repository at `http://repo1.maven.org/maven2/org/apache/activemq/activemq-rar/5.9.0/`. You will also need the ActiveMQ broker, which you can download from `https://activemq.apache.org/activemq-590-release.html`. Simply extract the binary distribution and run the `/apache-activemq-5.9.0/bin/activemq.bat` file to start the broker.

Installing the ActiveMQ resource adapter

Resource adapters (.rar) can be deployed using either WildFly management instruments or by copying the resource adapter into the deployments directory for standalone servers. Before doing this, we need to configure the Resource adapter in your server configuration. This can be done by adding the configuration to the JCA subsystem or (suggested choice) by creating a JCA descriptor of the external resource.

JCA descriptors can be created by using an utility contained in JBoss' JCA implementation named **IronJacamar** (http://www.jboss.org/ironjacamar). Within IronJacamar 1.1 or later distributions (accessible at http://www.jboss.org/ironjacamar/downloads), you can find a resource adapter information tool (rar-info.bat) that can be used to create the resource adapter deployment descriptor by generating a report file containing all the necessary information.

The rar-info.bat tool can be found in the doc/as folder of your IronJacamar distribution. So let's move to this folder:

```
$ cd doc/as
```

Now issue the following command, which assumes that you have saved your resource adapter in the /usr/doc folder:

```
rar-info.bat /usr/doc/activemq-rar-5.9.0.rar
```

Troubleshooting the rar-info shell

The rar-info command shell includes a set of libraries that are used to execute the main utility class. In order to inspect the JMS adapter, however, you need to manually edit the shell file and add jboss-jms-api_2.0_spec-1.0.0.Final and jboss-transaction-api_1.2_spec-1.0.0.Final.jar to the classpath. Those JAR files are contained in the main folder under JBOSS_HOME/modules/system/layers/base/javax/jms/api/ and JBOSS_HOME/modules/system/layers/base/javax/transaction/api/. Simply add paths for them in the rar-info.bat file (separated by character); for example, refer to the following (assuming the jars are in the same directory as rar-info.bat):

```
java -classpath ironjacamar-as.jar;..\..\lib\ironjacamar-
common-spi.jar;..\..\lib\jboss-logging.jar;..\..\lib\jboss-
common-core.jar;..\..\lib\ironjacamar-spec-api.jar;..\..\
lib\jandex.jar;..\..\lib\ironjacamar-common-impl.jar;..\..\
lib\ironjacamar-common-api.jar;..\..\lib\ironjacamar-core-
impl.jar;..\..\lib\ironjacamar-core-api.jar;..\..\lib\
ironjacamar-validator.jar;..\..\lib\jandex.jar;..\..\lib\
validation-api.jar;..\..\lib\hibernate-validator.jar;jboss-
jms-api_2.0_spec-1.0.0.Final.jar;jboss-transaction-api_1.2_
spec-1.0.0.Final.jar org.jboss.jca.as.rarinfo.Main %*
```

This will generate a file called `activemq-rar-5.9.0-report.txt`, which will provide you with the required information to construct your own JBoss' JCA configuration file that needs to be named `ironjacamar.xml`. Feel free to check out its contents.

In the following code, you can find a sample `ironjacamar.xml` file that defines a new queue (`java:jboss/activemq/queue/TicketQueue`):

```
<ironjacamar>
    <connection-definitions>
        <connection-definition class-name="org.apache.activemq.ra.
ActiveMQManagedConnectionFactory" jndi-name="java:jboss/activemq/
TopicConnectionFactory" pool-name="TopicConnectionFactory">
        <pool>
            <min-pool-size>1</min-pool-size>
            <max-pool-size>200</max-pool-size>
            <prefill>false</prefill>
        </pool>
        <security>
          <application />
        </security>
        <timeout>
          <blocking-timeout-millis>30000</blocking-timeout-millis>
          <idle-timeout-minutes>3</idle-timeout-minutes>
        </timeout>
        <validation>
          <background-validation>false</background-validation>
          <use-fast-fail>false</use-fast-fail>
        </validation>
      </connection-definition>
      <connection-definition class-name="org.apache.activemq.ra.Ac
tiveMQManagedConnectionFactory" jndi-name="java:jboss/activemq/
QueueConnectionFactory" pool-name="QueueConnectionFactory">
        <pool>
            <min-pool-size>1</min-pool-size>
            <max-pool-size>200</max-pool-size>
            <prefill>false</prefill>
        </pool>
        <security>
          <application />
        </security>
        <timeout>
          <blocking-timeout-millis>30000</blocking-timeout-millis>
          <idle-timeout-minutes>3</idle-timeout-minutes>
        </timeout>
```

```
            <validation>
              <background-validation>false</background-validation>
              <use-fast-fail>false</use-fast-fail>
            </validation>
        </connection-definition>
        </connection-definitions>
         <admin-objects>
        <admin-object class-name="org.apache.activemq.command.
  ActiveMQQueue" jndi-name="java:jboss/activemq/queue/TicketQueue">
            <config-property name="PhysicalName">
                   activemq/queue/TicketQueue
              </config-property>
        </admin-object>
        </admin-objects>
    </ironjacamar>
```

As you can see, this file contains the definition of ActiveMQ connection factories along with the mapping of JMS administration objects, which will be imported by the resource adapter. The `ironjacamar.xml` file needs to be copied into the `META-INF` folder of `activemq-rar-5.9.0.rar` (you can open the RAR file using the compressed files manager of your choice, for example, 7-Zip).

> **Additional configuration requirements of the resource adapter**
>
> Along with the `ironjacamar.xml` file, there is another configuration file that is contained in the `META-INF` folder of your `activemq-rar-5.9.0.rar` file. The `ra.xml` file is the standard JCA configuration file and describes the resource-adapter-related attribute's type and its deployment properties. We, however, do not need to alter its contents for our basic sample.

Now that we have completed the configuration, let's deploy the resource adapter (`activemq-rar-5.9.0.rar`) into our WildFly and check that the JCA factories and objects have been correctly bound to the application server. After the deployment, you should see the following similar messages in WildFly's console:

```
19:52:51,521 INFO  [org.jboss.as.connector.deployment] (MSC service
thread 1-5) JBAS010401: Bound JCA AdminObject [java:jboss/activemq/queue/
TicketQueue]

19:52:51,521 INFO  [org.jboss.as.connector.deployment] (MSC service
thread 1-5) JBAS010401: Bound JCA ConnectionFactory [java:jboss/jms/
TopicConnectionFactory]

19:52:51,521 INFO  [org.jboss.as.connector.deployment] (MSC service
thread 1-8) JBAS010401: Bound JCA ConnectionFactory [java:jboss/jms/
ConnectionFactory]
```

```
19:52:51,542 INFO  [org.jboss.as.server] (DeploymentScanner-threads - 1)
JBAS018559: Deployed "activemq-rar-5.9.0.rar" (runtime-name : "activemq-
rar-5.9.0.rar")
```

Consuming ActiveMQ messages

Well done! The hardest part is done. Now in order to consume JMS messages sent by the ActiveMQ broker, we will add a @ResourceAdapter annotation to a message-driven bean. This MDB will intercept bookings from the ActiveMQ broker. In order to be able to use the @ResourceAdapter annotation, we will need to add a JBoss-specific dependency to our pom.xml:

```
<dependency>
    <groupId>org.jboss.ejb3</groupId>
    <artifactId>jboss-ejb3-ext-api</artifactId>
    <version>2.1.0</version>
    <scope>provided</scope>
</dependency>
```

Our new annotated message bean is presented as follows (note that the property destinationType is the destination now):

```
@MessageDriven(name = "MDBService", activationConfig = {
    @ActivationConfigProperty(propertyName = "destination",
            propertyValue = "java:jboss/activemq/queue/
TicketQueue"),
    @ActivationConfigProperty(propertyName = "destinationType",
            propertyValue = "javax.jms.Queue"),}
)
@ResourceAdapter(value="activemq-rar-5.9.0.rar")
public class BookingQueueReceiver implements MessageListener {

    @Inject
    private Logger logger;

    @Override
    public void onMessage(Message message) {
        try {
            final String text = message.getBody(String.class);
            logger.info("Received message " + text);
        } catch (JMSException ex) {
            logger.severe(ex.toString());
        }
    }
}
```

Once a message is received, it is written to a console. This means that it is time to deploy our application. If your ActiveMQ broker is running, you should see the following similar messages during the deployment phase:

```
19:59:59,452 INFO  [org.apache.activemq.ra.ActiveMQEndpointWorker]
(ServerService Thread Pool -- 65) Starting

19:59:59,458 INFO  [org.apache.activemq.ra.ActiveMQEndpointWorker]
(default-threads - 1) Establishing connection to broker [tcp://
localhost:61616]

19:59:59,573 INFO  [javax.enterprise.resource.webcontainer.jsf.config]
(MSC service thread 1-5) Initializing Mojarra 2.2.5-jbossorg-3 20140128-
1641 for context '/ticket-agency-jms'

19:59:59,618 INFO  [org.apache.activemq.ra.ActiveMQEndpointWorker]
(default-threads - 1) Successfully established connection to broker
[tcp://localhost:61616]

20:00:00,053 INFO  [org.wildfly.extension.undertow] (MSC service thread
1-5) JBAS017534: Registered web context: /ticket-agency-jms

20:00:00,081 INFO  [org.jboss.as.server] (DeploymentScanner-threads - 1)
JBAS018559: Deployed "ticket-agency-jms.war" (runtime-name : "ticket-
agency-jms.war")
```

Now it is time to test our connection using the ActiveMQ console, which will send a message straight to the ActiveMQ broker. ActiveMQ 5.9.0 is equipped with a bundled **hawt.io** console. It is a pluggable web dashboard that can be configured to administer various applications. One of them is ActiveMQ. And, one of the benefits of using this console is that you can deploy it on almost any JVM-based container, including WildFly. Check out `http://hawt.io/` along with the ActiveMQ plugin (`http://hawt.io/plugins/activemq/`) for more information.

> From Version 5.10.0, ActiveMQ is not prebundled with hawt.io anymore. You can prepare your own hawt.io console by following the guidelines available at `http://hawt.io/getstarted/index.html`; installing the ActiveMQ plugin; or (which we strongly recommend) using Version 5.9.0 in your samples, which is conveniently preconfigured.

Go to `http://localhost:8161/hawtio/` and log in using the `admin/admin` credentials:

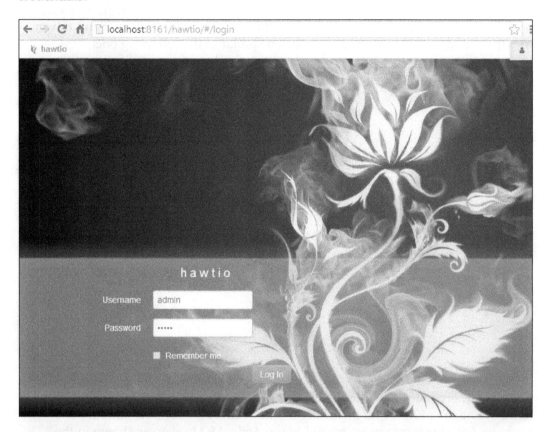

After the login, you should see the hawt.io web console. It is worth noting that it was created using Twitter Bootstrap, the same front-end framework that we are using in our application.

Select the first tab (ActiveMQ) and you should see a tree that represents the current configuration of the broker. Find the node `localhost/Queue/`. When you expand it, you should see the queue we defined earlier in our resource adapter: `java_jboss/activemq/queue/TicketQueue`. After selecting it, you can choose the **Send** tab on the right-hand side. You should see a screen similar to the following one:

Enter the desired message into the big text area in the center and click on the **Send Message** button. After switching to our WildFly console, we should see a log entry with the message we passed to the ActiveMQ broker, as shown in the following screenshot:

```
ndpointWorker] (default-threads - 5) Establishing connection to broker [tcp://localhost:61616]
ndpointWorker] (default-threads - 5) Successfully established connection to broker [tcp://localhost:61616]
tainer.jsf.config] (MSC service thread 1-7) Initializing Mojarra 2.2.5-jbossorg-3 20140128-1641 for context '/ticket
(MSC service thread 1-7) JBAS017534: Registered web context: /ticket-agency-jms
Scanner-threads - 1) JBAS018565: Replaced deployment "ticket-agency-jms.war" with deployment "ticket-agency-jms.war"
pter6.jms.BookingQueueReceiver] (default-threads - 7) Received message This is a message from ActiveMQ!
```

Congratulations! If you have gone successfully through this example, you have just mastered a real-world integration scenario. To make the sample more realistic, you could improve the message bean so that it would book tickets if the message were to contain the required information (for example, message 55,10 would book a seat with ID 55 for 10$). Feel free to experiment!

Summary

In this chapter, we discussed JBoss' message-oriented middleware that allows you to loosely couple heterogeneous systems together while typically providing reliability, transactions, and many other features.

We saw how to configure JMS destinations using the web console and create some message-driven beans, which are the standard way to consume messages from within the EJB container.

We will now move on to another component, which is typically used for integrating heterogeneous systems — web services.

7
Adding Web Services to Your Applications

In the previous chapter, we discussed the Java Messaging Service API, which is commonly used to develop loosely coupled applications and a common integration pattern for Java-to-Java systems. In this chapter, you will learn about web services that are defined by W3C as software systems, and designed to support interoperable machine-to-machine interaction over a network.

What makes web services different from other forms of distributed computing is that information is exchanged using only simple and nonproprietary protocols. This means the services can communicate with each other regardless of location, platform, or programming language. Essentially, web services protocols provide a platform-independent way to perform **Remote Procedure Calls (RPCs)**.

The focus of this chapter will be on the two chief web services standards, **JAX-WS (JSR 224)** and **JAX-RS (JSR 339)**, and how they are implemented in WildFly. As you can imagine, there is a lot of ground to cover, so we will quickly get our hands dirty with the following topics:

- A short introduction to SOAP-based web services
- Creating, deploying, and using the JBoss JAX-WS implementation (Apache CXF)
- A quick overview of REST web services
- How to create, deploy, and use services using the JBoss JAX-RS implementation (RESTEasy)
- Integrating JAR-RS with an external non-Java application

Developing SOAP-based web services

As stated, web services are based on the exchange of messages using nonproprietary protocol messages. The messages themselves are not sufficient to define the web service platform. We actually need a list of standard components, including the following:

- A language used to define the interfaces provided by a web service in a manner that is not dependent on the platform on which it is running or the programming language used to implement it

- A common standard format to exchange messages between web service **providers** and web service **consumers**

- A registry within which service definitions can be placed

The **Web Service Description Language**, also known as **WSDL**, (http://www.w3.org/TR/wsdl) is the de facto standard to provide a description of a web service contract exposed to clients. In particular, a WSDL document describes a web service in terms of the operations that it provides, and the data types that each operation requires as inputs and can return in the form of results.

Communication between the service provider and service consumer happens by means of XML messages that rely on the SOAP specification.

A basic SOAP message consists of an envelope that may contain any number of headers and a body. These parts are delimited by XML elements called envelope, header, and body, which belong to a namespace defined by the SOAP specification. The following figure depicts the basic structure of a SOAP message:

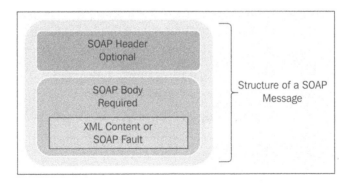

Strategies to build SOAP-based web services

As we have just discussed, the service description is provided by a commonly used document interface named WSDL that exposes the services as a collection of networks, endpoints, and ports, using the XML format.

You may logically be inclined to think that it is necessary to state the corresponding programming interfaces at the beginning of the contract of a service and then produce them.

Actually, you can follow two approaches to develop your SOAP web services:

- **Top-down**: This development strategy involves creating a web service from a WSDL file. The top-down approach is likely to be used when creating web services from scratch. It is the preferred choice of pure web service engineers because it is business-driven, that is, the contract is defined by business people and so the software is designed to fit the web service contract.
- **Bottom-up**: This approach requires the WSDL file to be generated by the programming interfaces. It is likely to be used when we have existing applications that we want to expose as web services. As this approach does not require a deep knowledge of the WSDL syntax, it is the easiest choice if you want to turn your Java classes or EJB into web services.

As the audience of this book is composed mainly of Java developers with little or no knowledge of WSDL basics, we will focus primarily on the bottom-up approach.

Designing top-down web services, on the other hand, will require you to integrate the basic web services notions provided with this chapter with a comprehensive awareness of the WSDL standard.

JBoss SOAP-based web services stack

All JAX-WS functionalities provided on top of WildFly are currently served through a proper integration of the JBoss web services stack with most of the **Apache CXF** project.

Apache CXF is an open source web service framework that provides an easy-to-use, standard-based programming model to develop both SOAP and REST web services. The integration layer (JBossWS-CXF in short hereafter) allows us to perform the following:

- Use standard web services APIs (including JAX-WS) on a WildFly Application Server; this is performed internally by leveraging Apache CXF, without requiring the user to deal with it
- Leverage Apache CXF's advanced native features on top of a WildFly Application Server without the need for the user to deal with all the required integration steps to run the application in such a container

Therefore, the focus of the next section will be on developing JAX-WS web services using the built-in Apache CXF configuration. If you want to further expand your knowledge about Apache CXF's native features, you can refer to the official documentation that is available at `http://cxf.apache.org/`.

A brief look at the JAX WS architecture

When a SOAP message sent by the client enters the web service runtime environment, it is captured by a component named **server endpoint listener**, which, in turn, uses the **Dispatcher** module to deliver the SOAP message to that service.

At this point, the HTTP request is converted internally into a SOAP message. The message content is extracted from the transport protocol and processed through the handler chain configured for the web service.

SOAP message handlers are used to intercept SOAP messages as they make their way from the client to the endpoint service and vice versa. These handlers intercept SOAP messages for both the request and response of the web service.

The next step is unmarshalling the SOAP message into Java objects. This process is governed by WSDL to Java Mapping and XML to Java Mapping. The former is performed by the JAX-WS engine, and it determines which endpoint to invoke from the SOAP message. The latter, performed by the JAXB libraries, deserializes the SOAP message so that it is ready to invoke the endpoint method.

Finally, the deserialized SOAP message reaches the actual web service implementation and the method is invoked.

Once the call is completed, the process is reversed. The return value from the web service method is marshalled into a SOAP response message using JAX-WS WSDL to Java mapping and JAXB 2.0 XML to Java mapping.

The JAXB provides a fast and convenient way to bind XML schemas and Java representations, making it easy for Java developers to incorporate XML data and process functions in Java applications. As part of this process, JAXB provides methods to unmarshal XML instance documents into Java content trees, and then marshal Java content trees back into XML instance documents. JAXB also provides a way to generate XML schema from Java objects.

Next, the outbound message is processed by handlers before returning it to the dispatcher and endpoint listener that will transmit the message as an HTTP response.

The following diagram describes how data flows from a web service client to a web service endpoint and back:

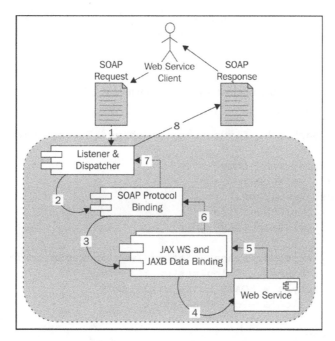

Coding SOAP web services with WildFly

In the first deliverable, we will show how easily you can turn a plain Java class into a web service. The newly created service will then be tested using a simple Eclipse-based testing GUI. The second part of this section will draw your attention to how EJBs can be exposed as web service endpoints by enhancing your ticket application with a web service.

Developing a POJO web service

We will start developing web services, using our project from *Chapter 4*, *Learning Context and Dependency Injection* (`ticket-agency-cdi`) as a base. We will omit the current JSF-based web layer for now. You can safely remove all of the JSF-related classes and configurations. If you encounter any problems, remember that you'll find a fully working project in the code examples, upon completion of this chapter.

Our first class will not be related to our ticket application, but it will just demonstrate how to create a web service from a POJO class named `CalculatePowerWebService`. This class has a method named `calculatePower`, which returns the power of an argument, as shown in the following highlighted code:

```
package com.packtpub.wflydevelopment.chapter7.boundary;

public class CalculatePowerWebService {

    public double calculatePower(double base, double exponent) {
        return Math.pow(base, exponent);
    }
}
```

Now, we will turn this simple class into a web service by adding the mandatory `@WebService` annotation:

```
package com.packtpub.wflydevelopment.chapter7.webservice;

import javax.jws.WebMethod;
import javax.jws.WebParam;
import javax.jws.WebResult;
import javax.jws.WebService;
import javax.jws.soap.SOAPBinding;

@WebService(targetNamespace = "http://www.packtpub.com/",
        serviceName = "CalculatePowerService")
@SOAPBinding(style = SOAPBinding.Style.RPC)
public class CalculatePowerWebService {

    @WebMethod
    @WebResult(name = "result")
    public double calculatePower(@WebParam(name = "base") double base,
                                 @WebParam(name = "exponent") double
exponent) {
        return Math.pow(base, exponent);
    }
}
```

Inside the @WebService annotation, you can specify additional elements, such as the targetNamespace element that declares the namespace used for the WSDL elements generated by the web service. If you don't specify this element, the web service container will use the Java package name to generate a default XML namespace.

You can also use the serviceName element to specify the service name. The name specified using serviceName is used to generate the name attribute in the service element in the WSDL interface. If you don't specify the serviceName element, the server will generate it using the default value, which is the bean class name appended with the service.

In the next row, we state that the web service is of the type **Remote Procedure Call** using the @javax.jws.SOAPBinding annotation. The possible values are DOCUMENT and RPC, the first one being the default value.

> The choice between the RPC and Document style boils down to the different ways we can construct services using these two styles. The body of an RPC-style SOAP message is constructed in a specific way, which is defined in the SOAP standard. This is built on the assumption that you want to call the web service just like you would call a normal function or method that is part of your application code.
>
> Therefore, the RPC is more tightly coupled because if you make any changes in the message structure, you'll need to change all the clients and servers processing this kind of message.
>
> A document-style web service, on the other hand, contains no restrictions for how the SOAP body must be constructed. It allows you to include whatever XML data you want and also a schema for this XML. Therefore, the document style is probably more flexible, but the effort to implement the web service and clients may be slightly more.
>
> In the end, the likelihood of change is a factor that one has to consider when choosing whether to use RPC- or Document-style web services.

Attaching the @WebMethod attribute to a public method indicates that you want the method exposed as part of the web service.

The @WebParam annotation is used to specify the parameter's name that needs to be exhibited in the WSDL. You should always consider using a WebParam annotation, especially when using multiple parameters, otherwise the WSDL will use the default argument parameter (in this case, arg0), which is meaningless for web service consumers.

The @WebResult annotation is quite similar to @WebParam in the sense that it can be used to specify the name of the value returned by the WSDL.

Your web service is now complete. In order to deploy your web service, run the following Maven goal, which will package and deploy your web service to your running WildFly instance:

```
mvn package wildfly:deploy
```

WildFly will provide a minimal output on the console; this will inform you that the web service project has been deployed and the WSDL file has been generated:

```
14:25:37,195 INFO  [org.jboss.weld.deployer] (MSC service thread 1-11)
JBAS016005: Starting Services for CDI deployment: ticket-agency-ws.war

14:25:37,198 INFO  [org.jboss.ws.cxf.metadata] (MSC service thread
1-11) JBWS024061: Adding service endpoint metadata: id=com.packtpub.
wflydevelopment.chapter7.boundary.CalculatePowerWebService

 address=http://localhost:8080/ticket-agency-ws/CalculatePowerService

 implementor=com.packtpub.wflydevelopment.chapter7.boundary.
CalculatePowerWebService

 serviceName={http://www.packtpub.com/}CalculatePowerService

 portName={http://www.packtpub.com/}CalculatePowerWebServicePort

 annotationWsdlLocation=null

 wsdlLocationOverride=null

 mtomEnabled=false
```

From the short log, you can pick up some useful information. For example, the first line states that the web service has been bound in the endpoint registry as {`http://www.packtpub.com/`}`CalculatePowerService`. Next is the information about the web context path, which, by default, has the same name as your project, that is, `ticket-agency-ws`. The last piece of information is about the web service address, which is `http://localhost:8080/ticket-agency-ws/CalculatePowerService`. By appending the `?wsdl` suffix to the end of the address, you can inspect the web service contract.

The `data` directory contains a versioned list of all the generated WSDLs. So, you might find the entire history of your web services published by `ticket-agency-ws` in `JBOSS_HOME/standalone/data/wsdl/ticket-agency-ws.war`.

Inspecting the web service from the console

You can inspect the web services subsystem by moving to the web admin console and navigating to **Runtime** | **Status** | **Subsystems** | **Web Services**.

Here, you can gather some useful information about the services deployed. In fact, the most useful option is the list of endpoint contracts available, which is needed when developing our clients. The following screenshot shows a view of the web service endpoints from the console:

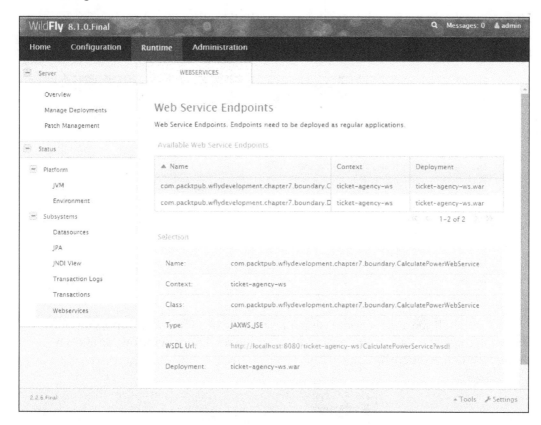

Particularly, in the lower part of the screen, you can read the web service endpoint address that bears the web application context name and registered name for the web service. In our case, it is `http://localhost:8080/ticket-agency-ws/CalculatePowerService?wsdl`.

Testing our simple web service

Since our first web service is not yet connected to our ticketing system, we will use an external client application to test our web service. One of the best tools to test web services is **SoapUI**.

SoapUI is a free, open source, cross-platform functional testing solution with an easy-to-use graphical interface and enterprise-class features. This tool allows you to create and execute automated, functional, regression, compliance, and load tests easily and rapidly. SoapUI is also available as an Eclipse plugin.

Here, we will use the SoapUI standalone application. Run it and create a new SOAP project providing the URL to the service WSDL, as shown in the following screenshot:

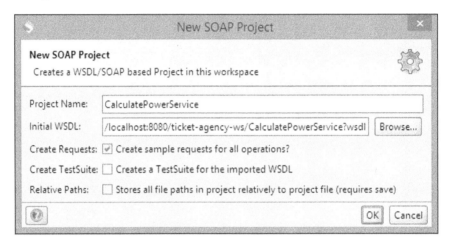

After this, you'll see a view containing a few windows. The most important ones show the request logs and the project view in the navigator window, as shown in the following screenshot:

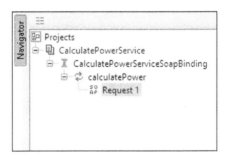

As you can see, your service operations have been automatically discovered. Double-click on the **Request 1** tree element; the SoapUI request window will appear where you can enter the named parameters. Enter the two arguments for the web service, as shown in the following screenshot:

```
<soapenv:Envelope xmlns:soapenv="http://schemas.xmlsoap.org/soap/envelope/" xmlns:pac="http://www.packtpub.com/">
  <soapenv:Header/>
  <soapenv:Body>
    <pac:calculatePower>
      <base>3</base>
      <exponent>2</exponent>
    </pac:calculatePower>
  </soapenv:Body>
</soapenv:Envelope>
```

Click on the **Submit** button on the toolbar and check the result in the SOAP response window:

```
<soap:Envelope xmlns:soap="http://schemas.xmlsoap.org/soap/envelope/">
  <soap:Body>
    <ns1:calculatePowerResponse xmlns:ns1="http://www.packtpub.com/">
      <result>9.0</result>
    </ns1:calculatePowerResponse>
  </soap:Body>
</soap:Envelope>
```

EJB3 Stateless Session Bean (SLSB) web services

The JAX-WS programming model supports the same set of annotations on EJB3 Stateless Session Bean as it does on POJO endpoints. Now that we already have some web service muscle, we will engineer one of the examples introduced in this book.

Our main web service class will be named `DefaultTicketWebService` and will use some of the core classes that we described in *Chapter 3, Introducing Java EE 7 – EJBs*, such as `TheatreBox`, which will keep in memory the ticket bookings and the `Seat` class as the model. The business methods of our web service will be described by a **Service Endpoint Interface (SEI)** named `TicketWebService`:

```
package com.packtpub.wflydevelopment.chapter7.boundary;

import javax.jws.WebService;
import java.util.List;


@WebService
```

```
public interface TicketWebService {

    List<SeatDto> getSeats();

    void bookSeat(int seatId);
}
```

 Writing the service interface is always a good practice as it gives a proper client-side view of our Service methods. The implementation class can then implement the methods defined in the interface.

We will now implement the interface by providing the business logic to the interface methods in the `DefaultTicketWebService` class:

```
package com.packtpub.wflydevelopment.chapter7.boundary;

import javax.inject.Inject;
import javax.jws.WebMethod;
import javax.jws.WebParam;
import javax.jws.WebResult;
import javax.jws.WebService;
import java.io.Serializable;
import java.util.List;
import java.util.stream.Collectors;

@WebService(targetNamespace = "http://www.packtpub.com/", serviceName
= "TicketWebService")
public class DefaultTicketWebService implements TicketWebService,
Serializable {

    @Inject
    private TheatreBox theatreBox;

    @WebMethod
    @WebResult(name = "listSeats")
    public List<SeatDto> getSeats() {
        return theatreBox.getSeats()
                        .stream()
                        .map(SeatDto::fromSeat)
                        .collect(Collectors.toList());

    }
```

```
@WebMethod
public void bookSeat(@WebParam(name = "seatId") int seatId) {
    theatreBox.buyTicket(seatId);
}
}
```

As you can see, the implementation class contains the getSeats method, which returns the list of seats that are self-generated when the TheatreBox object is initialized. The bookSeat method will be able to book seats for your web service clients as well.

Now deploy your web service and verify on the console that it has been correctly registered:

```
00:43:12,033 INFO  [org.jboss.ws.cxf.metadata] (MSC service thread
1-13) JBWS024061: Adding service endpoint metadata: id=com.packtpub.
wflydevelopment.chapter7.boundary.DefaultTicketWebService

 address=http://localhost:8080/ticket-agency-ws/TicketWebService

 implementor=com.packtpub.wflydevelopment.chapter7.boundary.
DefaultTicketWebService

 serviceName={http://www.packtpub.com/}TicketWebService

 portName={http://www.packtpub.com/}DefaultTicketWebServicePort

 annotationWsdlLocation=null

 wsdlLocationOverride=null

 mtomEnabled=false
```

Developing a web service consumer

The web service consumer of the TicketWebService class will be coded using the standard Java SE classes. We want to show here how to use these standard APIs. For this reason, you can just add a class named TicketWebServiceTestApplication to your current or a separate project in the package com.packtpub.wflydevelopment.chapter7.webservice:

```
package com.packtpub.wflydevelopment.chapter7.webservice;

import com.packtpub.wflydevelopment.chapter7.boundary.SeatDto;
import com.packtpub.wflydevelopment.chapter7.boundary.
TicketWebService;

import javax.xml.namespace.QName;
import javax.xml.ws.Service;
import java.net.MalformedURLException;
import java.net.URL;
```

```java
import java.util.Collection;
import java.util.List;
import java.util.logging.Logger;

public class TicketWebServiceTestApplication {

    private static final Logger logger = Logger.getLogger(TicketWebSer
viceTestApplication.class.getName());

    public static void main(String[] args) throws
MalformedURLException {
        final int seatId = 1;
        logger.info("TEST SOAP WS Service");
        final URL wsdlURL = new URL("http://localhost:8080/ticket-
agency-ws/TicketWebService?wsdl");
        final QName SERVICE_NAME = new QName("http://www.packtpub.
com/", "TicketWebService");
        final Service service = Service.create(wsdlURL, SERVICE_NAME);
        final TicketWebService infoService = service.
getPort(TicketWebService.class);

        logger.info("Got the Service: " + infoService);

        infoService.bookSeat(seatId);
        logger.info("Ticket Booked with JAX-WS Service");

        final List<SeatDto> list = infoService.getSeats();

        dumpSeatList(list);
    }

    private static void dumpSeatList(Collection<SeatDto> list) {
        logger.info("================= Available Ticket List
================");
        list.stream().forEach(seat -> logger.info(seat.toString()));
    }
}
```

The service WSDL URL and name are needed for retrieval of the Service object. Finally, the getPort method will return a proxy to your web service that can be used to test two basic operations: booking a seat and checking from the Seat list if the seat has actually been reserved.

This small standalone class has shown how it is possible to use SOAP-based services from the client-side perspective.

The most interesting part, however, is at the bottom of the Maven output, where the `Ticket` list is dumped after booking one seat, as depicted in the following command line:

```
apr 01, 2014 1:08:44 AM com.packtpub.wflydevelopment.chapter7.webservice.
TicketWebServiceTestApplication main

INFO: TEST SOAP WS Service

apr 01, 2014 1:08:44 AM com.packtpub.wflydevelopment.chapter7.webservice.
TicketWebServiceTestApplication main

INFO: Got the Service: JAX-WS RI 2.2.9-b130926.1035 svn-revision#8c29a9a
53251ff741fca1664a8221dc876b2eac8: Stub for http://localhost:8080/ticket-
agency-ws/TicketWebService

apr 01, 2014 1:08:44 AM com.packtpub.wflydevelopment.chapter7.webservice.
TicketWebServiceTestApplication main

INFO: Ticket Booked with JAX-WS Service

apr 01, 2014 1:08:44 AM com.packtpub.wflydevelopment.chapter7.webservice.
TicketWebServiceTestApplication dumpSeatList

INFO: ================= Available Ticket List =================

apr 01, 2014 1:08:44 AM com.packtpub.wflydevelopment.chapter7.webservice.
TicketWebServiceTestApplication lambda$dumpSeatList$0

INFO: SeatDto [id=1, name=Stalls, price=40, booked=true]

apr 01, 2014 1:08:44 AM com.packtpub.wflydevelopment.chapter7.webservice.
TicketWebServiceTestApplication lambda$dumpSeatList$0

INFO: SeatDto [id=2, name=Stalls, price=40, booked=false]

...
```

Developing REST-based web services

JAX-RS 2.0 (JSR-339 can be found at `https://jcp.org/en/jsr/detail?id=339`) is a JCP specification that provides a Java API for RESTful web services in the HTTP protocol. It is a major refresh from the old Version 1.1. Some of the new features are the client API, HATEOAS support, and asynchronous calls.

In their simplest form, RESTful web services are networked applications that manipulate the state of system resources. In this context, resource manipulation means resource creation, retrieval, updatation, and deletion (CRUD). However, RESTful web services are not limited to just these four basic data manipulation concepts. On the contrary, RESTful web services can execute logic at the server level but remember that every result must be a resource representation of the domain.

The main difference with SOAP web services is that REST asks developers to use HTTP methods explicitly and in a way that's consistent with the protocol definition. This basic REST design principle establishes a **one-to-one** mapping between CRUD operations and HTTP methods.

Therefore, with the delineated roles for resources and representations, we can now map our CRUD actions to the HTTP methods POST, GET, PUT, and DELETE as follows:

Action	HTTP protocol equivalent
RETRIEVE	GET
CREATE	POST
UPDATE	PUT
DELETE	DELETE

Accessing REST resources

As we said, REST resources can be accessed using actions that map an equivalent HTTP request. In order to simplify the development of REST applications, you can use simple annotations to map your actions; for example, in order to retrieve some data from your application, you can use something similar to the following:

```
@Path("/users")
public class UserResource {

    @GET
    public String handleGETRequest() { . . .}

    @POST
    public String handlePOSTRequest(String payload) { . . . }
}
```

The first annotation, @Path, in our example is used to specify the URI that is assigned to this web service. Subsequent methods have their specific @Path annotation so that you can provide a different response according to the URI requested.

Then, we have an @GET annotation that maps an HTTP GET request and an @POST annotation that handles an HTTP POST request. So, in this example, if we were to request for a web application bound to the example web context, an HTTP GET request to the URL http://host/example/users would trigger the handleGETRequest method; on the other hand, an HTTP POST request to the same URL would conversely invoke the handlePOSTRequest method.

JBoss REST web services

Having understood the basics of REST services, let's see how we can develop a RESTful web service using WildFly. The application server includes an out-of-the-box RESTEasy library that is a portable implementation of the JSR-339 specification. RESTEasy can run in any servlet container; however, it is perfectly integrated with WildFly, thus making the user experience nicer in that environment.

Besides the server-side specification, in the past, RESTEasy has been innovative in bringing JAX-RS to the client through the RESTEasy **JAX-RS Client Framework**. However, the latest version of the JAX-RS specification comes with a client API, which we can use in every JAX-RS implementation.

Activating JAX-RS

RESTEasy is bundled with WildFly, so you need very little effort to get started. You have two choices. The first one is to use the @ApplicationPath annotation in a class that extends javax.ws.rs.core.Application:

```
@ApplicationPath("/rest")
public class JaxRsActivator extends Application {


}
```

The second choice is less popular and used to configure the application using a web.xml file:

```
<?xml version="1.0" encoding="UTF-8"?>
<web-app xmlns="http://java.sun.com/xml/ns/j2ee" xmlns:xsi="http://
www.w3.org/2001/XMLSchema-instance"
    xsi:schemaLocation="http://java.sun.com/xml/ns/j2ee http://java.
sun.com/xml/ns/j2ee/web-app_3_0.xsd" version="3.0">
    <servlet>
        <servlet-name>javax.ws.rs.core.Application</servlet-name>
        <load-on-startup>1</load-on-startup>
    </servlet>
    <servlet-mapping>
        <servlet-name>javax.ws.rs.core.Application</servlet-name>
        <url-pattern>/rest/*</url-pattern>
    </servlet-mapping>
</web-app>
```

This simply means that if we were to deploy our former example, the HTTP GET method, http://host/example/rest/users would trigger our getUser business method, while the same URL will place a request through the handlePOSTRequest method using a POST request.

Adding REST to our ticket example

With all the configurations in place, we can now add a simple REST web service to our `Ticket Web Service` project, which will provide the same functionalities as our SOAP web service.

So add a new class to your project and name it `SeatsResource`. The code for this is as follows:

```
package com.packtpub.wflydevelopment.chapter7.boundary;

@Path("/seat")
@Produces(MediaType.APPLICATION_JSON)
@RequestScoped
public class SeatsResource {

    @Inject
    private TheatreBooker theatreBooker;

    @Inject
    private TheatreBox theatreBox;

    @GET
    public Collection<SeatDto> getSeatList() {
        return theatreBox.getSeats()
                .stream()
                .map(SeatDto::fromSeat)
                .collect(Collectors.toList());
    }

    @POST
    @Path("/{id}")
    public Response bookPlace(@PathParam("id") int id) {
        try {
            theatreBooker.bookSeat(id);
            return Response
             .ok(SeatDto.fromSeat(theatreBox.getSeat(id)))
             .build();
        } catch (Exception e) {
            final Entity<String> errorMessage = Entity
                                        .json(e.getMessage());
            return Response.status(Response.Status.BAD_REQUEST)
                    .entity(errorMessage).build();
        }
    }
}
```

If you have understood our earlier section well, this code will be almost intuitive to you. We have included two methods here, just like the SOAP alter ego; the former one is named `getSeatList`, which is bound to an HTTP GET request and produces the list of `Seats`. The list is returned using a JSON representation that is pretty common when returning Java objects to the client.

The grammar for JSON objects is simple and requires the grouping of the data definition and data values; it is as follows:

- Elements are enclosed within curly brackets (`{` and `}`)
- Values of elements come in pairs with the structure of `name:value` and are comma separated
- Arrays are enclosed within square brackets (`[` and `]`)

That's all there is to it (for the full JSON grammar description, visit `http://www.json.org/`).

The second method included in this class is `bookPlace`, which will be used to invoke the corresponding `bookSeat` class of our EJB. This method, on the other hand, is bound to the following HTTP POST method:

```
@POST
@Path("/{id}")
public Response bookPlace(@PathParam("id") int id)
```

You might be thinking that this `Path` expression seems a bit weird, but all it does is map a URI parameter (included in the `Path` expression) to a method parameter. In short, the parameter that is included in the URL will be passed to the method in the `ID` variable.

The previous method also returns a JSON-formatted string that is encoded and decoded using Jackson (by default, it is possible to create your own message body providers!), a library that transforms POJOs to JSON (and vice versa).

Before we proceed, we need to extend our sample with a new resource account, which will allow us to check the cash status and optionally reset it:

```
package com.packtpub.wflydevelopment.chapter7.boundary;

@Path("/account")
@Produces(MediaType.APPLICATION_JSON)
@RequestScoped
public class AccountResource {

    @Inject
```

```
        private TheatreBooker theatreBooker;

    @GET
    public AccountDto getAccount() {
        return AccountDto
                .fromAccount(theatreBooker.getCurrentAccount());
    }

    @POST
    public Response renew() {
        theatreBooker.createCustomer();
        return Response
        .ok(AccountDto.fromAccount(theatreBooker.getCurrentAccount()))
        .build();
    }
}
```

The account representation is available, as shown in the following code:

```
package com.packtpub.wflydevelopment.chapter7.entity;

public class Account {

    private final int balance;

    public Account(int initialBalance) {
        this.balance = initialBalance;
    }

    public Account charge(int amount) {
        final int newBalance = balance - amount;
        if (newBalance < 0) {
            throw new IllegalArgumentException("Debit value on
account!");
        }
        return new Account(newBalance);
    }

    public int getBalance() {
        return balance;
    }

    @Override
    public String toString() {
        return "Account [balance = " + balance + "]";
    }
}
```

The last step is to update our `TheatreBooker` class to use our new account representation:

```
private Account currentAccount;

@PostConstruct
public void createCustomer() {
    currentAccount = new Account(100);
}

public void bookSeat(int seatId) {
    logger.info("Booking seat " + seatId);
    final int seatPrice = theatreBox.getSeatPrice(seatId);

    if (seatPrice > currentAccount.getBalance()) {
        throw new IllegalArgumentException("Not enough money!");
    }

    theatreBox.buyTicket(seatId);
    currentAccount = currentAccount.charge(seatPrice);

    logger.info("Seat booked.");
}

public Account getCurrentAccount() {
    return currentAccount;
}
```

 The newest version of JAX-RS also supports server-side asynchronous responses. Thanks to the `@Suspended` annotation and the `AsyncResponse` class, you can use a separate (possibly delayed) thread to handle a request call.

Adding filters

JAX-RS allows us to define filters and interceptors for both the client and server. They allow the developer to address cross-cutting concerns, such as security, auditing, or compression. Basically, you can treat filters and interceptors as extension points.

Filters are used mainly on headers of requests and responses. For example, you can block a request based on its header fields or log only failed requests. On the contrary, interceptors deal with message bodies, for example, you can sign or compress the messages. Interceptors also come in two flavors: one for reading (they are executed when a message is translated into a POJO, for example JSON to `SeatDto`) and one for writing (they are used for POJO to message translation).

We can add a simple server-side logging filter to our application by creating the following class:

```java
package com.packtpub.wflydevelopment.chapter7.controller;

import java.io.IOException;
import java.util.logging.Logger;

import javax.inject.Inject;
import javax.ws.rs.container.ContainerRequestContext;
import javax.ws.rs.container.ContainerRequestFilter;
import javax.ws.rs.container.ContainerResponseContext;
import javax.ws.rs.container.ContainerResponseFilter;
import javax.ws.rs.ext.Provider;

@Provider
public class LoggingRestFilter implements ContainerRequestFilter,
ContainerResponseFilter {

    @Inject
    private Logger logger;

    @Override
    public void filter(ContainerRequestContext requestContext,
ContainerResponseContext responseContext)
            throws IOException {
        logger.info(responseContext.getStatusInfo().toString());
    }

    @Override
    public void filter(ContainerRequestContext requestContext) throws
IOException {
        logger.info(requestContext.getMethod() + " on " +
requestContext.getUriInfo().getPath());
    }
}
```

As you can see, we implement two pretty straightforward interfaces: `ContainerRequestFilter` and `ContainerResponseFilter`. We simply log some information about the HTTP request and response. To activate the filter, we use the `@Provider` annotation; without additional configuration, the filter will work for every REST resource in our application. Additionally, if we would like to reject a request in the filter, there is a `requestContext.abortWith` method.

The client side has two corresponding interfaces: `ClientRequestFilter` and `ClientResponseFilter`. The implementations, however, must be registered manually.

Now the REST service is complete and we can start deploying it in the usual way:

```
mvn package wildfly:deploy
```

If you followed all the steps so far, the `http://localhost:8080/ticket-agency-ws/rest/seat` GET method issued by your browser should print out the list of available seats:

```
[{"id":0,"name":"Stalls","price":40,"booked":false},{"id":1,"name":"St
alls","price":40,"booked":false},{"id":2,"name":"Stalls","price":40,"b
ooked":false},{"id":3,"name":"Stalls","price":40,"booked":false},{"id"
:4,"name":"Stalls","price":40,"booked":false},

. . . . . .
```

Going to `http://localhost:8080/ticket-agency-ws/rest/account` will result in:

```
{"balance":100}
```

You should also see some log statements from our filter in the console, for instance:

```
19:52:45,906 INFO    [com.packtpub.wflydevelopment.chapter7.controller.
LoggingRestFilter] (default task-10) GET on /seat

19:52:45,909 INFO    [com.packtpub.wflydevelopment.chapter7.controller.
LoggingRestFilter] (default task-10) OK

20:29:04,275 INFO    [com.packtpub.wflydevelopment.chapter7.controller.
LoggingRestFilter] (default task-14) GET on /account

20:29:04,313 INFO    [com.packtpub.wflydevelopment.chapter7.controller.
LoggingRestFilter] (default task-14) OK
```

Consuming our REST service

Connecting to a RESTful web service takes no more work than directly connecting to the service through an HTTP connection. For this reason, you can use plenty of APIs to access your REST services, such as the JDK `URLConnection` class or Jakarta Commons HttpClient API, since we have a standardized client available in JAX-RS.

If you want to retrieve the list of `Seats` from your REST service, your code should look like this:

```
Client restclient = ClientBuilder.newClient();
WebTarget seatResource = restclient.target(APPLICATION_URL + "seat");
Collection<SeatDto> seats = seatResource.request().get(new GenericType
<Collection<SeatDto>>() {});
```

The previous code will simply perform a GET action to the REST service that is deployed as part of the `ticket-agency-ws` web application. RESTEasy (using Jackson) will transform the JSON objects.

The following standalone sample will get the data from the account and seat resources and attempt to book all of the available seats:

```
public class RestServiceTestApplication {
    private static final String APPLICATION_URL =
"http://localhost:8080/ticket-agency-ws/rest/";

    private WebTarget accountResource;
    private WebTarget seatResource;

    public static void main(String[] args) {
        new RestServiceTestApplication().runSample();
    }

    public RestServiceTestApplication() {
        Client restclient = ClientBuilder.newClient();

        accountResource = restclient.target(APPLICATION_URL +
"account");
        seatResource = restclient.target(APPLICATION_URL + "seat");
    }

    public void runSample() {
        printAccountStatusFromServer();

        System.out.println("=== Current status: ");
```

```
        Collection<SeatDto> seats = getSeatsFromServer();
        printSeats(seats);

        System.out.println("=== Booking: ");
        bookSeats(seats);

        System.out.println("=== Status after booking: ");
        Collection<SeatDto> bookedSeats = getSeatsFromServer();
        printSeats(bookedSeats);

        printAccountStatusFromServer();
    }

    private void printAccountStatusFromServer() {
        AccountDto account = accountResource.request().get(AccountDto.
class);
        System.out.println(account);
    }

    private Collection<SeatDto> getSeatsFromServer() {
        return seatResource.request().get(new GenericType<Collection<S
eatDto>>() { });
    }

    private void printSeats(Collection<SeatDto> seats) {
        seats.forEach(System.out::println);
    }

    private void bookSeats(Collection<SeatDto> seats) {
        for (SeatDto seat : seats) {
            try {
                String idOfSeat = Integer.toString(seat.getId());
                seatResource.path(idOfSeat).request().post(Entity.
json(""), String.class);
                System.out.println(seat + " booked");
            } catch (WebApplicationException e) {
                Response response = e.getResponse();
                StatusType statusInfo = response.getStatusInfo();
                System.out.println(seat + " not booked (" +
statusInfo.getReasonPhrase() + "):" response.readEntity(JsonObject.
class). getString("entity"));
            }
        }
    }
}
```

In the highlighted fragments, you can see the REST calls used to retrieve the data and booking seats. Our `post` call requires an ID to be specified; we do that by using the `path` method of the `request` builder. It is also possible to make the call asynchronously, using the `async` method and a `Future` object:

```
Future<Collection<SeatDto>> future = seatResource.request()
        .async().get(new GenericType<Collection<SeatDto>>() {});
```

We can use the new `CompletableFuture` class from Java 8 to be notified about the completion of a request:

```
CompletableFuture.<Collection<SeatDto>> supplyAsync(() -> {
    try {
        return future.get();
    } catch (Exception e) {
        e.printStackTrace();
        throw new IllegalArgumentException(e);
    }
}).thenAccept(seats -> seats.forEach(System.out::println));
```

After receiving the data, we simply print it out. Another option is to simply create an `InvocationCallback` class and pass it as a second argument to the `get` method.

Compiling our ticket example

Our sample can reside in a separate Maven module or you can leave it with the server content (although it is not a good practice). In order to compile our client project with the REST web service, we need to import the JAX-RS API that is included in the application server libraries. We will need the following dependencies in our standalone application:

```
<properties>
    . . .
    <version.resteasy-client>3.0.6.Final</version.resteasy-client>
</properties>

<dependencies>
    <dependency>
        <groupId>org.jboss.resteasy</groupId>
        <artifactId>resteasy-client</artifactId>
        <version> ${version.resteasy-client}</version>
    </dependency>

    <dependency>
```

```
            <groupId>org.jboss.resteasy</groupId>
            <artifactId>resteasy-json-p-provider</artifactId>
            <version> ${version.resteasy-client}</version>
        </dependency>

        <dependency>
            <groupId>org.jboss.resteasy</groupId>
            <artifactId>resteasy-jackson-provider</artifactId>
            <version> ${version.resteasy-client}</version>
        </dependency>

        <dependency>
            <groupId>com.packtpub.wflydevelopment.chapter7</groupId>
            <artifactId>ticket-agency-ws</artifactId>
            <version>1.0</version>
        </dependency>
    </dependencies>
</dependencies>
```

If you have any problems with the creation of the POM file, you can look it up in the samples that are distributed with this book.

Now simply run your application, and you should see something similar to the following console output:

```
AccountDto [balance=100]
=== Current status:
SeatDto [id=1, name=Stalls, price=40, booked=false]
SeatDto [id=2, name=Stalls, price=40, booked=false]
SeatDto [id=3, name=Stalls, price=40, booked=false]
SeatDto [id=4, name=Stalls, price=40, booked=false]
SeatDto [id=5, name=Stalls, price=40, booked=false]
SeatDto [id=6, name=Circle, price=20, booked=false]
SeatDto [id=7, name=Circle, price=20, booked=false]
...
```

Adding AngularJS

Our samples for the REST integration are not very spectacular. However, because we expose the functionality of our application via a REST API, it is easy to create a non-Java GUI, which can be used to control the application.

To create a GUI that uses only the REST API to communicate with our Java backend, we will use a popular JavaScript framework: AngularJS (http://angularjs.org/). We won't get into too much detail of the JavaScript code. The most interesting part for us is the usage of our REST API, which we currently consume only in a Java application.

As seen in *Chapter 5*, *Combining Persistence with CDI*, we will use WebJars. This time, apart from Bootstrap, we need the AngularJS (preferably in Version 3.x) and Angular UI Bootstrap package (http://angular-ui.github.io/bootstrap/):

```
<dependency>
    <groupId>org.webjars</groupId>
    <artifactId>bootstrap</artifactId>
    <version>3.2.0</version>
</dependency>
<dependency>
    <groupId>org.webjars</groupId>
    <artifactId>angularjs</artifactId>
    <version>1.3.0-rc.1</version>
</dependency>
<dependency>
    <groupId>org.webjars</groupId>
    <artifactId>angular-ui-bootstrap</artifactId>
    <version>0.11.0-2</version>
</dependency>
```

 Remember that all the files that are required to run this sample are available with the code attached to this book.

We will need an index.html file to start our work and an empty scripts directory to store our logic. Our directory structure should currently look like this:

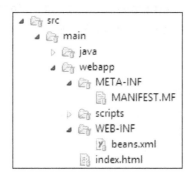

In the `index.html` file, we need to add all the required libraries along with our well-known Bootstrap structure:

```
<!doctype html>
<html lang="en" ng-app="ticketApp">
<head>
    <meta charset="utf-8">
    <title>Ticket Service</title>
    <link rel="stylesheet" href=""webjars/bootstrap/3.2.0/css/
bootstrap.css">
    <link rel="stylesheet" href=""webjars/bootstrap/3.2.0/css/
bootstrap-theme.css">
    <style>
        body {
            padding-top: 60px;
        }
    </style>
</head>
<body>

<div class="navbar navbar-inverse navbar-fixed-top" role="navigation">
</div>

<div class="container" ng-controller="SeatCtrl">
    <footer>
        <p class="text-muted">&copy; Packt Publishing 2014</p>
    </footer>
</div>

<script src="webjars/angularjs/1.3.0-rc.1/angular.js"></script>
<script src="webjars/angularjs/1.3.0-rc.1/angular-resource.js"></
script>
<script src="webjars/angularjs/1.3.0-rc.1/angular-route.js"></script>
<script src="webjars/angular-ui-bootstrap/0.11.0/ui-bootstrap-tpls.
js"></script>

<script src="scripts/app.js"></script>
<script src="scripts/controllers/seat.js"></script>
<script src="scripts/services/seatservice.js"></script>
<script src="scripts/services/accountservice.js"></script>
</body>
</html>
```

You may have also noticed two strange-looking attributes in the `html` tags: `ng-app` and `ng-controller`. These are AngularJS directives that point to the web page being an AngularJS application, and that the container div will use a `SeatCtrl` controller.

Now, we will need the following files placed in our `scripts` directory. The first one is the initialization file `app.js`:

```
'use strict';
angular.module('ticketApp', [ 'ngResource', 'ngRoute', 'ui.bootstrap'
])
    .config(function ($routeProvider) {
        $routeProvider.when('/', {
            controller: 'SeatCtrl'
        }).otherwise({
            redirectTo: '/'
        });
    });
```

Next we will initialize the address of our seat resource in `scripts/services/seatservice.js`:

```
'use strict';
angular.module('ticketApp').service('SeatService',
    function SeatService($resource) {
        return $resource('rest/seat/:seatId', {
            seatId: '@id'
        }, {
            query: {
                method: 'GET',
                isArray: true
            },
            book: {
                method: 'POST'
            }
        });
    });
```

As you can see, we mapped our REST URL to the JavaScript code along with two HTTP methods: GET and POST. They will be called by the controller to communicate with the server; the same goes for our account resource, as shown in the following code:

```
'use strict';
angular.module('ticketApp').service('AccountService',
    function AccountService($resource) {
        return $resource('rest/account', {}, {
```

```
        query: {
            method: 'GET',
            isArray: false
        },
        reset: {
            method: 'POST'
        }
    });
});
```

Finally, we create a simple controller to place our logic at `scripts/controllers/seat.js`:

```
'use strict';
angular.module('ticketApp').controller(
    'SeatCtrl',
    function ($scope, SeatService, AccountService) {
        $scope.seats = SeatService.query();
        $scope.account = AccountService.query();

        $scope.alerts = [];

        $scope.bookTicket = function (seat) {
            seat.$book({}, function success() {
                $scope.account.$query();
            }, function err(httpResponse) {
                $scope.alerts.push({
                    type: 'danger',
                    msg: 'Error booking ticket for seat '
                        + httpResponse.config.data.id + ': '
                        + httpResponse.data.entity
                });
            });
        };
        $scope.closeAlert = function (index) {
            $scope.alerts.splice(index, 1);
        };
        $scope.clearWarnings = function () {
            $scope.alerts.length = 0;
        };
        $scope.resetAccount = function () {
            $scope.account.$reset();
        };
    });
```

The highlighted portions of code are calls to the services we defined previously. For instance, `$scope.seats = SeatService.query()` will issue a GET request to retrieve a list of seats in the JSON format. The case for `seat.$book` is similar; it will issue a POST request to book a specific seat.

Our whole JavaScript logic is now in place. One final move is to place some HTML code bound to it in our `index.html` file. Insert the following code in the `index.html` file, inside the `content` div:

```
<alert ng-repeat="alert in alerts" type="alert.type"
        close="closeAlert($index)">{{alert.msg}}
</alert>

<div class="panel panel-default">
    <div class="panel-heading">
        <h3 class="panel-title">Ticket booking</h3>
    </div>
    <div class="panel-body">
        <p>
            Remaining money: <span class="badge">{{account.balance}}</span>
        </p>
        <br/>

        <button type="button" class="btn btn-primary btn-xs"
                ng-click="clearWarnings()">Clear warnings
        </button>

        <button type="button" class="btn btn-warning btn-xs"
                ng-click="resetAccount()">Reset account
        </button>
    </div>
    <table class="table table-hover table-striped">
        <thead><th>ID</th><th>Name</th><th>Price</th><th>Booked<//
th>    <th>Book</th></thead>
        <tbody>
        <tr ng-repeat="seat in seats">
            <td>{{seat.id}}</td>
            <td>{{seat.name}}</td>
            <td>${{seat.price}}</td>
            <td><span
                    class="glyphicon glyphicon-{{seat.booked ?
'ok' :'remove'}}"></span></td>
            <td>
                <button type="button"
                        class="btn btn-primary {{seat.booked?
'disabled' :''}} btn-xs" ng-click="bookTicket(seat)">Book
```

```
            </button>
          </td>
        </tr>
        </tbody>
    </table>
```

The code is similar to the JSF tables we created in the earlier chapters. What is important to us is that the {{ }} symbols are used by AngularJS to bind the displayed data with a variable in a controller, which, in fact, is a representation of our REST endpoints.

Additionally, the ng-click directives are bound to the appropriate methods in the controller. The bookTicket method issues a seat.$book call, which is propagated as a POST request to our backend.

We can now deploy our application to the server. After going to http://localhost:8080/ticket-agency-ws/index.html in your browser, you should see your application running, as shown in the following screenshot:

You can use the developer's tools in Chrome (or FireBug in Mozilla Firefox) to inspect the `rest` calls that are done against the server; simply press *F12* and switch to the **Network** tab:

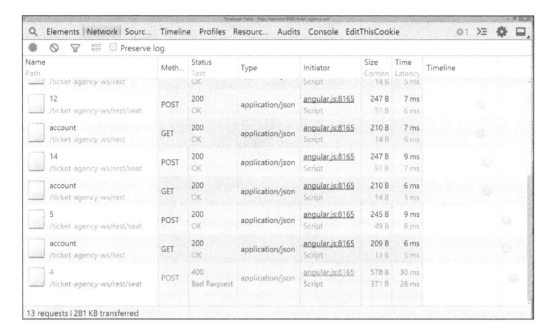

Congratulations! You have just created a modern Internet application and combined it with a REST API that was earlier used by a standalone console application!

Choosing between SOAP and REST services

The choice of adopting SOAP rather than REST depends on your application's requirements. SOAP web services are exposed using their own well-defined protocol and focus on exposing pieces of application logic as services. So if your requirement is to consume business services that are exposed using a well-defined and negotiated contract (between the service consumer and service provider), SOAP web services are a perfect match.

On the other hand, if you need to access some server resources using stateless HTTP invocations and as little as possible of the navigation bar of your browser, you should probably go with RESTful web services.

That being said, there may still be some scenarios that could fit both the options, and you are free to choose whichever web service suits your requirements the best. Recently, REST has gained popularity, thanks to its interoperability. We use only the HTTP protocol and JSON, which almost every language can handle. Therefore, a REST API developed using Java EE can be used by a wide variety of clients along with mobile devices. Often, this feature is a deal breaker when it comes to designing a system.

Summary

In this chapter, we introduced some of the basic web services concepts so that you could get acquainted with these technologies before using them to enhance your ticket application.

Then, we went through SOAP-based web services that are based on a contract between the service and client defined by the WSDL file. SOAP web services are an excellent option to integrate systems when you have well-defined, abstract operations exposed using standard XML files.

Then, we discussed REST services. The key to the REST methodology is to write web services using an interface that is already well known and widely used: the URI. The twist here is to identify the key system resources (this can be entities, collections, or anything else the designer thinks is worthy of having its own URI) and expose them using standard methods that are mapped to standard methods. In this case, the HTTP verbs are mapped to resource-specific semantics.

We created two applications that use our REST API: one console-based and one written purely in JavaScript using AngularJS. Both of these use the same REST endpoints and the second one knows only about JSON; it has no idea about the Java classes underneath (or even about Java).

We discussed application server resources a lot. In the next chapter, we will explore another approach for client-server communication: WebSockets.

8
Adding WebSockets

WebSockets are one of the biggest additions in Java EE 7. In this chapter, we will explore the new possibilities that they provide to a developer. In our ticket booking applications, we already used a wide variety of approaches to inform the clients about events occurring on the server side. These include the following:

- JSF polling
- Java Messaging Service (JMS) messages
- REST requests
- Remote EJB requests

All of them, besides JMS, were based on the assumption that the client will be responsible for asking the server about the state of the application. In some cases, such as checking whether someone else has not booked a ticket during our interaction with the application, this is a wasteful strategy; the server is in the position to inform clients when it is needed. What's more, it feels like the developer must hack the HTTP protocol to get a notification from a server to the client. This is a requirement that has to be implemented in most web applications, and therefore, deserves a standardized solution that can be applied by the developers in multiple projects without much effort.

WebSockets are changing the game for developers. They replace the request-response paradigm in which the client always initiates the communication with a two-point bidirectional messaging system. After the initial connection, both sides can send independent messages to each other as long as the session is alive. This means that we can easily create web applications that will automatically refresh their state with up-to-date data from the server. You probably have already seen this kind of behavior in Google Docs or live broadcasts on news sites. Now we can achieve the same effect in a simpler and more efficient way than in earlier versions of Java Enterprise Edition. In this chapter, we will try to leverage these new, exciting features that come with WebSockets in Java EE 7 thanks to JSR 356 (`https://jcp.org/en/jsr/detail?id=356`) and HTML5.

In this chapter, you will learn the following topics:

- How WebSockets work
- How to create a WebSocket endpoint in Java EE 7
- How to create an HTML5/AngularJS client that will accept push notifications from an application deployed on WildFly

An overview of WebSockets

A WebSocket session between the client and server is built upon a standard TCP connection. Although the WebSocket protocol has its own control frames (mainly to create and sustain the connection) coded by the Internet Engineering Task Force in the RFC 6455 (http://tools.ietf.org/html/rfc6455), the peers are not obliged to use any specific format to exchange application data. You may use plaintext, XML, JSON, or anything else to transmit your data. As you probably remember, this is quite different from SOAP-based WebServices, which had bloated specifications of the exchange protocol. The same goes for RESTful architectures; we no longer have the predefined verb methods from HTTP (GET, PUT, POST, and DELETE), status codes, and the whole semantics of an HTTP request.

This liberty means that WebSockets are pretty low level compared to the technologies that we have used up to this point, but thanks to this, the communication overhead is minimal. The protocol is less verbose than SOAP or RESTful HTTP, which allows us to achieve higher performance. This, however, comes with a price. We usually like to use the features of higher-level protocols (such as horizontal scaling and rich URL semantics), and with WebSockets, we would need to write them by hand. For standard CRUD-like operations, it would be easier to use a REST endpoint than create everything from scratch.

What do we get from WebSockets compared to the standard HTTP communication? First of all, a direct connection between two peers. Normally, when you connect to a web server (which can, for instance, handle a REST endpoint), every subsequent call is a new TCP connection, and your machine is treated like it is a different one every time you make a request. You can, of course, simulate a stateful behavior (so that the server will recognize your machine between different requests) using cookies and increase the performance by reusing the same connection in a short period of time for a specific client, but basically, it is a workaround to overcome the limitations of the HTTP protocol.

Once you establish a WebSocket connection between a server and client, you can use the same session (and underlying TCP connection) during the whole communication. Both sides are aware of it and can send data independently in a full-duplex manner (both sides can send and receive data simultaneously). Using plain HTTP, there is no way for the server to spontaneously start sending data to the client without any request from its side. What's more, the server is aware of all of its connected WebSocket clients, and can even send data between them!

The current solution that includes trying to simulate real-time data delivery using HTTP protocol can put a lot of stress on the web server. Polling (asking the server about updates), long polling (delaying the completion of a request to the moment when an update is ready), and streaming (a Comet-based solution with a constantly open HTTP response) are all ways to hack the protocol to do things that it wasn't designed for and have their own limitations. Thanks to the elimination of unnecessary checks, WebSockets can heavily reduce the number of HTTP requests that have to be handled by the web server. The updates are delivered to the user with a smaller latency because we only need one round-trip through the network to get the desired information (it is pushed by the server immediately).

All of these features make WebSockets a great addition to the Java EE platform, which fills the gaps needed to easily finish specific tasks, such as sending updates, notifications, and orchestrating multiple client interactions. Despite these advantages, WebSockets are not intended to replace REST or SOAP WebServices. They do not scale so well horizontally (they are hard to distribute because of their stateful nature), and they lack most of the features that are utilized in web applications. URL semantics, complex security, compression, and many other features are still better realized using other technologies.

How do WebSockets work

To initiate a WebSocket session, the client must send an HTTP request with an `Upgrade: websocket` header field. This informs the server that the peer client has asked the server to switch to the WebSocket protocol.

 You may notice that the same happens in WildFly for Remote EJBs; the initial connection is made using an HTTP request, and is later switched to the remote protocol thanks to the `Upgrade` mechanism. The standard `Upgrade` header field can be used to handle any protocol, other than HTTP, which is accepted by both sides (the client and server). In WildFly, this allows you to reuse the HTTP port (`80/8080`) for other protocols and therefore minimise the number of required ports that should be configured.

If the server can "understand" the WebSocket protocol, the client and server then proceed with the handshaking phase. They negotiate the version of the protocol, exchange security keys, and if everything goes well, the peers can go to the data transfer phase. From now on, the communication is only done using the WebSocket protocol. It is not possible to exchange any HTTP frames using the current connection. The whole life cycle of a connection can be summarized in the following diagram:

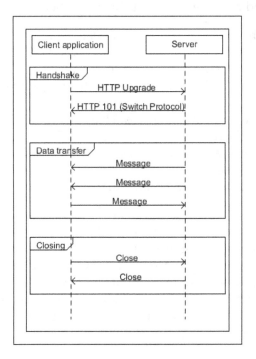

A sample HTTP request from a JavaScript application to a WildFly server would look similar to this:

```
GET /ticket-agency-websockets/tickets HTTP/1.1
Upgrade: websocket
Connection: Upgrade
Host: localhost:8080
Origin: http://localhost:8080
Pragma: no-cache
Cache-Control: no-cache
Sec-WebSocket-Key: TrjgyVjzLK4Lt5s8GzlFhA==
```

```
Sec-WebSocket-Version: 13

Sec-WebSocket-Extensions: permessage-deflate; client_max_window_bits,
x-webkit-deflate-frame

User-Agent: Mozilla/5.0 (Windows NT 6.3; WOW64) AppleWebKit/537.36
(KHTML, like Gecko) Chrome/34.0.1847.116 Safari/537.36

Cookie: [45 bytes were stripped]
```

We can see that the client requests an upgrade connection with WebSocket as the target protocol on the URL /ticket-agency-websockets/tickets. It additionally passes information about the requested version and key.

If the server supports the request protocol and all the required data is passed by the client, then it would respond with the following frame:

```
HTTP/1.1 101 Switching Protocols

X-Powered-By: Undertow 1

Server: Wildfly 8

Origin: http://localhost:8080

Upgrade: WebSocket

Sec-WebSocket-Accept: ZEAab1TcSQCmv8RsLHg4RL/TpHw=

Date: Sun, 13 Apr 2014 17:04:00 GMT

Connection: Upgrade

Sec-WebSocket-Location: ws://localhost:8080/ticket-agency-websockets/
tickets

Content-Length: 0
```

The status code of the response is 101 (switching protocols) and we can see that the server is now going to start using the WebSocket protocol. The TCP connection initially used for the HTTP request is now the base of the WebSocket session and can be used for transmissions. If the client tries to access a URL, which is only handled by another protocol, then the server can ask the client to do an upgrade request. The server uses the 426 (upgrade required) status code in such cases.

> The initial connection creation has some overhead (because of the HTTP frames that are exchanged between the peers), but after it is completed, new messages have only 2 bytes of additional headers. This means that when we have a large number of small messages, WebSocket will be an order of magnitude faster than REST protocols simply because there is less data to transmit!

If you are wondering about the browser support of WebSockets, you can look it up at http://caniuse.com/websockets. All new versions of major browsers currently support WebSockets; the total coverage is estimated (at the time of writing) at 74 percent. You can see this in the following screenshot:

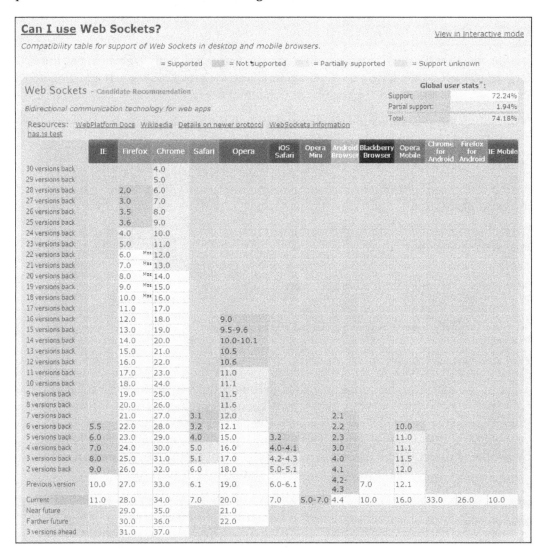

After this theoretical introduction, we are ready to jump into action. We can now create our first WebSocket endpoint!

Creating our first endpoint

Let's start with a simple example:

```
package com.packtpub.wflydevelopment.chapter8.boundary;

import javax.websocket.EndpointConfig;
import javax.websocket.OnOpen;
import javax.websocket.Session;
import javax.websocket.server.ServerEndpoint;
import java.io.IOException;

@ServerEndpoint("/hello")
public class HelloEndpoint {

    @OnOpen
    public void open(Session session, EndpointConfig conf) throws
IOException {
        session.getBasicRemote().sendText("Hi!");
    }
}
```

Java EE 7 specification has taken into account developer friendliness, which can be clearly seen in the given example. In order to define your WebSocket endpoint, you just need a few annotations on a **Plain Old Java Object (POJO)**. The first annotation `@ServerEndpoint("/hello")` defines a path to your endpoint. It's a good time to discuss the endpoint's full address. We placed this sample in the application named `ticket-agency-websockets`. During the deployment of application, you can spot information in the WildFly log about endpoints creation, as shown in the following command line:

```
02:21:35,182 INFO  [io.undertow.websockets.jsr] (MSC service thread
1-7) UT026003: Adding annotated server endpoint class com.packtpub.
wflydevelopment.chapter8.boundary.FirstEndpoint for path /hello

02:21:35,401 INFO  [org.jboss.resteasy.spi.ResteasyDeployment] (MSC
service thread 1-7) Deploying javax.ws.rs.core.Application: class com.
packtpub.wflydevelopment.chapter8.webservice.JaxRsActivator$Proxy$_$$_
WeldClientProxy

02:21:35,437 INFO  [org.wildfly.extension.undertow] (MSC service thread
1-7) JBAS017534: Registered web context: /ticket-agency-websockets
```

The full URL of the endpoint is `ws://localhost:8080/ticket-agency-websockets/hello`, which is just a concatenation of the server and application address with an endpoint path on an appropriate protocol.

The second used annotation @OnOpen defines the endpoint behavior when the connection from the client is opened. It's not the only behavior-related annotation of the WebSocket endpoint. Let's look to the following table:

Annotation	Description
@OnOpen	The connection is open. With this annotation, we can use the Session and EndpointConfig parameters. The first parameter represents the connection to the user and allows further communication. The second one provides some client-related information.
@OnMessage	This annotation is executed when a message from the client is being received. In such a method, you can just have Session and for example, the String parameter, where the String parameter represents the received message.
@OnError	There are bad times when an error occurs. With this annotation, you can retrieve a Throwable object apart from standard Session.
@OnClose	When the connection is closed, it is possible to get some data concerning this event in the form of the CloseReason type object.

There is one more interesting line in our HelloEndpoint. Using the Session object, it is possible to communicate with the client. This clearly shows that in WebSockets, two-directional communication is easily possible. In this example, we decided to respond to a connected user synchronously (getBasicRemote()) with just a text message *Hi!* (sendText (String)). Of course, it's also possible to communicate asynchronously and send, for example, sending binary messages using your own binary bandwidth saving protocol. We will present some of these processes in the next example.

Expanding our client application

It's time to show how you can leverage the WebSocket features in real life. In the previous chapter, *Chapter 7, Adding Web Services to Your Applications*, we created the ticket booking application based on the REST API and AngularJS framework. It was clearly missing one important feature: the application did not show information concerning ticket purchases of other users. This is a perfect use case for WebSockets!

Since we're just adding a feature to our previous app, we will only describe the changes we will introduce to it.

In this example, we would like to be able to inform all current users about other purchases. This means that we have to store information about active sessions. Let's start with the registry type object, which will serve this purpose. We can use a `Singleton` session bean for this task, as shown in the following code:

```
@Singleton
public class SessionRegistry {

    private final Set<Session> sessions = new HashSet<>();

    @Lock(LockType.READ)
    public Set<Session> getAll() {
        return Collections.unmodifiableSet(sessions);
    }

    @Lock(LockType.WRITE)
    public void add(Session session) {
        sessions.add(session);
    }

    @Lock(LockType.WRITE)
    public void remove(Session session) {
        sessions.remove(session);
    }
}
```

We could use `Collections.synchronizedSet` from standard Java libraries but it's a great chance to remember what we described in *Chapter 3, Introducing Java EE 7 – EJBs*, about container-based concurrency. In `SessionRegistry`, we defined some basic methods to add, get, and remove sessions. For the sake of collection thread safety during retrieval, we return an unmodifiable view.

We defined the registry, so now we can move to the endpoint definition. We will need a POJO, which will use our newly defined registry as shown:

```
@ServerEndpoint("/tickets")
public class TicketEndpoint {

    @Inject
    private SessionRegistry sessionRegistry;

    @OnOpen
    public void open(Session session, EndpointConfig conf) {
```

```
            sessionRegistry.add(session);
    }

    @OnClose
    public void close(Session session, CloseReason reason) {
            sessionRegistry.remove(session);
    }

    public void send(@Observes Seat seat) {
            sessionRegistry.getAll().forEach(session -> session.
getAsyncRemote().sendText(toJson(seat)));
    }

    private String toJson(Seat seat) {
            final JsonObject jsonObject = Json.createObjectBuilder()
                    .add("id", seat.getId())
                    .add("booked", seat.isBooked())
                    .build();
            return jsonObject.toString();
    }
}
```

Our endpoint is defined in the /tickets address. We injected a SessionRepository to our endpoint. During @OnOpen, we add Sessions to the registry, and during @OnClose, we just remove them. Message sending is performed on the CDI event (the @Observers annotation), which is already fired in our code during TheatreBox.buyTicket(int). In our send method, we retrieve all sessions from SessionRepository, and for each of them, we asynchronously send information about booked seats. We don't really need information about all the Seat fields to realize this feature. That's the reason why we don't use the automatic JSON serialization we know from the last chapter here. Instead, we decided to use a minimalistic JSON object, which provides only the required data. To do this, we used the new Java API for JSON Processing (JSR-353). Using a fluent-like API, we're able to create a JSON object and add two fields to it. Then, we just convert JSON to the string, which is sent in a text message.

Because in our example we send messages in response to a CDI event, we don't have (in the event handler) an out-of-the-box reference to any of the sessions. We have to use our sessionRegistry object to access the active ones. However, if we would like to do the same thing but, for example, in the @OnMessage method, then it is possible to get all active sessions just by executing the session.getOpenSessions() method.

These are all the changes required to perform on the backend side. Now, we have to modify our AngularJS frontend to leverage the added feature. The good news is that JavaScript already includes classes that can be used to perform WebSocket communication! There are a few lines of code we have to add inside the module defined in the seat.js file, which are as follows:

```
var ws = new WebSocket("ws://localhost:8080/ticket-agency-websockets/
tickets");
ws.onmessage = function (message) {
    var receivedData = message.data;
    var bookedSeat = JSON.parse(receivedData);

    $scope.$apply(function () {
        for (var i = 0; i < $scope.seats.length; i++) {
            if ($scope.seats[i].id === bookedSeat.id) {
                $scope.seats[i].booked = bookedSeat.booked;
                break;
            }
        }
    });
};
```

The code is very simple. We just create the WebSocket object using the URL to our endpoint, and then we define the onmessage function in that object. During the function execution, the received message is automatically parsed from the JSON to JavaScript object. Then, in $scope.$apply, we just iterate through our seats, and if the ID matches, we update the booked state. We have to use $scope.$apply because we are touching an Angular object from outside the Angular world (the onmessage function). Modifications performed on $scope.seats are automatically visible on the website. With this, we can just open our ticket booking website in two browser sessions, and see that when one user buys a ticket, the second users sees almost instantly that the seat state is changed to *booked*.

We can enhance our application a little to inform users if the WebSocket connection is really working. Let's just define onopen and onclose functions for this purpose:

```
ws.onopen = function (event) {
    $scope.$apply(function () {
        $scope.alerts.push({
            type: 'info',
            msg: 'Push connection from server is working'
        });
    });
};
```

```
ws.onclose = function (event) {
    $scope.$apply(function () {
        $scope.alerts.push({
            type: 'warning',
            msg: 'Error on push connection from server '
        });
    });
};
```

To inform users about a connection's state, we push different types of alerts. Of course, again we're touching the Angular world from the outside, so we have to perform all operations on Angular from the $scope.$apply function.

Running the described code results in the notification, which is visible in the following screenshot:

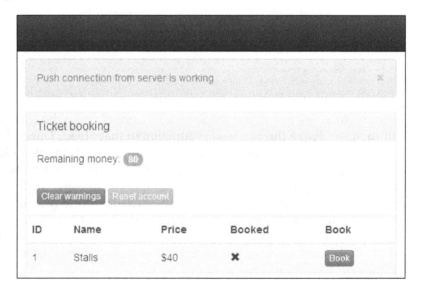

However, if the server fails after opening the website, you might get an error as shown in the following screenshot:

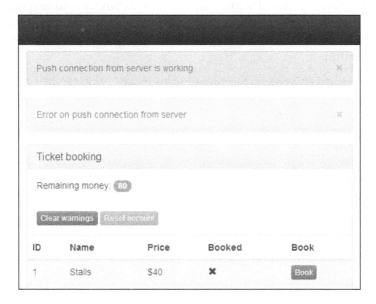

Transforming POJOs to JSON

In our current example, we transformed our `Seat` object to JSON manually. Normally, we don't want to do it this way; there are many libraries that will do the transformation for us. One of them is GSON from Google. Additionally, we can register an `encoder/decoder` class for a WebSocket endpoint that will do the transformation automatically. Let's look at how we can refactor our current solution to use an encoder.

First of all, we must add GSON to our classpath. The required Maven dependency is as follows:

```
<dependency>
    <groupId>com.google.code.gson</groupId>
    <artifactId>gson</artifactId>
    <version>2.3</version>
</dependency>
```

Next, we need to provide an implementation of the `javax.websocket.Encoder.Text` interface. There are also versions of the `javax.websocket.Encoder.Text` interface for binary and streamed data (for both binary and text formats). A corresponding hierarchy of interfaces is also available for decoders (`javax.websocket.Decoder`). Our implementation is rather simple. This is shown in the following code snippet:

```
public class JSONEncoder implements Encoder.Text<Object> {

    private Gson gson;

    @Override
    public void init(EndpointConfig config) {
        gson = new Gson(); [1]
    }

    @Override
    public void destroy() {
        // do nothing
    }

    @Override
    public String encode(Object object) throws EncodeException {
        return gson.toJson(object); [2]
    }
}
```

First, we create an instance of GSON in the `init` method; this action will be executed when the endpoint is created. Next, in the `encode` method, which is called every time, we send an object through an endpoint. We use JSON command to create JSON from an object. This is quite concise when we think how reusable this little class is. If you want more control on the JSON generation process, you can use the `GsonBuilder` class to configure the `Gson` object before creation. We have the encoder in place. Now it's time to alter our endpoint:

```
@ServerEndpoint(value = "/tickets", encoders={JSONEncoder.class}) [1]
public class TicketEndpoint {

    @Inject
    private SessionRegistry sessionRegistry;

    @OnOpen
    public void open(Session session, EndpointConfig conf) {
```

```
        sessionRegistry.add(session);
    }

    @OnClose
    public void close(Session session, CloseReason reason) {
        sessionRegistry.remove(session);
    }

    public void send(@Observes Seat seat) {
        sessionRegistry.getAll().forEach(session -> session.
getAsyncRemote().sendObject(seat));   [2]
    }
}
```

The first change is done on the `@ServerEndpoint` annotation. We have to define a list of supported encoders; we simply pass our `JSONEncoder.class` wrapped in an array. Additionally, we have to pass the endpoint name using the `value` attribute.

Earlier, we used the `sendText` method to pass a string containing a manually created JSON. Now, we want to send an object and let the encoder handle the JSON generation; therefore, we'll use the `getAsyncRemote().sendObject()` method. And that's all. Our endpoint is ready to be used. It will work the same as the earlier version, but now our objects will be fully serialized to JSON, so they will contain every field, not only `id` and `booked`.

After deploying the server, you can connect to the WebSocket endpoint using one of the Chrome extensions, for instance, the `Dark WebSocket` terminal from the Chrome store (use the `ws://localhost:8080/ticket-agency-websockets/tickets` address). When you book tickets using the web application, the WebSocket terminal should show something similar to the output shown in the following screenshot:

```
19:25:37  command: /connect ws://localhost:8080/ticket-agency-websockets/tickets
19:25:38    system: connection established, ws://localhost:8080/ticket-agency-websockets/tickets
19:25:47 received: {"id":4,"name":"Stalls","price":40,"booked":true}
19:25:47 received: {"id":6,"name":"Circle","price":20,"booked":true}
19:25:48 received: {"id":7,"name":"Circle","price":20,"booked":true}
19:25:48 received: {"id":8,"name":"Circle","price":20,"booked":true}
19:25:54  command: /disconnect
19:25:54    system: connection closed, ws://localhost:8080/ticket-agency-websockets/tickets
19:25:58                                                                    send    menu
```

Of course, it is possible to use different formats other than JSON. If you want to achieve better performance (when it comes to the serialization time and payload size), you may want to try out binary serializers such as **Kryo** (`https://github.com/EsotericSoftware/kryo`). They may not be supported by JavaScript, but may come in handy if you would like to use WebSockets for other clients too. **Tyrus** (`https://tyrus.java.net/`) is a reference implementation of the WebSocket standard for Java; you can use it in your standalone desktop applications. In that case, besides the encoder (which is used to send messages), you would also need to create a decoder, which can automatically transform incoming messages.

An alternative to WebSockets

The example we presented in this chapter is possible to be implemented using an older, lesser-known technology named **Server-Sent Events** (**SSE**). SSE allows for one-way communication from the server to client over HTTP. It is much simpler than WebSockets but has a built-in support for things such as automatic reconnection and event identifiers. WebSockets are definitely more powerful, but are not the only way to pass events, so when you need to implement some notifications from the server side, remember about SSE.

Another option is to explore the mechanisms oriented around the Comet techniques. Multiple implementations are available and most of them use different methods of transportation to achieve their goals. A comprehensive comparison is available at `http://cometdaily.com/maturity.html`.

Summary

In this chapter, we managed to introduce the new low-level type of communication. We presented how it works underneath and compares to SOAP and REST introduced in the previous chapter. We also discussed how the new approach changes the development of web applications.

Our ticket booking application was further enhanced to show users the changing state of the seats using push-like notifications. The new additions required very little code changes in our existing project when we take into account how much we are able to achieve with them. The fluent integration of WebSockets from Java EE 7 with the AngularJS application is another great showcase of flexibility, which comes with the new version of the Java EE platform.

In the next chapter, you will learn more about WildFly administration and management, so that we can explore more system-wide features of Java EE 7 in the following chapters.

9
Managing the Application Server

So far, we have covered many Java Enterprise examples and deployed them on the application server. We will now dive headlong into the vast and varied ocean of instruments that are available to manage the application server. The purpose of this chapter is to teach you how to use these instruments to administer and monitor all the resources available on the application server.

Here is the list of topics we will cover in this chapter:

- An introduction to the WildFly **Command-line Interface** (CLI)
- How to create scripts with the CLI
- How to programmatically manage your server resources using scripting languages and WildFly's client API
- How to enforce role-based security for administrators

Entering the WildFly CLI

A CLI is a complete management tool that can be used to start and stop servers, deploy and undeploy applications, configure system resources, and perform other administrative tasks. Operations in it can be executed in an atomic way or in batch modes, allowing you to run multiple tasks as a group.

Launching the CLI

If you are using Windows, you can start the CLI by entering the following command from the JBOSS_HOME/bin folder using the Command Prompt:

```
jboss-cli.bat
```

Alternatively, enter the following command if you are using Linux:

```
./jboss-cli.sh
```

Once the CLI has started, you can connect to the managed server instance using the `connect` command, which by default connects to `localhost` and the `9990` port:

```
[disconnected /] connect
[standalone@localhost:9990 /]
```

If you want to connect to another address or port, you can simply pass it to the `connect` command, as follows:

```
[disconnected /] connect 192.168.1.1
[standalone@192.168.1.1:9990 /]
```

It is also possible to launch a CLI in the connected mode; this allows it to be connected automatically and to possibly specify the commands to be executed. For example, the following `shell` command automatically connects to a WildFly instance and issues a `shutdown` command:

```
> jboss-cli.bat --connect command=:shutdown
{"outcome" => "success"}
```

CLI is especially useful for the automation of your software development process—**Continuous Integration** (**CI**) and production environment management systems can automatically control the life cycle of your application server with tools such as Chef (`https://www.getchef.com/`) or Puppet (`http://puppetlabs.com/`). It might be handy if you would like to minimize the number of manual tasks that are required to be done to deploy an application.

Connecting from remote hosts

Starting from the 7.1.0 Beta release of the application server, security is enabled on AS management interfaces by default to prevent unauthorized remote access to the application server. Although local clients of the application server are still allowed to access management interfaces without any authentication, remote clients need to enter a username/password pair to access a CLI. Here's an example session that successfully connects to a remote host with the IP address `10.13.2.255`:

```
[disconnected /] connect 10.13.2.255
Authenticating against security realm: ManagementRealm
Username: administrator
Password:
[standalone@10.13.2.255:9990 /]
```

Please refer to *Chapter 2, Your First Java EE Application on WildFly*, for more information about creating a user with the add-user.sh shell command.

Using a CLI in the graphical mode

An interesting option available for the command-line interface is the graphical mode, which can be activated by adding the --gui parameter to the shell script:

```
jboss-cli.bat --gui
```

Here's how CLI looks in the graphical mode:

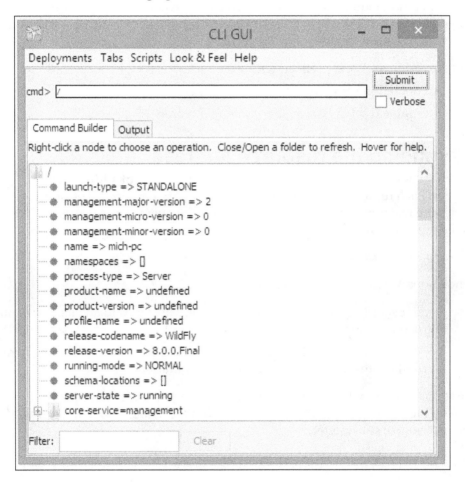

As described in the label, the resource will expand when you click on a folder; on the other hand, if you right-click on a node, you can fire an operation on it. The graphical mode could be useful to explore the possible configuration values or if you are not a big fan of console tools.

The next section discusses how to construct CLI commands, which can be executed either in the terminal mode or the graphical mode.

Constructing CLI commands

All CLI operation requests allow you to have low-level interactions with the server management model. They provide a controlled way to edit the server configurations. An operation request consists of three parts:

- An address that is prefixed with /
- An operation name that is prefixed with :
- An optional set of parameters contained within ()

Determining the resource address

The server configuration is presented as a hierarchical tree of addressable resources. Each resource node offers a different set of operations. The address specifies the resource node on which to perform the operation. An address uses the following syntax:

`/node-type=node-name`

The notations are explained as follows:

- `node-type`: This is the resource node type. This maps to an element name in the server configuration.
- `node-name`: This specifies the resource node name. This maps to the name attribute of the element in the server configuration.

Separate each level of the resource tree with a slash (/). So, for example, the following CLI expression identifies the ExampleDS data source registered in the data source subsystem:

`/subsystem=datasources/data-source=ExampleDS`

Performing operations on resources

Once you have identified a resource, you can perform operations on the resource. An operation uses the following syntax:

```
:operation-name
```

So in the previous example, you can query the list of available resources for your nodes by adding the read-resource command at the end of it:

```
/subsystem=datasources/:read-resource
{
    "outcome" => "success",
    "result" => {
        "data-source" => {"ExampleDS" => undefined},
        "jdbc-driver" => {"h2" => undefined},
        "xa-data-source" => undefined
    }
}
```

If you want to query for a specific attribute of your node, you can use the read-attribute operation instead. For example, the following code shows how to read the enabled attribute from the data source:

```
/subsystem=datasources/data-source=ExampleDS/:read-
attribute(name=enabled)
{
    "outcome" => "success",
    "result" => false
}
```

> Apart from the operations on a specific resource, you can also perform a set of commands that are available on every path of your WildFly subsystem, such as cd or ls commands. These commands are pretty much equivalent to their Unix shell counterparts, and they allow you to navigate through the WildFly subsystems. Other important additions are the deploy and undeploy commands that, as you might guess, allow you to manage the deployment of applications. These key commands are discussed in the *Deploying applications using the CLI* section of this chapter.

The CLI, however, is not just about querying attributes from the WildFly subsystems; you can also set attributes or create resources. For example, if you were to set the HTTP port of the HTTP connector, you will have to use the corresponding `write` attribute on HTTP's socket binding interface, shown as follows:

```
/socket-binding-group=standard-sockets/socket-binding=http/:write-
attribute(name=port,value=8080)
{
    "outcome" => "success",
    "response-headers" => {
        "operation-requires-reload" => true,
        "process-state" => "reload-required"
    }
}
```

Apart from the operations that we have seen so far, which can be performed on every resource of your subsystems, there can be special operations that can be performed exclusively on one resource. For example, within the naming subsystem, you will be able to issue a `jndi-view` operation that will display the list of JNDI bindings, as shown in the following code snippet:

```
/subsystem=naming/:jndi-view
{
    "outcome" => "success",
    "result" => {"java: contexts" => {
        "java:" => {
            "TransactionManager" => {
                "class-name" => "com.arjuna.ats.jbossatx.jta.
                TransactionManagerDelegate",
                "value" => "com.arjuna.ats.jbossatx.jta.
                TransactionManagerDelegate@afd978"
            },
    . . .
}
```

Using the tab completion helper

Getting to know all the available commands in the CLI is a pretty hard task; this management interface includes an essential feature, the tab completion. Suppose the cursor is positioned at the beginning of an empty line; now if you type in / and press the *Tab* key, you will get the following list of all the available node types:

```
[standalone@localhost:9990 /] /
core-service            extension               socket-binding-group
deployment              interface               subsystem
deployment-overlay      path                    system-property
```

After selecting the node type, you want to enter into the tree of resources, so type = and press the *Tab* key again. This will result in a list of all the following node names available for the chosen node type:

```
[standalone@localhost:9990 /] /subsystem=
batch                    jdr                      resource-adapters
datasources              jmx                      sar
deployment-scanner       jpa                      security
ee                       jsf                      threads
ejb3                     logging                  transactions
infinispan               mail                     undertow
io                       naming                   webservices
jaxrs                    pojo                     weld
jca                      remoting
```

After you have finished with the node path, adding a colon (:) at the end of the node path and pressing the *Tab* key will display all the available operation names for the selected node, which is shown as follows:

```
[standalone@localhost:9990 /] /subsystem=deployment-scanner/
scanner=default:
add                            read-resource
read-attribute                 read-resource-description
read-children-names            remove
read-children-resources        resolve-path
read-children-types            undefine-attribute
read-operation-description     whoami
read-operation-names           write-attribute
```

To see all the parameters of the add operation (after the operation name), press the *Tab* key:

```
[standalone@localhost:9990 /] /subsystem=deployment-
scanner/scanner=default:read-attribute(
include-defaults=    name=
```

Choose the parameter you want and specify its value after =:

```
[standalone@localhost:9990 /] /subsystem=deployment-
scanner/scanner=default:read-attribute(name=
runtime-failure-causes-rollback     scan-enabled
relative-to                         scan-interval
path                                auto-deploy-zipped
auto-deploy-exploded                deployment-timeout
auto-deploy-xml
```

Finally, when all the parameters have been specified, add) and press *Enter* to issue the following command:

```
[standalone@localhost:9990 /] /subsystem=deployment-

scanner/scanner=default:read-attribute(name=scan-enabled)
{
    "outcome" => "success",
    "result" => true
}
```

Deploying applications using the CLI

Deploying an application (in the standalone mode) can be easily performed by copying the application's archives into the `deployment` folder of your server distribution. That's a pretty handy option; however, we would like to stress the advantage of using a CLI, which offers a wide choice of additional options when deploying and also provides the opportunity to deploy applications remotely.

All it takes to deploy an application's archive is a connection to the management instance, either local or remote, and by issuing of the `deploy` shell command. When used without arguments, the `deploy` command provides a list of applications that are currently deployed, as shown in the following command:

```
[disconnected /] connect
[standalone@localhost:9990 /] deploy ExampleApp.war
```

If you feed a resource archive such as a WAR file to the shell, it will deploy it on the standalone server right away, as shown in the following command:

```
[standalone@localhost:9990 /] deploy ../MyApp.war
```

By default, a CLI uses the `JBOSS_HOME/bin` file as a source for your deployment archives. You can, however, use absolute paths when specifying the location of your archives; the CLI expansion facility (using the *Tab* key) makes this option fairly simple:

```
[standalone@localhost:9990 /] deploy c:\deployments\MyApp.war
```

Redeploying the application requires an additional flag to be added to the `deploy` command. Use the `-f` argument to force the application's redeployment:

```
[standalone@localhost:9990 /] deploy -f ../MyApp.war
```

Undeploying the application can be done through the `undeploy` command, which takes the application that is deployed as an argument. This is shown in the following command:

```
[standalone@localhost:9990 /] undeploy MyApp.war
```

By checking the WildFly configuration file (for example, `standalone.xml` or `domain.xml`), you will notice that the deployment element for your application has been removed.

Deploying applications to a WildFly domain

When you are deploying an application using the domain mode, you will have to specify to which server group the deployment is associated with. The CLI lets you choose between the following two options:

- Deploy to all server groups
- Deploy to a single server group

We will discuss these choices in two separate sections.

Deploying to all server groups

If this option is chosen, the application will be deployed to all the available server groups. The `--all-server-groups` flag can be used for this purpose. For example, refer to the following code:

```
[domain@localhost:9990 /] deploy ../application.ear --all-server-
groups
```

If, on the other hand, you want to undeploy an application from all the server groups that belong to a domain, you will have to issue the `undeploy` command as shown in the following command:

```
[domain@localhost:9990 /] undeploy application.ear --all-relevant-
server-groups
```

You might have noticed that the `undeploy` command uses the `--all-relevant-server-group` instead of the `--all-server-group`. The reason for this difference is that the deployment might not be enabled on all the server groups; therefore, by using this option, you will actually undeploy it from all the server groups in which the deployment is enabled.

Deploying to a single server group

The other option lets you perform a selective deployment of your application only on the server groups you indicate:

```
[domain@localhost:9990 /] deploy application.ear --server-
groups=main-server-group
```

You are not limited to a single server group, and you can separate multiple server groups with a comma (,). For example, refer to the following code:

```
[domain@localhost:9990 /] deploy application.ear --server-
groups=main-server-group,other-server-group

Successfully deployed application.ear
```

The tab completion feature will help you to complete the value for the list of --server-groups selected for deployment.

Now, suppose we want to undeploy the application from just one server group. In this case, there can be two possible outcomes. If the application is available just on that server group, you will successfully complete the undeployment as shown in the following command:

```
[domain@localhost:9990 /] undeploy wflyproject.war --server-
groups=main-server-group
```

On the other hand, if your application is available on other server groups, the following error will be returned by the CLI:

```
Undeploy failed: {"domain-failure-description" => {"Composite
operation failed and was rolled back. Steps that failed:" =>
{"Operation step-3" => "Cannot remove deployment wflyproject.war from
the domain as it is still used by server groups [other-server-
group]"}}}
```

It seems that something went wrong. As a matter of fact, when you are removing an application from a server group, the domain controller will verify that any other server group will not refer to the application; otherwise, the previous command will fail.

You can, however, instruct the domain controller to undeploy the application without deleting the content as well. This is shown in the following command:

```
[domain@localhost:9990 /] undeploy application.ear --server-
groups=main-server-group --keep-content
```

Creating CLI scripts

As a program developer, you might be interested to know that a CLI can execute commands in a non-interactive way by adding them to a file, just as a shell script. In order to execute the script, you can launch the CLI with the `--file` parameter as in the following example (for Windows):

```
jboss-cli.bat --file=test.cli
```

The equivalent command for Unix users will be as follows:

```
./jboss-cli.sh --file=test.cli
```

In the next section, we will look at some useful scripts that can be added to your administrator toolbox.

Deploying an application to several WildFly nodes

The earlier JBoss AS releases used to ship with a `farm` folder, which would trigger a deployment to all the nodes that are part of a JBoss cluster. This option is not included anymore with JBoss AS7 and WildFly, but resurrecting a farm deployment is just a matter of following a few CLI instructions.

In the following example, we are deploying an application to the default server address (127.0.0.1 and port 9990) and to another server instance that is bound to the same address but to port 10190:

```
connect
deploy /usr/data/example.war
connect 127.0.0.1:10190
deploy /usr/data/example.war
```

Restarting servers in a domain

A common requirement for the domain administrator is to restart the application server nodes, for example, when some server libraries are updated. CLI provides a handy shortcut to stop and start all the servers that are part of a server group:

```
connect
/server-group=main-server-group:start-servers
/server-group=main-server-group:stop-servers
```

If you prefer a more granular approach, you can start the single server nodes as shown in the following example, which shows how you can apply conditional execution logic in your CLI scripts:

```
connect

if (result == "STARTED") of /host=master/server-config=server-
one:read-attribute(name=status)

/host=master/server-config=server-one:stop

end-if


if (result == "STARTED") of /host=master/server-config=server-
two:read-attribute(name=status)

/host=master/server-config=server-two:stop

end-if

/host=master/server-config=server-one:start


/host=master/server-config=server-two:start
```

In the `if end-if` part of the code, we are checking for the server's status attribute. If the status is **STARTED**, the application servers are stopped and then restarted.

Installing a data source as a module

In WildFly, you can use the `module` command in order to install a new module. We already did something similar in *Chapter 5, Combining Persistence with CDI*. Now, you can fully automate a data source creation as shown in the following example:

```
connect


module add --name=org.postgresql --resources= postgresql-9.3-1101.jdbc41.
jar  --dependencies=javax.api,javax.transaction.api


/subsystem=datasources/jdbc-driver=postgresql:add(driver-module-
name=org.postgresql,driver-name=postgresql,driver-class-
name=org.postgresql.Driver)


/subsystem=datasources/data-source=PostgreSQLDS:add(jndi-
name=java:jboss/datasources/PostgreSQLDS , driver-
name=postgresql, connection-
url=jdbc:postgresql://localhost:5432/ticketsystem,user-
name=jboss,password=jboss)
```

The first line of the script, after the connection, installs a new module named `org.postgresql` in your server modules' directory, including the PostgreSQL JDBC driver and the required dependencies.

The second line installs the JDBC driver for the `org.postgresql` module into the `datasources/jdbc-driver` subsystem.

Finally, a data source is added to `jndi java:jboss/datasources/PostgreSQLDS` with the required URL and credentials.

Adding JMS resources

Adding a new JMS destination is quite easy since it does not require a lengthy set of commands. However, it is sometimes your application that needs to set up lots of JMS destinations in order to work, so why not create a script for it too? The following is a tiny script that adds a JMS queue to the server configuration:

```
connect
jms-queue add  --queue-address=queue1 --entries=queues/queue1
```

The following is the corresponding script you can use to create a JMS topic:

```
connect
jms-topic add  --topic-address=topic1 --entries=topics/topic1
```

Using advanced languages to create powerful CLI scripts

So far, we have learned how to write CLI shell commands to manage the application server's resources. This approach has the advantage that you can easily access every server resource easily and quickly, thanks to the built-in autocompletion feature. If, on the other hand, you want to perform some sophisticated logic around your commands, then you need to find some other alternatives.

If you are a shell guru, you might easily resort to some bash scripting in order to capture the output of the CLI and use the rich set of Unix/Linux tools to perform some administrative actions.

Supplying a short overview of the bash functionalities might be an amusing exercise; however, if we do this, we would move away from the scope of this book. We will instead document some built-in functionalities such as the following:

- In the first section, we will show how to use a CLI remote client API from within a Python script

- In the next section, we will use the raw management API to execute CLI commands from within Java applications

There are multiple use cases in which the JBoss CLI scripts could be useful. A script could be used to configure a developer's machine, a test environment, or as an initial configuration for production. In many cases, the configuration needed to start a full-blown enterprise application may be nontrivial; you might need to use a specific port configuration to cluster tests or your own security domain. You might also need your continuous integration server to do this for you. Besides this, it's better to have an automatic configuration script than set up the configuration manually every time, which is just a waste of time and a potential source of bugs.

Using scripting languages to wrap CLI execution

JBoss AS 7 has introduced a new CLI remote API that acts as a facade for the CLI public API. The core class that acts as a bridge between these two APIs is the `scriptsupport.CLI` class that is contained in the `JBOSS_HOME/bin/client/jboss-cli-client.jar` file.

Thanks to this API, you can execute CLI commands using lots of different languages such as Jython, Groovy, or JavaScript. Since Jython is also the de facto management standard for other application servers, such as Oracle, WebLogic, and WebSphere, we will use it to perform some basic management tasks.

 Jython is an implementation of Python for JVM. Jython is extremely useful because it provides the productivity features of a mature scripting language while running on a JVM. Unlike a Python program, a Jython program can run in any environment that supports a JVM.

Jython is invoked using the `jython` script, which is a short script that invokes your local JVM, running the Java class file, `org.python.util.jython`.

The first thing you need to do in order to get started is download the Jython installer from `http://www.jython.org/downloads.html`.

Run the installer with the following command:

```
java -jar jython-installer-2.5.3.jar
```

Next, add the JYTHON_HOME/bin folder (for example, C:\jython2.5.3\bin) to the system path and add the jboss-cli-client.jar file to the system, CLASSPATH. For example, in Windows, use the given command:

```
set JYTHON_HOME= C:\jython2.5.3
set PATH=%PATH%;%JYTHON_HOME%\bin

set CLASSPATH=%CLASSPATH%;%JBOSS_HOME%\bin\client\jboss-cli-
client.jar;.
```

Here's the same command for Linux:

```
export PATH=$PATH:/usr/data/jython2.5.3/bin
export CLASSPATH=$CLASSPATH$:%JBOSS_HOME%/bin/client/jboss-cli-
client.jar
```

Ok, now we will create our first script that will basically return the JNDI view of our application server.

 Be aware that Jython, just like Python, uses indentation to determine the code structure instead of using braces or keywords. Therefore, do not use them randomly. An IDE might help you with this—for Python you can use, for example, Vim with python-mode (https://github.com/klen/python-mode) or Eclipse with the PyDev extension (http://pydev.org/).

Create a file named script.py containing the following code:

```python
from org.jboss.as.cli.scriptsupport import CLI

cli = CLI.newInstance()
cli.connect()

cli.cmd("cd /subsystem=naming")

result = cli.cmd(":jndi-view")
response = result.getResponse()

print 'JNDI VIEW ======================= '
print response
cli.disconnect()
```

Now execute the script with the following code:

```
jython script.py
```

As you can see, the code is very self-explanatory; we are importing the `org.jboss.as.cli.scriptsupport.CLI` class, which is used to send commands and read the response. Then, we are connecting to the local WildFly instance and issuing a `:jndi-view` command.

> The connect command can be used to connect to a remote WildFly host as well by adding the following parameters: `connect (String controllerHost, int controllerPort, String username, String password)`.

The response variable is `org.jboss.dmr.ModelNode`. This can be further inspected as shown in the following example, which goes in to some depth about platform MBeans, to get some memory statistics:

```
from org.jboss.as.cli.scriptsupport import CLI

cli = CLI.newInstance()
cli.connect()

cli.cmd("cd /core-service=platform-mbean/type=memory/")

result = cli.cmd(":read-resource(recursive=false,proxies=false,inclu
de-runtime=true,include-defaults=true)")

response = result.getResponse()
enabled = response.get("result").get("heap-memory-usage")

used = enabled.get("used").asInt()

if used > 512000000:
    print "Over 1/2 Gb Memory usage "
else:
    print 'Low usage!'

cli.disconnect()
```

In the previous example, we tracked the resources contained in `/core-service=platform-mbean/type=memory`. The available resources are, however, child resources of the two kinds of available heap memory areas (`heap-memory-usage` and `non-heap-memory-usage`), as shown by the following code:

```
[standalone@localhost:9990 /] /core-service=platform-mbean/
type=memory:read-resource(recursive=false,proxies=false,
include-runtime=true,include-defaults=true)
{
    "outcome" => "success",
    "result" => {
        "heap-memory-usage" => {
            "init" => 67108864L,
            "used" => 59572256L,
            "committed" => 170852352L,
            "max" => 477233152L
        },
        "non-heap-memory-usage" => {
            "init" => 24313856L,
            "used" => 90491328L,
            "committed" => 90701824L,
            "max" => 369098752L
        },
        "object-pending-finalization-count" => 0,
        "verbose" => false
    }
}
```

Using just the `get` command of the `ModelNode` object, you can refer to the child resources of the memory type and reach all the single attributes. Once you have got the attributes, it's easy to cast them to an integer using the `asInt()` function of the `ModelNode` object and use the cool Python constructs to alert your administrator.

Using the raw management API to manage the application server

If you don't feel like learning a scripting language to manage the application server, you can still use the raw management API from within your Java classes. Don't be influenced by the fact that we left this option as the last one; in fact, using the native management API is not difficult at all since it is based on very few classes and has little compile-time and runtime dependencies on the WildFly API.

For this reason, you can use the management API as well from any Java EE application by simply adding the following dependencies to the META-INF/ MANIFEST.MF file of your application:

```
Dependencies: org.jboss-as-controller-client,org.jboss.dmr
```

The core API named **detyped management API** is quite simple; the primary class is org.jboss.dmr.ModelNode, which we already mentioned in the Jython section. A ModelNode class is essentially just a wrapper around a value; the value is typically a basic JDK type that can be retrieved using the getType() method of ModelNode.

In addition to the jboss-dmr API, the other module that is used to connect to the management API is jboss-as-controller-client.

 You don't need to download any of these libraries since both of these modules are included in the application server since release 7.

Reading management model descriptions via the raw management API

Using the **detyped management API** is not too different from its scripting language counterpart; at first, you need to create a management client that can connect to your target process's native management socket (which can be an individual standalone mode server, or in a domain mode environment, the domain controller):

```
ModelControllerClient client =
ModelControllerClient.Factory.create(InetAddress.getByName
("localhost"), 9990);
```

Next, you need to create an operation request object using the org.jboss.dmr. ModelNode class, as shown in the following command:

```
final ModelNode operation = new ModelNode();
operation.get("operation").set("jndi-view");

final ModelNode address = operation.get("address");
address.add("subsystem", "naming");

operation.get("recursive").set(true);
operation.get("operations").set(true);

final ModelNode returnVal = client.execute(operation);
logger.info(returnVal.get("result").toString());
```

As you can see, `ModelNode` objects can be chained in order to reach an operation (in the example, the JNDI view), which is available on a node path (in our case, the naming subsystem).

Once you have added the `ModelNode` attributes, you can issue the `execute` commands on your node, which will in turn return `ModelNode` where the result of the operation will be stored.

In the samples, you can find a fully working project containing these management examples.

Creating your resource watches using the detyped API

Now that you have learned the basics of the **detyped management API**, we will illustrate a concrete example; our goal will be to monitor a server resource (the number of active JDBC connections for a data source) using an EJB. You can use this pattern to create your own server watches that can be integrated with your application environment. This is shown in the following code snippet:

```
package com.packtpub.wflydevelopment.chapter9;

import org.jboss.as.controller.client.ModelControllerClient;
import org.jboss.dmr.ModelNode;

import javax.ejb.Schedule;
import javax.ejb.Stateless;
import java.io.Closeable;
import java.net.InetAddress;
import java.util.logging.Level;
import java.util.logging.Logger;

@Stateless
public class WatchMyDB {

    private final static Logger logger = Logger.getLogger(WatchMyDB.
class.getName());

    @Schedule(dayOfWeek = "*", hour = "*", minute = "*", second =
            "*/30", year = "*", persistent = false)
    public void backgroundProcessing() {
        ModelControllerClient client = null;
        try {
            client = ModelControllerClient.Factory
    .create(InetAddress.getByName("localhost"), 9990);
```

```java
            final ModelNode operation = new ModelNode();
            operation.get("operation").set("read-resource");
            operation.get("include-runtime").set(true);
            final ModelNode address = operation.get("address");
            address.add("subsystem", "datasources");
            address.add("data-source", "ExampleDS");
            address.add("statistics", "pool");
            final ModelNode returnVal = client.execute(operation);

            final ModelNode node2 = returnVal.get("result");
            final String stringActiveCount =
              node2.get("ActiveCount").asString();

            if (stringActiveCount.equals("undefined")) {
                return; // Connection unused
            }
            int activeCount = Integer.parseInt(stringActiveCount);

            if (activeCount > 50) {
                alertAdministrator();
            }
        } catch (Exception exc) {
            logger.log(Level.SEVERE, "Exception !", exc);
        } finally {
            safeClose(client);
        }
    }

    public void safeClose(final Closeable closeable) {
        if (closeable != null) {
            try {
                closeable.close();
            } catch (Exception e) {
                logger.log(Level.SEVERE, "Exception closing the
client! ", e);
            }
        }
    }

    private void alertAdministrator() {
        // Implement it !
    }
}
```

We will not rehash the basic concepts about EJB Timers, which have been discussed in *Chapter 3*, *Introducing Java EE 7 – EJBs*. We suggest that you have a look at the highlighted section of the code, which shows how you can chain your `ModelNode` objects in order to reach the attribute that we are going to monitor (the `activeCount` attribute of the `ExampleDS` datasource).

Once you have the value of the `activeCount` attribute, we leave it to your imagination to envision all the possible actions you can undertake!

It is worth noting that there are additional means of monitoring WildFly. One of them is using the `hawt.io` plugin for JBoss (`http://hawt.io/plugins/jboss/`). We already tried this for ActiveMQ when we were developing MessageBeans. Another tool is Jolokia (`http://www.jolokia.org/`), which exposes JMX beans over HTTP. So, if you are not into writing your own monitors, there are other options worth exploring.

Role-based security

In JBoss 7, a logged-in administrator has unlimited power over every configuration aspect of a running server. This could be a problem in a production environment when multiple users have access to the server to do different tasks. One user could only be interested in deploying new applications, another should only be able to restart the server, and there could be one who should not be able to change anything (for example, a monitoring agent sending data about the execution of an application).

To support these kinds of requirements, WildFly brings two access control strategies:

- Simple, which is the all-or-nothing approach known from JBoss AS 7 and EAP in versions earlier than 6.2 (every authenticated administrator has full access to the application server). This is the default strategy.

- Role based access control (RBAC), which allows you to assign administrative users to specific management roles.

Let's navigate to `http://localhost:8080/console` and log in with our administrator password. The upper menu contains a tab named **Administration**. This is used to configure the access control mechanism. Once you click on it (you should see a message box informing you that RBAC is not yet enabled), we will see three subtabs: **Users**, **Groups**, and **Roles**. Let's take a closer look at each of these objects.

Users are defined using the `add-user.bat` (`.sh`) scripts in the `JBOSS_HOME/bin` directory. We have already defined one before the first time we accessed the JBoss console. The created user, however, requires some additional information in order to determine his or her security level. The easiest way to achieve this is to organize them into groups. The assignment can be done via the user creation scripts or by the `mgmt-groups.properties` files in the WildFly's configuration directory. Another way to do this is to define a security realm connected to an external source (an LDAP server for instance). We will talk more about security realms in the next chapter. For now, you can create a user assigned to a group named `TestGroup`.

A group is mapped to a set of security roles to provide specific permissions. For example, we can create user groups for developers and junior administrators and map them to a subset of desired roles. A user can be part of multiple groups, so there is also a possibility to exclude a role for a specific group so that no other group could grant it.

Finally, we have roles that cover multiple areas of the server's functionality. Every role has a set of permissions assigned and some of them are additionally constrained (for instance, to allow you to configure modifications in only specific subsystems such as data sources). A list of built-in roles is available in the following table:

Role	Permissions	Sensitive data (passwords and auditing)
Monitor	Read-only access to configuration and runtime state.	No access.
Operator	All permissions of **Monitor**. This role can restart the server, control JMS destination, and database connection pools. It cannot modify the configuration.	No access.
Maintainer	All permissions of **Operator**. This role can modify the configuration (including deploying new applications).	No access.
Deployer	All permissions of **Maintainer**, but with restrictions on deploying new applications (cannot change the configuration of the server).	No access.
Administrator	All permissions of **Maintainer**.	Read/write access. No access to the audit system.
Auditor	All permissions of **Monitor**.	Read-only access. Full access to the auditing system.

Role	Permissions	Sensitive data (passwords and auditing)
Super User	Everything is permitted. The administrator known from JBoss AS 7 and the simple strategy in WildFly. Also, this is the default role for a local user (connecting from a localhost).	Full access.

Besides relying on the group-role mapping mechanism, you have another option to assign users to roles. You can use the **Administration/Users** screen in the admin console to directly assign a user to a role (be sure to select **Include** as the type). Assign the SuperUser role now to your current user using the **Add** button. Additionally, you can use **Administration/Groups** to add our newly created TestGroup to, for instance, the Monitor role.

Our configuration is now in place; try and check it out. To switch to the RBAC strategy, we will need to issue the following command using the CLI interface:

```
/core-service=management/access=authorization:write-
attribute(name=provider, value=rbac)
```

Reload the server and log in to the web console again using the account you designed as SuperUser.

We are testing the web console, but the RBAC mechanism also works for the CLI. Note that the CLI will allow you to access it from localhost as long as you have the $local user allowed in your security realm:

```
<security-realm name="ManagementRealm">
  <authentication>
    <local default-user="$local" allowed-users="*"/>
    <properties path="mgmt-users.properties" relative-
to="jboss.server.config.dir"/>
  </authentication>
  <authorization map-groups-to-roles="false">
    <properties path="mgmt-groups.properties"
relative-
to="jboss.server.config.dir"/>
  </authorization>
</security-realm>
```

If you wish to disable it, simply remove this line.

If you are wondering what your current role is, you can click on **Username** in the upper-right corner of the screen. You should see a bit of information about the currently logged-in administrator in the following screenshot:

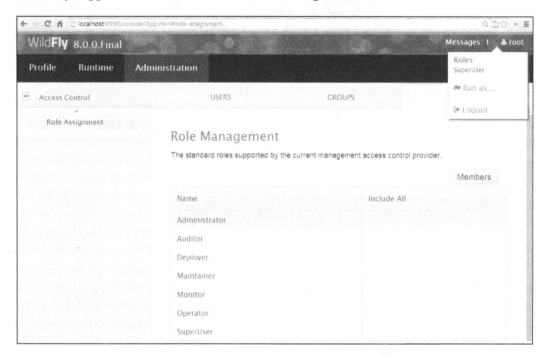

In the preceding screenshot, we can see that the user root is logged in as a `SuperUser` role. Besides having the possibility to do everything with the application server, the `SuperUser` role has one additional feature. It can impersonate other roles using **Run as...**, which can be useful if you want to check what are the limitations of another role. Feel free to check them out right now. For instance, as a `Monitor`, you should not be able to alter any settings in the admin console.

You can also relogin with the user you've created earlier, which is assigned to `TestGroup`. It should have the **Monitor** role shown in the upper-right corner of the screen.

Auditing administrative operations

WildFly introduces an audit-log feature that allows the administrators to track the configuration changes made on the server. The feature is initially disabled but can be useful in some scenarios, so let's take a short look at it.

The audit-log configuration consists of three parts:

- **Formatter**: This formats the log output. By default, it's based on JSON.
- **Handler**: This handles the output. By default, it is a file-based handler, but it is possible to use a TCP or UDP to send the logs to a remote server.
- **Logger**: This controls the login process.

Detailed configuration can be found in the official WildFly documentation at `https://docs.jboss.org/author/display/WFLY8/Audit+logging`.

The audit log is disabled by default. To enable it, we must issue the following CLI command:

```
/core-service=management/access=audit/logger=audit-log:write-
attribute(name=enabled, value=true)
```

Now you can try to do any administrative action using the web console (for instance, disabling a data source). After this, you should find a trace of it in `JBOSS_HOME/standalone/data/audit-log.log` (along with information about switching the audit logging on).

Patching a running instance

The newest version of the JBoss Application Server comes with a patching utility that allows you to automatically update parts of the server with newer versions. Currently, the patching is done using a CLI. Any patch can be reverted, and the administrator is able to track the history of patches.

A patch can be applied by simply calling the `patch apply <file path>` (without -) command. A complementary command is `patch rollback --patch-id = id`, a patch-rollback command. To obtain information about the installed patches, simply call `patch info`. Patches are distributed by teams responsible for specific WildFly subsystems. Visit their websites if you need a patch for a specific module.

Summary

In this chapter, we covered the application server's management API from a developer's perspective, which will enable you to write your own scripts to monitor the health of your application server.

The most effective tool for monitoring the application server is the command-line interface. However, if you want to spice it up with some typical programming logic, you can resort to some other alternatives such as scripting languages or the raw management API.

We also explored some of the new, advanced features that were introduced with WildFly. You now know how to restrict access to your management console and how to audit the changes done to the configuration.

We have now completed our review of management. In the next chapter, we are going to discuss clustering, which is the environment where critical applications are deployed.

10
Securing WildFly Applications

In the previous chapter, we described how to manage your application server. The next stop in our journey will be learning about security, which is a key element of any Enterprise application. You must be able to control and restrict who is permitted to access your applications and what operations users may perform.

The Java Enterprise Edition specification defines a simple role-based security model for Enterprise JavaBeans and web components. The implementation of WildFly security is delivered by the **Picketbox** framework (formerly known as JBoss Security), which is part of the application server and provides the authentication, authorization, auditing, and mapping capabilities for Java applications.

Here is the list of topics we will cover in this chapter:

- A short introduction to the Java security API
- The foundation of the WildFly security subsystem
- Defining and applying login modules to secure Java EE applications
- Using the **Secure Sockets Layer (SSL)** protocol to encrypt the traffic

Approaching the Java security API

Java EE security services provide a robust and easily configurable security mechanism to authenticate users and authorize access to application functions and the associated data. To better understand the topics related to security, we should first lay out some basic definitions:

- **Authentication**: This is the process by which you can verify who is currently executing an application, regardless of whether it is an EJB or a servlet (and so on). Authentication is usually performed by means of a Login module contained in a web/standalone application. The Java EE specification provides only general requirements that must be met by all compliant containers. This means that every application server provides its own authentication mechanisms, which is a problem when it comes to portability of applications and their configuration.

- **Authorization**: This is the process by which you can verify if a user has the right (permission) to access system resources or invoke certain operations. Authorization, therefore, presupposes that authentication has occurred; it would be impossible to grant any access control if you don't know who the user is first. Java EE specification provides means to authorize a user's actions. The authorization declarations are usually portable between different application servers. The difference between authentication and authorization is depicted in the following diagram:

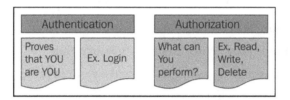

In Java EE, the containers are responsible for providing application security. A container basically provides two types of security: declarative and programmatic. Let's take a look at both of them:

- **Declarative security**: This expresses an application component's security requirements by means of deployment descriptors. Because deployment descriptor information is contained in an external file, it can be changed without the need to modify the source code.

  For example, Enterprise JavaBeans components use an EJB deployment descriptor, which must be named ejb-jar.xml and placed in the META-INF folder of the EJB JAR file.

Web components use a web application deployment descriptor named `web.xml`, which is located in the `WEB-INF` directory.

 Since the release of Java EE 5, you can apply declarative security by means of annotations just like we have for other key APIs (EJB, web services, and so on). Annotations are specified within a class file, and when the application is deployed, the application server translates this information internally.

- **Programmatic security**: This is embedded in an application and used to make security decisions. It can be used when declarative security alone is not sufficient to express the security model of an application. The Java EE security API allows the developer to test whether or not the current user has access to a specific role, using the following calls:

  - `isUserInRole()` for servlets and JSPs (adopted in `javax.servlet.http.HttpServletRequest`)
  - `isCallerInRole()` for EJBs (adopted in `javax.ejb.SessionContext`)

Additionally, there are other API calls that provide access to the user's identity, which are as follows:

  - `getUserPrincipal()` for servlets and JSPs (adopted in `javax.servlet.http.HttpServletRequest`)
  - `getCallerPrincipal()` for EJBs (adopted in `javax.ejb.SessionContext`)

Using these APIs, you can develop arbitrarily complex authorization models.

The WildFly security subsystem

WildFly security qualifies as an extension to the application server and is included, by default, both in standalone and domain servers using the following code:

```
<extension module="org.jboss.as.security"/>
```

WildFly defines security policies using two terms: security realms and security domains. Security realms are configuration sets mapped to external connectors (for example, EJB remoting and management interface). They allow every connection type to have its own appropriate authentication and authorization properties defined. For instance, both management and application realms define two separate files, which store the allowed usernames. Additionally, the application realm contains a reference to a file that defines user role.

The configuration defined in the security realm is then passed to a security domain requested by the deployed application. The security domain defines a set of login modules that are responsible for checking the user's credentials and creating a security principal representing the client (along with a set of roles for the requester).

The following is an extract from the default security subsystem contained in the server configuration file, which contains the RealmDirect login that will be used in the next section to secure the Ticket example application:

```
<subsystem xmlns="urn:jboss:domain:security:1.2">
    <security-domains>
        <security-domain name="other" cache-type="default">
            <authentication>
                <login-module code="Remoting" flag="optional">
                    <module-option name="password-stacking"
                     value="useFirstPass"/>
                </login-module>
                <login-module code="RealmDirect" flag="required">
                    <module-option name="password-stacking"
                     value="useFirstPass"/>
                </login-module>
            </authentication>
        </security-domain>
        <security-domain name="jboss-web-policy" cache-
            type="default">
            <authorization>
                <policy-module code="Delegating" flag="required"/>
            </authorization>
        </security-domain>
        <security-domain name="jboss-ejb-policy" cache-
            type="default">
            <authorization>
                <policy-module code="Delegating" flag="required"/>
            </authorization>
        </security-domain>
    </security-domains>
</subsystem>
```

Configuration files are defined in the security realm using the following code:

```
<security-realm name="ApplicationRealm">
    <authentication>
        <local default-user="$local" allowed-users="*"/>
            <properties path="application-users.properties"
                relative-to="jboss.server.config.dir"/>
```

```
        </authentication>
      <authorization>
          <properties path="application-roles.properties" relative-
              to="jboss.server.config.dir"/>
      </authorization>
    </security-realm>
```

As you can see, the configuration is pretty short as it relies largely on default values, especially for high-level structures such as the security management area. By defining your own security management options, you could, for example, override the default authentication/authorization managers with your implementations. Since it is likely that you will not need to override these interfaces, we will rather concentrate on the `security-domain` element, which is the core aspect of WildFly security.

A security domain can be thought of as a Customs Office for foreigners. Before the request crosses WildFly borders, the security domain performs all the required authentication and authorization checks and eventually notifies if he/she can proceed or not.

Security domains are generally configured at server startup and subsequently bound into the JNDI tree under the key `java:/jaas/`. Within the security domain, you can configure login authentication modules so that you can easily change your authentication provider by simply changing its `login-module` element.

There are several implementations of login modules available out of the box; there is obviously not enough room here to describe in detail the features of each module, though we will offer a comprehensive description of some popular options, such as:

- The `RealmDirect` login module, which can be used for basic file-based authentication
- The `Database` login module, which checks user credentials against a relational database

> Should you need further information about login modules, check out the WildFly documentation at:
>
> - `https://docs.jboss.org/author/display/`
>   `WFLY8/Security+subsystem+configuration`
> - `https://docs.jboss.org/author/display/`
>   `WFLY8/Security+Realms`

Setting up your first login module

In the following section, we will demonstrate how to secure an application using the `RealmDirect` security domain, which was introduced earlier. The `RealmDirect` login module is based on the following two files:

- `application-users.properties`: This contains the list of usernames and passwords

- `application-roles.properties`: This contains the mapping between the users and their roles

These files are located in the application server configuration folder and they are updated each time you add a new user via the `add-user.sh/add-user.cmd` script. For our purpose, we will create a new application user named `demouser`, which belongs to the role `Manager`, as shown in the following screenshot:

Once the user is added, the `application-users.properties` file will contain the username and the MD5 encoding of the password, shown as follows:

```
demouser=9e21f32c593ef5248e7d6b2aab28717b
```

Conversely, the `application-roles.properties` file will contain the roles granted to the `demouser` username once logged in:

```
demouser=Manager
```

Using the login module in the Ticket web application

We can now apply the `RoleDirect` login module in the Ticket web application described in *Chapter 4, Learning Context and Dependency Injection* (you could pick the version from another chapter if you like). We will first show how to provide a BASIC web authentication, and then we will show a slightly more complex example using FORM-based authentication.

 BASIC-access authentication is the simplest way to provide a username and password when making a request through a browser.

It works by sending an encoded string containing the user credentials. This Base64-encoded string is transmitted and decoded by the receiver, resulting in colon-separated username and password strings. When it comes to safety, BASIC authentication is usually not the best solution. The password can be stolen during the transmission, so SSL is a must in order to protect it.

Turning on web authentication requires the `security-constraints` element to be defined in the web application configuration file (`web.xml`), as shown in the following code snippet:

```
<web-app xmlns="http://xmlns.jcp.org/xml/ns/javaee"
         xmlns:xsi="http://www.w3.org/2001/XMLSchema-instance"
         xsi:schemaLocation="http://xmlns.jcp.org/xml/ns/javaee
             http://xmlns.jcp.org/xml/ns/javaee/web-app_3_1.xsd"
         version="3.1">

. . . . . .

    <security-constraint>
        <web-resource-collection>
            <web-resource-name>HtmlAuth</web-resource-name>
            <description>application security constraints
            </description>
            <url-pattern>/*</url-pattern>
            <http-method>GET</http-method>
            <http-method>POST</http-method>
        </web-resource-collection>
```

```
      <auth-constraint>
          <role-name>Manager</role-name>
      </auth-constraint>
  </security-constraint>
  <login-config>
      <auth-method>BASIC</auth-method>
  </login-config>

  <security-role>
      <role-name>Manager</role-name>
  </security-role>
</web-app>
```

This configuration will add a security constraint on any JSP/servlet of the web application that will restrict access to users authenticated with the role `Manager`. All login modules shown in the earlier section define this role, so you can just use the login module that suits your needs best.

From Java EE 7, there are two more methods to express your security constraints. Firstly, you can use a new container provided role: `**`. It indicates that you are referring to any authenticated user, without taking its roles into account.

The second one is the `deny-http-uncovered-methods` tag, which can be used in a `web.xml` file to forbid access to every HTTP method that is not covered by a separate security constraint.

The next configuration tweak needs to be performed on the JBoss web deployment's descriptor, `WEB-INF/jboss-web.xml`. You need to declare the security domain here, which will be used to authenticate the users. Since we are using `RealmDirect`, which is part of the other built-in login module, we will need to include the `java:/jaas/other` context information:

```
<jboss-web>
      <security-domain>java:/jaas/other</security-domain>
</jboss-web>
```

The following diagram illustrates the whole configuration sequence applied to a `Database` login module:

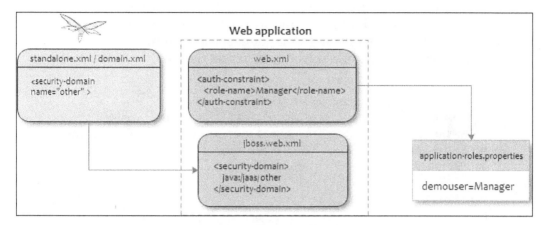

Once you have deployed your application, the outcome should be a blocking pop up requesting user authentication. The window will look a little different on every browser and its appearance cannot be changed.

Logging in with `demouser` username and the valid password will grant access to the application with the `Manager` role.

Switching to FORM-based security

FORM-based authentication lets developers customize the authentication user interface, adapting it, for example, to your company's standards. Configuring it in your application requires you to basically modify just the `login-config` stanza of the security section of your `web.xml` file. Within it, we will define a login landing page (`login.xhtml`) and an error page (`error.xhtml`), in case the login fails. The code snippet for it is as follows:

```
<login-config>
    <auth-method>FORM</auth-method>
    <form-login-config>
        <form-login-page>/faces/login.xhtml</form-login-page>
        <form-error-page>/faces/error.xhtml</form-error-page>
    </form-login-config>
</login-config>
```

The login form must contain fields to enter a username and password. These fields must be named j_username and j_password, respectively. The authentication form should post these values to the j_security_check logical name. All these names beginning with j_ are standardized by the Java Servlet specification — we just need to follow the convention in order to let the automatic mechanisms work. Here's a simple login.xhtml page, which can be used to pass the required values to the security system:

```
<?xml version='1.0' encoding='UTF-8' ?>
<!DOCTYPE html PUBLIC "-//W3C//DTD XHTML 1.0 Transitional//EN"
        "http://www.w3.org/TR/xhtml1/DTD/xhtml1-transitional.dtd">
<html xmlns="http://www.w3.org/1999/xhtml"
      xmlns:h="http://xmlns.jcp.org/jsf/html">
<head>
    <title>FORM based Login</title>
</head>
<body>
<form method="post" action="j_security_check" name="loginForm">
    <h:panelGrid columns="2">
        <h:outputLabel id="userNameLabel" for="j_username"
            value="Username:"/>
        <h:inputText id="j_username" autocomplete="off"/>
        <h:outputLabel id="passwordLabel" for="j_password"
            value="Password:"/>
        <h:inputSecret id="j_password" autocomplete="off"/>

        <div/>
        <h:panelGroup>
            <h:commandButton type="submit" value="Login"/>
            <h:commandButton type="reset" value="Clear"/>
        </h:panelGroup>
    </h:panelGrid>
</form>
</body>
</html>
```

For the sake of brevity, we won't include the error page, which will simply alert that the user entered an incorrect combination of username and password. The expected outcome is the following login screen, which will intercept all user access to your application and grant access to the default home page if the username and password credentials are correct.

Creating a Database login module

The `UserRoles` login module is a good starting point to learn how to put together all the pieces required to secure a web application. In real-world cases, there are better alternatives to protect your applications, such as the `Database` login module. A database security domain follows the same logic exposed in the earlier example; it just stores the credentials within the database. In order to run this example, we will refer to a data source defined in *Chapter 5, Combining Persistence with CDI* (bound at the JNDI name `java:jboss/datasources/wflydevelopment`), which needs to be deployed on the application server:

```
<security-domain name="dbdomain" cache-type="default">
    <authentication>
        <login-module code="Database" flag="required">
            <module-option name="dsJndiName" value="
            java:jboss/datasources/wflydevelopment"/>
            <module-option name="principalsQuery" value="select
            passwd from USERS where login=?"/>
            <module-option name="rolesQuery" value="select
            role 'Roles' from USER_ROLES where login=?"/>
        </login-module>
    </authentication>
</security-domain>
```

In order to get this configuration working, you have to first create the required tables and insert some sample data in it using the following queries:

```
CREATE TABLE USERS(login VARCHAR(64) PRIMARY KEY, passwd
    VACHAR(64));
CREATE TABLE USER_ROLES(login VARCHAR(64), role VARCHAR(32));
INSERT into USERS values('admin', 'admin');
INSERT into USER_ROLES values('admin', 'Manager');
```

As you can see, the `admin` user will map again to the `Manager` role. One caveat of this configuration is that it uses clear text passwords in the database; so before rolling this module into production, you should consider adding additional security to your login module. Let's see how to do this in the next section.

Encrypting passwords

Storing passwords in the database as a clear text string is not considered a good practice; as a matter of fact, a database has even more potential security holes than a regular filesystem. Imagine, for example, that a DBA added a public synonym for some tables, forgetting that one of those tables held sensitive information such as application passwords, as shown in the following screenshot! You then need to be sure that no potential attackers will ever be able to deliver the following query.

	login [PK] characte	passwd character varying(64)
1	admin	admin
*		

Fortunately, securing application passwords is relatively easy; you can add a few extra options to your login module, specifying that the stored passwords are encrypted using a message digest algorithm. For example, in the Database login module, you should add the following highlighted options at the bottom:

```
<login-module code="Database" flag="required">
    <module-option name="dsJndiName"
        value="java:jboss/datasources/wflydevelopment"/>
    <module-option name="principalsQuery" value="select passwd
        from USERS where login=?"/>
    <module-option name="rolesQuery" value="select role, 'Roles'
        from USER_ROLES where login=?"/>
    <module-option name="hashAlgorithm" value="SHA-256"/>
    <module-option name="hashEncoding" value="BASE64"/>
</login-module>
```

Here, we specified that the password will be hashed against an SHA hash algorithm; alternatively, you can use any other algorithm allowed by your JCA provider.

> For an excellent introduction to hashing algorithms, refer to http://www.unixwiz.net/techtips/iguide-crypto-hashes.html.

For the sake of completeness, we include a small application as follows, which generates the Base64 hashed password that is to be inserted in Database:

```
public class Hash {

    public static void main(String[] args) throws Exception{
        String password = args[0];
        MessageDigest md = MessageDigest.getInstance("SHA-256");
```

```
byte[] passwordBytes = password.getBytes();
byte[] hash = md.digest(passwordBytes);
String passwordHash =
    Base64.getEncoder().encodeToString(hash);

System.out.println("password hash: "+passwordHash);
}
```

Running the main program with `admin` as the argument will generate the hash `jGl25bVBBBW96Qi9Te4V37Fnqchz/Eu4qB9vKrRIqRg=`. This hash will be your updated password, which needs to be updated in your database, as shown in the following screenshot. Update the password using the following code:

```
UPDATE USERS SET PASSWD =  'jGl25bVBBBW96Qi9Te4V37Fnqchz/
Eu4qB9vKrRIqRg=' WHERE LOGIN = 'admin';
```

You can update it with any SQL client of your choice.

	login [PK] characte	passwd character varying(64)
1	admin	jGl25bVBBBW96Qi9Te4V37Fnqchz/Eu4qB9vKrRIqRg=
*		

Using the Database login module in your application

Once you are done with the login module configuration, don't forget to reference it through the JBoss web deployment's descriptor, `WEB-INF/jboss-web.xml`:

```
<jboss-web>
    <security-domain>java:/jaas/dbdomain</security-domain>
</jboss-web>
```

Securing EJBs

Securing applications by means of a web login form is the most frequently used option in Enterprise applications. Nevertheless, the HTTP protocol is not the only choice available to access applications. For example, EJBs can be accessed by remote clients using the RMI-IIOP protocol. In such a case, you should further refine your security policies by restricting access to the EJB components, which are usually involved in the business layer of your applications.

How does security work at the EJB level?
Authentication must be performed before any EJB method is called. Authorization, on the other hand, occurs at the beginning of each EJB method call.

One vast area of improvement introduced in Java EE 5 concerns the use of annotations, which can also be used to perform the basic security checks. There are five available annotations, which are listed as follows:

- `@org.jboss.ejb3.annotation.SecurityDomain`: This specifies the security domain that is associated with the class/method.

- `@javax.annotation.security.RolesAllowed`: This specifies the list of roles permitted to access a method(s) in an EJB application.

- `@javax.annotation.security.RunAs`: This assigns a role dynamically to the EJB application during the invocation of the method. It can be used, for example, if we need to temporarily allow permission to access certain methods.

- `@javax.annotation.security.PermitAll`: This specifies that an EJB application can be invoked by any client. The purpose of this annotation is to widen security access to some methods in situations where you don't exactly know what role will access the EJB application (imagine that some modules have been developed by a third party and they access your EJB application with some roles that are not well identified).

- `@javax.annotation.security.DenyAll`: This specifies that an EJB application cannot be invoked by external clients. It has the same considerations as those for `@PermitAll`.

The following snippet is an example of how to secure the `TheatreBooker` SFSB, which we discussed in *Chapter 4, Learning Context and Dependency Injection*:

```
@RolesAllowed("Manager")
@SecurityDomain("dbdomain")
@Stateful
@Remote(TheatreBooker.class)
public class TheatreBooker implements TheatreBooker {

}
```

Be careful! There is more than one `SecurityDomain` API available. You have to include `org.jboss.ejb3.annotation.SecurityDomain`. The `@RolesAllowed` annotation, on the other hand, needs to import `javax.annotation.security.RolesAllowed`.

The JBoss-specific annotations can be found in the following maven dependency:

```
<groupId>org.jboss.ejb3</groupId>
<artifactId>jboss-ejb3-ext-api</artifactId>
<version>2.0.0</version>
<scope>provided</scope>
```

Annotations can also be applied at the method level; for example, if we want to secure just the `bookSeat` object of the `TheatreBookerBean` class, we will tag the `bookSeat` method as follows:

```
@RolesAllowed("Manager")
@SecurityDomain("dbdomain")
public String bookSeat(int seatId) throws SeatBookedException {

}
```

What if you don't want to use annotations to establish security roles? For example, if you have a security role that is used crosswise by all your EJB applications, perhaps it is simpler to use a plain old XML configuration instead of tagging all EJBs with annotations. In this scenario, you have to declare the security constraints first in the generic `META-INF/ejb-jar.xml` file, shown as follows:

```
<ejb-jar xmlns="http://java.sun.com/xml/ns/javaee" xmlns:xsi="http://
www.w3.org/2001/XMLSchema-instance"
  version="3.2"
  xsi:schemaLocation="http://java.sun.com/xml/ns/javaee http://java.
sun.com/xml/ns/javaee/ejb-jar_3_2.xsd">
  <assembly-descriptor>
    <method-permission>
      <role-name>Manager</role-name>
      <method>
        <ejb-name>*</ejb-name>
        <method-name>*</method-name>
      </method>
    </method-permission>
  </assembly-descriptor>
</ejb-jar>
```

Then, inside the `META-INF/jboss-ejb3.xml` configuration file, just add a reference to your security domain:

```xml
<?xml version="1.0" encoding="UTF-8"?>
<jboss:ejb-jar xmlns="http://java.sun.com/xml/ns/javaee"
   xmlns:jboss="http://www.jboss.com/xml/ns/javaee"
       xmlns:xsi="http://www.w3.org/2001/XMLSchema-instance"
   xmlns:s="urn:security:1.1" version="3.1" impl-version="2.0">
   <assembly-descriptor>
     <s:security>
       <ejb-name>*</ejb-name>
       <s:security-domain>dbdomain</s:security-domain>
     </s:security>
   </assembly-descriptor>
</jboss:ejb-jar>
```

Here's a snapshot illustrating the role configuration of the EJB file:

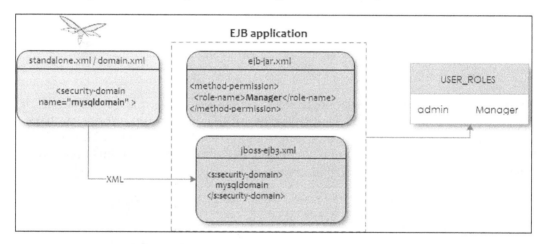

If you want to use a login module via EJB remoting, you must configure your security realm accordingly using the JAAS entry, as shown in the following code:

```
<security-realm name="ApplicationRealm">
  <authentication>
   <jaas name="dbdomain"/>
  </authentication>
</security-realm>
```

 Additionally, you should place the following entries in `jbossyourjboss-ejb-client-properties`:

```
remote.connection.default.username=admin
remote.connection.default.password=admin
remote.connectionprovider.create.options.org.xnio.
    Options.SSL_ENABLED=false
remote.connection.default.connect.options.org.xnio.
    Options.SASL_POLICY_NOPLAINTEXT=false
remote.connection.default.connect.options.org.xnio.
    Options.SASL_POLICY_NOANONYMOUS=true
```

These entries will ensure (besides passing the credentials), that the transmitted password will not be additionally hashed by the remoting mechanism.

Securing web services

Web service authorization can basically be carried out in two ways, depending on whether we are dealing with a POJO-based web service or an EJB-based web service. Security changes to POJO web services are identical to those we introduced for servlets/JSP, consistent in defining the `security-constraints` element in `web.xml` and the login modules in `jboss-web.xml`.

If you are using a web client to access your web service, it is all you need to get authenticated. If you are using a standalone client, you will need to specify the credentials in the JAX-WS Factory. The following is an example of how to access the secured `CalculatePowerService` instance, which was described in *Chapter 7, Adding Web Services to Your Applications*:

```
JaxWsProxyFactoryBean factory = new JaxWsProxyFactoryBean();

factory.getInInterceptors().add(new LoggingInInterceptor());
factory.getOutInterceptors().add(new LoggingOutInterceptor());
```

```
factory.setServiceClass(CalculatePowerWebService.class);
factory.setAddress("http://localhost:8080/pojoService");
factory.setUsername("admin");
factory.setPassword("admin");
CalculatePowerWebService client = (CalculatePowerWebService)
    factory.create();
```

What about EJB-based web services? The configuration is slightly different; since the security domain is not specified in web descriptors, we have to provide it by means of annotations:

```
@Stateless
@WebService(targetNamespace = "http://www.packtpub.com/", serviceName
    = "TicketWebService")
@WebContext(authMethod = "BASIC",
            secureWSDLAccess = false)
@SecurityDomain(value = "dbdomain")
@RolesAllowed("Manager")
public class TicketSOAPService implements TicketSOAPServiceItf,
    Serializable {


    . . . .

}
```

As you can see, the @org.jboss.ws.api.annotation.Webcontext annotation basically reflects the same configuration options as that of POJO-based web services, with BASIC authentication and unrestricted WSDL access.

 The @WebContext annotation can be found in the following dependency:

```
<dependency>
    <groupId>org.jboss.ws</groupId>
    <artifactId>jbossws-api</artifactId>
    <version>1.0.2.Final</version>
    <scope>provided</scope>
</dependency>
```

The @org.jboss.ejb3.annotation.SecurityDomain annotation should be familiar to you since we introduced it to illustrate how to secure an EJB. As you can see, it's a replacement for the information contained in the jboss-web.xml file, except that the security domain is referenced directly by dbdomain (instead of java:/jaas/dbdomain).

The previous security configuration can also be specified by means of the META-INF/ejb-jar.xml and META-INF/jboss-ejb3.xml file in case you prefer using standard configuration files.

To pass your login credentials to the web service, you can use the `RequestContext` object:

```
final TicketWebService infoService =
    service.getPort(TicketWebService.class);
Map<String, Object> requestContext = ((BindingProvider)
    infoService).getRequestContext();
requestContext.put(BindingProvider.USERNAME_PROPERTY, "admin");
requestContext.put(BindingProvider.PASSWORD_PROPERTY, "admin");
```

The username and password values will be passed to the login module defined in the security domain, just like in every other authentication method.

Securing the transport layer

If you were to create a mission-critical application with just the bare concepts you learned until now, you would be exposed to all sorts of security threats. For example, if you need to design a payment gateway, where the credit card information is transmitted by means of an EJB or servlet, using just the authorization and authentication stack is really not enough, as the sensitive information is still sent across a network and it could be disclosed by a hacker.

In order to prevent disclosure of critical information to unauthorized individuals or systems, you have to use a protocol that provides encryption of the information. Encryption is the conversion of data into a form that cannot be understood by unauthorized people. Conversely, decryption is the process of converting encrypted data back into its original form so that it can be understood.

The protocols used to secure the communication are SSL and TLS, the latter being considered a replacement for the older SSL.

 The differences between the two protocols are minor and very technical. In short, TLS uses stronger encryption algorithms and has the ability to work on different ports. For the rest of this chapter, we will refer to SSL for both protocols. Check out Wikipedia for more information on it: http://en.wikipedia.org/wiki/Transport_Layer_Security.

There are two basic techniques to encrypt information: symmetric encryption (also called secret-key encryption) and asymmetric encryption (also called public-key encryption).

Symmetric encryption is the oldest and best-known technique. It is based on a secret key, which is applied to the text of a message to change the content in a particular way. As long as both the sender and recipient know the secret key, they can encrypt and decrypt all messages that use this key. These encryption algorithms typically work fast and are well suited to encrypt blocks of messages at once.

One significant issue with symmetric algorithms is the requirement of a safe administrative organization to distribute keys to users. This generally results in increased overhead from the administrative aspect while the keys remain vulnerable to unauthorized disclosure and potential abuse.

For this reason, a mission-critical enterprise system usually relies on the asymmetric encryption algorithms, which tend to be easier to employ, manage, and are ultimately more secure.

Asymmetric cryptography, also known as **public-key cryptography**, is based on the concept that the key used to encrypt is not the same as the key that is used to decrypt the message. In practice, each user holds a couple of keys: the public key that is distributed to other parties and the private key that is kept as a secret. Each message is encrypted with the recipient's public key and can only be decrypted (by the recipient) with his private key, as shown in the following diagram:

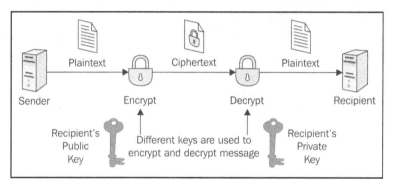

Using asymmetric encryption, you can be sure that your message cannot be disclosed to a third party. However, there is still one vulnerability.

Suppose you want to exchange some valuable information with a business partner and to that end are requesting his public key by telephone or email. A fraudulent user intercepts your e-mail or simply listens to your conversation and quickly sends you a fake mail with his public key. Now, even if your data transmission is secured, it will be directed to the wrong person!

In order to solve this issue, we need a document to verify that the public key belongs to a particular individual. This document is called a **digital certificate** or public-key certificate. A digital certificate consists of a formatted block of data that contains the name of the certificate holder (which may be either a user or system name) and the holder's public key, along with the digital signature of a **Certification Authority (CA)** for authentication. The CA attests that the sender's name is the one associated with the public key in the document.

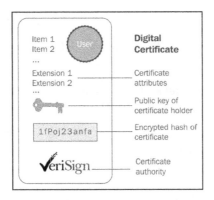

Public key certificates are commonly used to secure the interaction with websites. By default, the web browser ships with a set of predefined CAs; they are used to verify that the public certificate served to a browser when you enter a secure site has actually been issued by the owner of the website. In short, if you connect your browser to `https://www.abc.com` and your browser doesn't give any certificate warning, you can safely interact with the entity in charge of the site, that is, unless the site or your browser has been hacked. However, this is another story.

Simple authentication and client authentication

In the previous example, we depicted a simple authentication, (also called server authentication). In this scenario, the only party that needs to prove its identity is the server.

SSL, however, is able to perform mutual authentication (also called client or two-way authentication); here too, the server requests a client certificate during the SSL handshake over the network.

Client authentication requires a client certificate in the x.509 format from a CA. The x.509 format is an industry-standard format for SSL certificates. In the next section, we will explore which tools are available to generate digital certificates, and how to get your certificates signed by a CA.

Enabling the Secure Socket Layer on WildFly

WildFly uses the **Java Secure Socket Extension (JSSE)**, which is bundled in the Java SE to leverage the SSL/TLS communication.

An Enterprise application can be secured at two different locations: the HTTP level for web applications, and the RMI level for applications using EJB. HTTP communication is handled by the web subsystem within the `standalone.xml/ domain.xml` file. Securing the RMI transport is, on the other hand, not always a compelling requirement of your applications. Actually, in most production environments, WildFly is placed behind a firewall.

As you can see from the following diagram, this implies that your EJBs are not directly exposed to untrusted networks, which usually connect through the web server placed in a demilitarized zone:

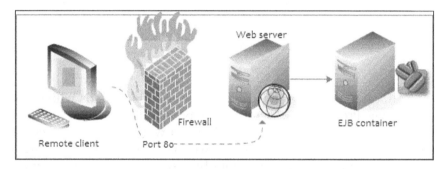

In order to get started with WildFly and SSL, we need a tool that generates a public/private key pair in the form of an x.509 certificate for use by the SSL server sockets. This is covered in the next section.

Certificate management tools

One tool that can be used to set up a digital certificate is **keytool**, a key and certificate management utility that ships with the Java SE. It enables users to administer their own public/private key pairs and associated certificates for use in self-authentication (where the user authenticates himself or herself to other users or services) or data integrity and authentication services, using digital signatures. It also allows users to cache the public keys (in the form of certificates) of their communicating peers.

The keytool stores the keys and certificates in a file termed keystore, a repository of certificates used to identify a client or server. Typically, a keystore contains a client or server's identity, which is protected by a password. Let's see an example of the keystore generation:

```
keytool -genkey -keystore wildfly.keystore -storepass mypassword -keypass
mypassword -keyalg RSA -validity 180  -alias wflyalias    -dname "cn=John
Smith,o=PackPub,c=GB"
```

This command creates the keystore named `wildfly.keystore` in the working directory, and assigns it the password `mypassword`. It generates a public/private key pair for the entity whose unique name has the common name `John Smith`, organization `PacktPub`, and two-letter country code `GB`.

The result of this action will be a self-signed certificate (using the RSA signature algorithm), which includes the public key and the unique name. This certificate will be valid for 180 days, and is associated with the private key in a keystore entry referred to by the alias `wflyalias`.

 A self-signed certificate is a certificate that has not been verified by a CA and thus, leaves you vulnerable to the classic man-in-the-middle attack. A self-signed certificate is only suitable for in-house use or for testing while you wait for your real certificate to arrive.

Securing the HTTP communication with a self-signed certificate

Now let's see how you can use this keystore file to secure your WildFly web channel. Open your server configuration file and locate the web subsystem.

Within the web subsystem, you have to first change the default `http-listener` and `socket-binding` to `https-listener` and `"https"`, and add the `security-realm` element to it. Next, you have to insert an `ssl` stanza within it, which contains the details of your `keystore` object (in our example, we dropped the file `jboss.keystore` into the server configuration directory):

```
<subsystem xmlns="urn:jboss:domain:undertow:1.0">
        <buffer-caches>
            <buffer-cache name="default" buffer-size="1024"
                buffers-per-region="1024" max-regions="10"/>
        </buffer-caches>
        <server name="default-server">
```

```
            <https-listener name="default" socket-binding="https"
                security-realm="EJBRealm"/>
            <host name="default-host" alias="localhost">
                <location name="/" handler="welcome-content"/>
                <filter-ref name="server-header"/>
                <filter-ref name="x-powered-by-header"/>
            </host>
        </server>
        <servlet-container name="default" default-buffer-
            cache="default" stack-trace-on-error="local-only">
            <jsp-config/>
        </servlet-container>
        // some more code
    </subsystem>
```

As you can see, we referenced EJBRealm in the configuration, but we still need to define it. We will do this in the next sections.

Generating the server and client certificates

Start by generating a public/private key pair for the entity whose unique name has the common name John Smith, organization PacktPub, and two-letter country code GB.

```
keytool -genkey -v -alias wflyAlias -keyalg RSA -keysize 1024 -keystore
wfly.keystore -validity 180 -keypass mypassword -storepass mypassword
-dname "cn=John Smith,o=PacktPub,c=GB"
```

Next, export the server's public key into a certificate named sslPublicKey.cer that uses the password mypassword.

```
keytool -export -keystore jboss.keystore -alias wflyAlias -file
sslPublicKey.cer -keypass mypassword -storepass mypassword
```

Now that we have finished configuring the server, we will generate a key pair for the client too. We will do this by using the alias ejbclientalias and the same properties as we did for the server's keystore object:

```
keytool -genkey -v -alias ejbclientalias -keyalg RSA -keysize 1024
-keystore jbossClient.keystore -validity 180 -keypass clientPassword
-storepass clientPassword -dname "cn=John Smith,o=PacktPub,c=GB"
```

The client public key will also be exported to a certificate named clientPublicKey. cer.

```
keytool -export -keystore jbossClient.keystore -alias ejbclientalias
-file clientPublicKey.cer -keypass clientPassword -storepass
clientPassword
```

Now, in order to complete the SSL handshake successfully, we need to first import the client's public key into the server's `truststore` object:

```
keytool -import -v -trustcacerts -alias ejbclientalias -file
clientPublicKey.cer -keystore jboss.keystore -keypass mypassword
-storepass mypassword
```

The server certificate also needs to be trusted by the client. You have two available options to solve this issue, as follows:

- Import the server certificate into the client's JDK bundle of certificates
- Create a new repository of certificates trusted by the client (`truststore`)

Importing the server certificate into the client JDK means executing a certificate import into the client's certified authorities.

```
keytool -import -v -trustcacerts -alias wflyAlias -file sslPublicKey.cer
-keystore C:\Java\jdk1.8.0_20\jre\lib\security\cacerts
```

We just have to replace the path we used with our actual JDK path and use the client store's password in order to complete this operation (the default value is `changeit`).

Otherwise, if you want to import the certificate into a newly created `truststore` object, just substitute the `cacerts` destination with your client's `truststore` object.

```
keytool -import -v -trustcacerts -alias wflyAlias -file sslPublicKey.
cer -keystore jbossClient.keystore -keypass clientPassword -storepass
clientPassword
```

> If you choose the latter option, you need to add the following properties to your client's JDK arguments, which will override the default JDK's `truststore` object:
>
> ```
> java -Djavax.net.ssl.trustStore=<truststorefile>
> -Djavax.net.ssl.trustStorePassword=<password>
> ```

Creating an SSL-aware security realm

Within WildFly, security realms are used to secure access to the management interfaces, HTTP interface, and remote JNDI and EJB access. Within a security realm, it is also possible to define an identity for the server; this identity can be used for both inbound connections to the server and outbound connections being established by the server.

Therefore, in order to enable SSL communication for our EJB communication and HTTP, we will define a security realm (named `EJBRealm`) that is bound to a server identity, which references the server's `keystore` object, shown as follows:

```
<security-realm name="EJBRealm">
<server-identities>
    <ssl>
      <keystore path="jboss.keystore" relative-
          to="jboss.server.config.dir" keystore-
            password="mypassword"/>
    </ssl>
  </server-identities>
  <authentication>
      <jaas name="ejb-security-domain"/>
  </authentication>
</security-realm>
```

Besides containing the location where SSL certificates are stored, this security realm also contains the authentication policy used by your EJBs, which is defined by the JAAS's security domain, named `ejb-security-domain`.

The following is a security domain definition, which is a simple file-based security domain containing the user credentials and roles in the files `ejb-users.properties` and `ejb-roles.properties`, respectively:

```
<security-domain name="ejb-security-domain" cache-type="default">
<authentication>
  <login-module code="Remoting" flag="optional">
    <module-option name="password-stacking" value="useFirstPass"/>
  </login-module>
  <login-module
  code="org.jboss.security.auth.spi.UsersRolesLoginModule"
  flag="required">
    <module-option name="defaultUsersProperties"
    value="${jboss.server.config.dir}/ejb-users.properties"/>
    <module-option name="defaultRolesProperties"
    value="${jboss.server.config.dir}/ejb-roles.properties"/>
    <module-option name="usersProperties"
    value="${jboss.server.config.dir}/ejb-users.properties"/>
```

```
        <module-option name="rolesProperties"
        value="${jboss.server.config.dir}/ejb-roles.properties"/>
        <module-option name="password-stacking" value="useFirstPass"/>
    </login-module>
</authentication>
</security-domain>
```

As you can imagine, you need to create the two property files, each with some values in them. For example, here's the `ejb-user.properties` file to be placed in the server configuration's folder:

```
adminUser=admin123
```

The following is the corresponding `ejb-roles.properties` file that grants the role `ejbRole` to the `adminUser` role:

```
adminUser=ejbRole
```

The last configuration effort would be to specify it in the `security-realm` attribute of your `remoting` connector's element:

```
<subsystem xmlns="urn:jboss:domain:remoting:2.0">
    <endpoint worker="default"/>
    <http-connector name="http-remoting-connector"
    connector-ref="default"
    security-realm="EJBRealm"/>
</subsystem>
```

Let's check the outcome of our work. First, we will try out the HTTPS connection.

You have to restart WildFly to activate the changes. You should see the following log at the bottom of your console, which informs you about the new HTTPS channel running on port 8443:

```
[org.wildfly.extension.undertow] (MSC service thread 1-9)
   JBAS017519: Undertow HTTP listener default listening on
   /127.0.0.1:8443
```

The following screen is what will be displayed by the Internet Explorer (don't try this at home) browser (the same kind of error message, with a different format, will be displayed by other browsers such as Firefox and Google Chrome) if you try to access the Ticket example using the secured channel (for example, `https://localhost:8443/ticket-agency-cdi`):

There is a problem with this website's security certificate.

The security certificate presented by this website was not issued by a trusted certificate authority.
The security certificate presented by this website was issued for a different website's address.

Security certificate problems may indicate an attempt to fool you or intercept any data you send to the server.

We recommend that you close this webpage and do not continue to this website.

Click here to close this webpage.

Continue to this website (not recommended).

More information

What happened? Once you establish a secure connection with the web server, the server certificate is sent to the browser. Since the certificate has not been signed by any recognized CA, the browser security sandbox warns the user about the potential security threat.

This is an in-house test so we can safely proceed by choosing **Continue to this website**. That's all you need to do in order to activate the Secure Socket Layer with a self-signed certificate.

Securing HTTP communication with a certificate signed by a CA

Having your certificate signed requires a **certificate-signing request** (CSR) to be issued to a CA, which will return a signed certificate to be installed on your server. This implies a cost for your organization, which depends on how many certificates you request, the encryption strength, and other factors.

Firstly, generate a CSR using the newly created `keystore` and keyentry:

```
keytool -certreq -keystore jboss.keystore -alias wflyalias -storepass
mypassword -keypass mypassword  -keyalg RSA  -file certreq.csr
```

This will create a new certificate request named `certreq.csr`, bearing the following format:

```
-----BEGIN NEW CERTIFICATE REQUEST-----
. . . . . .
-----END NEW CERTIFICATE REQUEST-----
```

The previous certificate needs to be transmitted to the CA. At the end of the enrollment phase, the CA will return a signed certificate, which needs to be imported into your keychain. The following code assumes you saved your CA certificate in a file named `signed_ca.txt`:

```
keytool -import -keystore jboss.keystore -alias testkey1 -storepass
mypassword -keypass mypassword -file signed_ca.txt
```

Now, your web browser will recognize your new certificate as being signed by a CA, so it won't complain about not being able to validate the certificate.

Securing EJB communication

EJB clients interact with the Enterprise EJB tier using the RMI-IIOP protocol. The RMI-IIOP protocol has been developed by Sun to combine the RMI programming model with the IIOP underlying transport.

Securing the EJB transport is required for applications that have strict secure policies, which cannot be carried out using clear text transmission. In order to do this, we need to be sure to complete the following steps:

1. First, generate the SSL certificates and then store the client's public key in the server's `keystore` object and the server's public key on the client's `truststore`; we've already done this in order to prepare our HTTPS connector.

2. Next, we need to create an SSL-aware security realm, which will be used by the `remoting` transport. We can use the one created for the HTTPS communication.

3. Finally, we need to apply some changes to our EJB application so that it actually uses the SSL secure channel. We will cover this in the next subsection.

Connecting to an SSL-aware security realm

As you saw in *Chapter 3, Introducing Java EE 7 – EJBs*, the RMI-IIOP connection properties are specified in the `jboss-ejb-client.properties` file, which needs to be tweaked a bit to enable SSL connections:

```
remote.connections=node1
remote.connection.node1.host=localhost
remote.connection.node1.port = 4447
remote.connection.node1.username=adminUser
remote.connection.node1.password=admin123
remote.connectionprovider.create.options.org.xnio.Options.SSL_ENABLED
    =true
remote.connection.node1.connect.options.org.xnio.Options.SSL_STARTTLS
    =true
remote.connection.node1.connect.options.org.xnio.Options.SASL_POLICY_
    NOANONYMOUS=true
```

The `SSL_ENABLED` option, when set to `true`, enables the `remoting` connector's SSL communication.

The `STARTTLS` option specifies whether to use the **Tunneled Transport Layer Security (TTLS)** mode at startup or when needed.

The `SASL_POLICY_NOANONYMOUS` option specifies whether **Simple Authentication and Security Layer (SASL)** mechanisms, which accept anonymous logins, are permitted.

Finally, since our security realm also includes an authentication security domain, we can choose to restrict access to some methods by specifying a `@RolesAllowed` annotation, which requires the role `ejbRole`:

```
@RolesAllowed("ejbRole")
public String bookSeat(int seatId)  throws SeatBookedException {
  . . . .
}
```

In order to activate the security domain on your EJBs, we need to mention it in the assembly descriptor of your `jboss-ejb3.xml` file:

```
<jboss:ejb-jar>
  <assembly-descriptor>
    <s:security>
      <ejb-name>*</ejb-name>
        <s:security-domain>ejb-security-domain</s:security-domain>
    </s:security>
  </assembly-descriptor>
</jboss:ejb-jar>
```

Now, redeploy the Ticket EJB example application, following the directions contained in *Chapter 3*, *Introducing Java EE 7 – EJBs*, and execute the client.

If the connection is successful, then you have configured a fully working and secured remoting connection.

Summary

We started this chapter by discussing the basic concepts of security and the difference between authentication and authorization.

WildFly uses the PicketBox framework sitting on top of the **Java Authentication and Authorization Service (JAAS)**, which secures all the Java EE technologies running in the application. The core section of the security subsystem is contained in the security-domain element that performs all the required **authorization** and **authentication** checks.

Then, we took a much closer look at the login modules, which are used to store the user credentials and their associated roles. In particular, you learned how to apply the file-based UserRoles login module and the Database login module. Each login module can be used by Enterprise applications in either a programmatic or declarative way. While programmatic security can provide a fine-grained security model, you should consider using declarative security, which allows a clean separation between the business layer and the security policies.

Finally, in the last section of this chapter, we covered how to encrypt the communication channel using the Secure Socket Layer and the certificates produced by the keytool Java utility.

In the next chapter, we are going to discuss clustering, which is the environment where critical applications are deployed.

11
Clustering WildFly Applications

In the previous chapters, we went through the most interesting aspects of developing Java Enterprise applications. Once you are ready to roll out your applications, it is important that you guarantee your customers a responsive and fault-tolerant environment. This requirement can be achieved through application server clustering.

WildFly clustering is not the product of a single library or specification, but rather a blend of technologies. In this chapter, we will first introduce some of the basics of clustered programming. Then, we will quickly move on to the cluster configuration and its setup, which will be required to deploy some clustered applications.

The following list is a preview of the topics that will be covered in this chapter:

- What clustering is and how WildFly implements it
- Setting up clusters in the standalone and domain mode
- Developing clustered Java EE 7 applications in order to achieve load balancing and high availability

Clustering basics

A cluster of application servers consists of multiple server instances (cluster nodes) running simultaneously and working together to provide increased scalability and reliability. The nodes that make up a cluster can be located either on the same machine or different machines. From the client's point of view, this is irrelevant because the cluster appears as a single server instance.

Introducing clustering in your applications will produce the following benefits:

- **Horizontal scalability (scaling out)**: Adding a new node to a cluster should allow the overall system to service a higher client load than that provided by a simple basic configuration. Ideally, it should be possible to service any given load simply by adding the appropriate number of servers or machines.

- **Load balancing**: In a clustered environment, the individual nodes that compose the cluster should each process a fair share of the overall client load. This can be achieved by distributing client requests across multiple servers, which is also known as load balancing.

- **High availability**: Applications running in a cluster can continue to do so when a server instance fails. This is achieved because applications are deployed on multiple nodes of the cluster, and so if a server instance fails, another server instance on which that component is deployed can continue with application processing.

WildFly clustering

Clustering is available in WildFly out of the box. There is no all-in-one library that deals with clustering, but rather a set of libraries that cover different kinds of aspects.

The following diagram shows the basic clustering architecture adopted by WildFly:

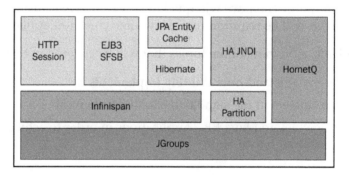

The backbone of JBoss clustering is the **JGroups** library, which provides communication between members of the cluster using a multicast transmission.

 Multicast is a protocol where data is transmitted simultaneously to a group of hosts that have joined the appropriate multicast group. You can think about multicast as a radio or television streaming where only those tuned to a particular frequency receive the streaming.

The next building block is **Infinispan**, which handles the consistency of your application across the cluster by means of a replicated and transactional JSR-107-compatible cache.

 JSR-107 specifies the API and semantics for temporary in-memory caching of Java objects, including object creation, shared access, spooling, invalidation, and consistency across JVMs.

Before diving into some cluster examples, we will first need to describe how to set up a cluster of WildFly nodes using the two available nodes: **standalone cluster** and **domain cluster**. If you don't remember the difference between the **standalone** and **domain** mode or what core **domain** elements are, you can revise the material from *Chapter 2, Your First Java EE Application on WildFly*.

Starting a cluster of standalone nodes

A standalone server starts as a single JVM process; therefore, we need to start each server using the `standalone.bat/standalone.sh` command, passing all the required parameters. In the following example, we are starting a cluster of two server nodes on two different boxes that are bound to the IP addresses `192.168.1.10` and `192.168.1.11`, respectively:

```
./standalone.sh -c standalone-ha.xml -b 192.168.1.10
./standalone.sh -c standalone-ha.xml -b 192.168.1.11
```

The `-c` parameter specifies the server configuration to be used; out of the box, the application server includes two standalone clustering configurations: `standalone-ha.xml` and `standalone-full-ha.xml`. The latter one also includes the messaging subsystem and other elements of the Java EE full profile; therefore, it has been named the *full* configuration.

The other parameter (`-b`) should sound familiar to older JBoss users, as it's still used to specify the server-binding address, which needs to be unique in order to avoid port conflicts.

In this other example, we are starting another cluster of two nodes on the same box using some additional parameters in order to avoid port conflicts:

```
./standalone.sh -c standalone-ha.xml -Djboss.node.name=node1
./standalone.sh -c standalone-ha.xml -Djboss.node.name=node2 -Djboss.
socket.binding.port-offset=200
```

As you can see, we had to specify two additional parameters: `jboss.node.name` in order to assign a unique server name to each node and a socket-binding port, which uses an offset of `200`. So, for example, the second node would respond to the HTTP channel on port `8280` instead of port `8080`.

 Don't be surprised if you don't see any message about clustering on your server console. Clustering modules are activated on demand, so first you need to deploy an application that is cluster-aware. In a few minutes, we will show you how.

Starting a cluster of domain nodes

In order to configure a cluster running on a domain of server nodes, you need to configure the main `domain.xml` file for your domain controller. Then, for every WildFly host that is a part of the cluster, you need to provide a `host.xml` configuration file, which describes the configuration of a single-server distribution.

The domain controller configuration

The `domain.xml` file is located at `JBOSS_HOME/domain/configuration/`. It includes the main domain configuration, which is shared by all server instances. In the `domain.xml` file, we will define the server group configurations specifying a profile that is compatible with clustering. Out of the box, a WildFly domain ships with four different profiles:

- `default`: This profile has the support of Java EE Web Profile and some extensions, such as RESTful web services, or support for **Enterprise JavaBeans (EJB)** 3 remote invocations
- `full`: This profile supports all the default subsystems contained in the default profile and the messaging subsystem
- `ha`: This profile corresponds to the `default` profile extended with clustering capabilities
- `full-ha`: This is the `full` profile with clustering capabilities

So, first specify a cluster-aware profile for your server groups in your `domain.xml` file. In our example, we have adopted the `full-ha` profile for both the server groups so that you can run the full Java EE stack on all your domain servers:

```
<server-groups>
    <server-group name="main-server-group" profile="full-ha">
        <jvm name="default">
            <heap size="64m" max-size="512m"/>
```

```
            </jvm>
            <socket-binding-group ref="full-ha-sockets"/>
        </server-group>
        <server-group name="other-server-group" profile="full-ha">
            <jvm name="default">
                <heap size="64m" max-size="512m"/>
            </jvm>
            <socket-binding-group ref="full-sockets"/>
        </server-group>
    </server-groups>
```

When using a full-ha profile, you need to configure HornetQ clustering security. You can just disable it, or you need to additionally set a completely random user credential for a JMS cluster. Find the profile settings in domain.xml, and add the following code to the messaging subsystem:

```
<subsystem xmlns="urn:jboss:domain:messaging:2.0">
    <hornetq-server>
        <cluster-user>randomUser</cluster-user>
        <cluster-password>randomPassword</cluster-password>
            . . .
    </hornetq-server>
</subsystem>
```

In addition to the domain.xml file, you need to check whether your domain controller's host.xml file contains a reference to the local host, as shown in the following code snippet:

```
<host name="master" xmlns="urn:jboss:domain:2.0">
    ...
    <domain-controller>
        <local/>
    </domain-controller>
    ...
</host>
```

The local stanza means that this host controller will take the role of a domain controller. For all other hosts controllers, you must specify the remote domain controller host and its port (in this example, we added some variables as placeholders). We will cover them in the next section.

Finally, you need to create a management user that will be used to establish a connection between the slave nodes and the domain controller. For this purpose, launch the `add-user.sh`/`add-user.cmd` script, which is located in the JBOSS_HOME/bin directory of your distribution:

```
What type of user do you wish to add?
 a) Management User (mgmt-users.properties)
 b) Application User (application-users.properties)
(a): a


Enter the details of the new user to add.
Using realm 'ManagementRealm' as discovered from the existing property
files.
Username : admin1234
Password recommendations are listed below. To modify these restrictions
edit the add-user.properties configuration file.
 - The password should not be one of the following restricted values
{root, admin, administrator}
 - The password should contain at least 8 characters, 1 alphabetic
character(s), 1 digit(s), 1 non-alphanumeric symbol(s)
 - The password should be different from the username
Password :
Re-enter Password :
What groups do you want this user to belong to? (Please enter a comma
separated list, or leave blank for none) [ ]:
About to add user 'admin1234' for realm 'ManagementRealm'
Is this correct yes/no? yes
Added user 'admin1234' to file 'D:\Dev\Servers\wildfly-8.1.0.Final\
standalone\configuration\mgmt-users.properties'
Added user 'admin1234' to file 'D:\Dev\Servers\wildfly-8.1.0.Final\
domain\configuration\mgmt-users.properties'
Added user 'admin1234' with groups  to file 'D:\Dev\Servers\wildfly-
8.1.0.Final\standalone\configuration\mgmt-groups.properties'
Added user 'admin1234' with groups  to file 'D:\Dev\Servers\wildfly-
8.1.0.Final\domain\configuration\mgmt-groups.properties'
Is this new user going to be used for one AS process to connect to
another AS process?
e.g. for a slave host controller connecting to the master or for a
Remoting connection for server to server EJB calls.
yes/no? yes
To represent the user add the following to the server-identities
definition <secret value="c2xvZHppYWsxMjM0" />
Press any key to continue . . .
```

As you can see from the preceding listing, you have to create a management user by specifying a username and password for it. You should answer the previous question with either `yes` or `y` to indicate that the user will be used to connect to the domain controller from the host controller. The generated secret value is the Base64-encoded password of the newly created user.

Now we can start the domain controller by specifying the address that will be used for public and management interfaces (in our example, `192.168.1.10`) with the following command:

```
domain.sh -host-config=host-master.xml -b 192.168.1.10 -Djboss.bind.
address.management=192.168.1.10
```

We have set the bind address of the physical network to the host configuration with the `jboss.bind.address.management` property. The management interface must be reachable for all the hosts in the domain in order to establish a connection with the domain controller.

Host configurations

After the domain controller is configured and started, the next step is to set up the other hosts that will connect to the domain controller. On each host, we also need an installation of WildFly, where we will configure the `host.xml` file. (As an alternative, you can name the host file as you like and start the domain with the `-host-config` parameter, for example, `./domain.sh -host-config=host-slave.xml`.)

The first thing is to choose a unique name for each host in our domain in order to avoid name conflicts. Otherwise, the default is the hostname of the server.

```
<host name="server1" xmlns="urn:jboss:domain:2.0">
    . . .
</host>
```

Also, you have to choose a unique name for the other host:

```
<host name="server2" xmlns="urn:jboss:domain:2.0">
    . . .
</host>
```

Next, we need to specify that the host controller will connect to a remote domain controller. We will not specify the actual IP address of the domain controller but leave it as a property named `jboss.domain.master.address`.

Additionally, we need to specify the username that will be used to connect to the domain controller. So let's add the user `admin1234`, which we created on the domain controller machine:

```
<domain-controller>
        <remote host="${jboss.domain.master.address}"
        port="${jboss.domain.master.port:9999}"
        username="admin1234"
        security-realm="ManagementRealm"/>
</domain-controller>
```

Finally, we need to specify the Base64 password for the server identity that we included in the `remote` element:

```
<management>
    <security-realms>
        <security-realm name="ManagementRealm">
            <server-identities>
                <secret value="QWxlc3NhbmRybzIh" />
            </server-identities>
            <authentication>
                <properties path="mgmt-users.properties"
                relative-to="jboss.domain.config.dir" />
            </authentication>
        </security-realm>
        <security-realm name="ApplicationRealm">
            <authentication>
                <properties path="application-users.properties"
                relative-to="jboss.domain.config.dir" />
            </authentication>
        </security-realm>
    </security-realms>
    <management-interfaces>
        <native-interface security-realm="ManagementRealm">
            <socket interface="management"
            port="${jboss.management.native.port:9999}" />
        </native-interface>
    </management-interfaces>
</management>
```

The final step is to configure the server nodes inside the host.xml file on both the hosts. So, on the first host, we will configure server-one and server-two to add them to main-server-group:

```
<servers>
        <server name="server-one" group="main-server-group"/>
        <server name="server-two" group="main-server-group"
        auto-start="false">
            <socket-bindings port-offset="150"/>
        </server>
</servers>
```

On the second host, we will configure server-three and server-four to add them to other-server-group:

```
<servers>
        <server name="server-three" group="other-server-group"/>
        <server name="server-four" group="other-server-group">
        auto-start="false">
            <socket-bindings port-offset="150"/>
        </server>
</servers>
```

Please note that the auto-start flag value indicates that the server instances will not be started automatically if the host controller is started.

For server-two and server-four, a port-offset value of 150 is configured to avoid port conflicts. Okay, now we are done with our configuration. Assuming that the first host has an IP address of 192.168.1.10, we can start the first host with the following code snippet:

```
domain.sh \
-host-conifg=host.xml
-b 192.168.1.10   \
-Djboss.domain.master.address=192.168.1.1 \
-Djboss.bind.address.management=192.168.1.10
```

The second host (192.168.1.11) can be started with the following code snippet:

```
domain.sh \
-host-conifg=host.xml
-b 192.168.1.11 \
-Djboss.domain.master.address=192.168.1.1 \
-Djboss.bind.address.management=192.168.1.11
```

Deploying clustered applications

If you have tried starting your standalone or domain set of cluster nodes, you will be surprised that there is no information at all about clustering in your server logging. Believe me, it is not a bug but a feature! One of the key features of WildFly is that only a minimal set of services is started; therefore, in order to see a cluster's live demonstration, you need to deploy a cluster-aware application. In order to trigger clustering libraries in your application, you can follow two approaches:

- If your application uses Enterprise JavaBeans, you don't have to do anything more. This area brings some important changes in WildFly. Now, by default, the data of all stateful session beans is replicated in HA profiles, and all stateless beans are clustered. If your application is deployed on a container started with the `standalone-ha.xml` configuration, all remote **Stateless Session Bean (SLSB)** support failover capabilities by default.

- If your application includes a web application archive, you can use the portable `<distributable />` element in your `web.xml` file.

Let's have a look at both the approaches, starting from clustering EJBs.

Creating HA Stateful Session Beans

Clustered **Stateful Session Beans (SFSB)** have built-in failover capabilities. This means that the state of `@Stateful` EJBs is replicated across the cluster nodes so that if one of the nodes in the cluster goes down, some other node will be able to take over the invocations addressed to it. It is possible to disable this feature for specific beans using the `@Stateful(passivationCapable=false)` annotation.

The following diagram depicts a typical exchange of information between the EJB client application and the remote EJB component:

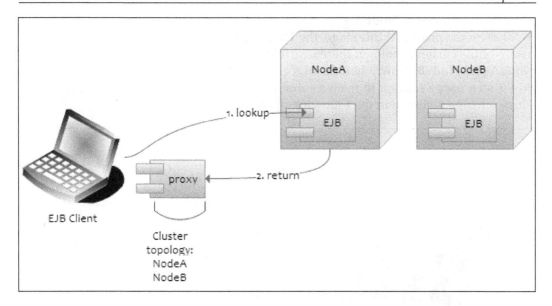

As you can see, after a successful lookup of an SFSB via **Java Naming and Directory Interface (JNDI)**, a proxy is returned to the client for subsequent method invocations.

> Since the EJB is clustered, it will return a session ID and along with it the *affinity* of that session, that is, the name of the cluster to which the stateful bean belongs to on the server side. This affinity will later help the EJB client to route the invocations on the proxy appropriately to a specific node in the cluster.

While this session creation request is going on, **NodeA** will also send back an asynchronous message that contains the cluster topology. The JBoss **EJB Client** implementation will take note of this topology information and will later use it to create connections to the nodes within the cluster and route invocations to those nodes, whenever necessary.

Now let's assume that **NodeA** goes down and the client application subsequently invokes on the proxy. At this stage, the **JBoss EJB Client** implementation will be aware of the cluster topology; therefore, it knows that the cluster has two nodes: **NodeA** and **NodeB**. Now when the invocation arrives, it detects that **NodeA** is down, so it uses a selector to fetch a suitable node from among the cluster nodes. This exchange is shown in the following diagram:

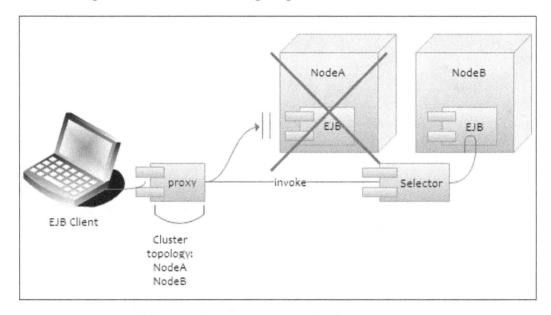

If a suitable node is found, the **JBoss EJB Client** implementation creates a connection to that node (in our case **NodeB**) and creates an EJB receiver out of it. At the end of this process, the invocation has now been effectively failed over to a different node within the cluster.

Clustering the Ticket example

In *Chapter 3, Introducing Java EE 7 – EJBs*, we discussed our ticket system example, which was built around the following:

- A stateful EJB to hold the session data
- A singleton EJB to store the cache of data
- A stateless EJB to perform some business methods

Let's see how to apply the necessary changes to start our application in a cluster context.

The stateless and stateful beans are ready to be clustered — no additional code is required; however, there's a pitfall. As a matter of fact, the singleton EJB that is used to hold the cache of a seat will be instantiated once in each JVM of the cluster. This means that if there's a server failure, the data in the cache will be lost and new data (inconsistent) will be used.

There are several alternatives to set up a cache in a clustered environment:

- Use a JBoss proprietary solution that deploys a clustered version of `SingletonService`, which exposes an HA singleton of `org.jboss.msc.service.Service` (an example of this approach is contained in the WildFly quickstart demo at `https://github.com/wildfly/quickstart/tree/master/cluster-ha-singleton`)

- Move your cache to a persistent storage, which means using JPA to store and read data from the cache (see *Chapter 5, Combining Persistence with CDI,* which includes a JPA-based example of our application)

- Use a distributed data cache such as Infinispan to store data, providing a failover and data consistency to your cache

Showing all the possible solution implementations would, however, make this section excessively long; therefore, we will illustrate how to use the last option, which can provide a good architectural pattern with the least amount of effort.

Turning your cache into a distributed cache

Infinispan is a distributed data grid platform that exposes a JSR-107-compatible cache interface in which you can store data and enhance it by providing additional APIs and features (such as transactional cache, data eviction and expiration, asynchronous operations on the cache, and more). Its primary interface is `javax.cache.Cache`, which is similar to the `java.util.ConcurrentMap` Java SE, with some modifications for distributed environments. In particular, it adds the ability to register, deregister, and list event listeners. Also, it defines a `CacheLoader` interface to load/store cached data. Cache instances can be retrieved using an appropriate `CacheManager` interface, which represents a collection of caches.

So here's our singleton `TheatreBox` class rewritten using the Infinispan API:

```
@Singleton
@Startup
@AccessTimeout(value = 5, unit = TimeUnit.MINUTES)
public class TheatreBox {

    private static final Logger logger =
            Logger.getLogger(TheatreBox.class);
```

```
    private Map<Integer, Seat> seats;

    @Resource(lookup = "java:jboss/infinispan/tickets")
    private EmbeddedCacheManager container;

    @PostConstruct
    public void setupTheatre() {
        try {
            this.cache = container.getCache();
            logger.info("Got Infinispan cache");

            int id = 0;
            for (int i = 0; i < 5; i++) {
                addSeat(new Seat(++id, "Stalls", 40));
                addSeat(new Seat(++id, "Circle", 20));
                addSeat(new Seat(++id, "Balcony", 10));
            }
            logger.info("Seat Map constructed.");
        } catch (Exception e) {
            logger.info("Error! " + e.getMessage());
        }
    }

    private void addSeat(Seat seat) {
        seats.put(seat.getId(), seat);
    }

    @Lock(READ)
    public Collection<Seat> getSeats() {
        return Collections.unmodifiableCollection(seats.values());
    }

    @Lock(READ)
    public int getSeatPrice(int seatId) throws NoSuchSeatException {
        return getSeat(seatId).getPrice();
    }

    @Lock(WRITE)
    public void buyTicket(int seatId) throws SeatBookedException,
        NoSuchSeatException {
        final Seat seat = getSeat(seatId);
        if (seat.isBooked()) {
            throw new SeatBookedException("Seat " + seatId + "
                already booked!");
```

```
        }
        addSeat(seat.getBookedSeat());
    }

    @Lock(READ)
    private Seat getSeat(int seatId) throws NoSuchSeatException {
        final Seat seat = cache.get(seatId);
        if (seat == null) {
            throw new NoSuchSeatException("Seat " + seatId + "
                does not exist!");
        }
        return seat;
    }
}
```

The first thing we want to stress on is the `@Resource` annotation, which injects an `EmbeddedCacheManager` instance. When the WildFly deployer encounters this annotation, your application will include a dependency on the requested cache container. Consequently, the cache container will automatically start during deployment and stop (including all caches) during undeployment of your application.

Subsequently, when the EJB is instantiated (see the method `start`, which is annotated as `@PostConstruct`), `org.infinispan.Cache` is created using `EmbeddedCacheManager` as a factory. This cache will be used to store our highly available set of data.

The operations performed against the distributed cache are quite intuitive: the `put` method is used to store instances of the `Seat` object in the cache and the corresponding `get` method is used to retrieve elements from it, just what you would do using an ordinary hashmap. The only difference is that in our clustered cache, every entry must be serializable. Be sure to mark `Seat` as `Serializable` and create a default constructor for it.

As far as application deployment is concerned, you need to state a dependency to the Infinispan API explicitly, which is not included as an implicit dependency in WildFly's class-loading policy. This is most easily done by adding the following line to your application's `META-INF/MANIFEST.MF`:

```
Dependencies: org.infinispan export
```

We additionally need to add the new cache container to the appropriate profile in our `domain.xml` file (in the Infinispan subsystem):

```
<cache-container name="tickets" default-cache="default" jndi-
    name="java:jboss/infinispan/tickets"
        module="deployment.ticket-agency-cluster.jar">
```

```
<transport lock-timeout="60000"/>
<replicated-cache name="default" batching="true" mode="SYNC">
<locking isolation="REPEATABLE_READ"/>
</replicated-cache>
</cache-container>
```

> In our sample, we are using the `seats.values()` call to get all the elements from our distributed map, which is in fact an instance of `org.infinispan.Cache`. This operation is normally discouraged in distributed caches (not replicated) and has its own limitations. Check out the Javadoc for this method at `https://docs.jboss.org/infinispan/6.0/apidocs/org/infinispan/Cache.html#values()` for more information. This is however, no longer the case for the newest version of Infinispan: `http://infinispan.org/infinispan-7.0/`.

Coding the cluster-aware remote client

The remote EJB client will not need any particular change in order to be able to achieve high availability.

We will only need to prepare a `jboss-ejb-client.properties` file, which will contain the list of servers that will be initially contacted (via remoting) by our client application:

```
remote.connectionprovider.create.options.org.xnio.Options
    .SSL_ENABLED=false
remote.connections=node1,node2
remote.connection.node1.host=localhost
remote.connection.node1.port = 8080
remote.connection.node1.connect.options.org.xnio.Options
    .SASL_POLICY_NOANONYMOUS=false
remote.connection.node2.host=localhost
remote.connection.node2.port = 8280
remote.connection.node2.connect.options.org.xnio.Options
    .SASL_POLICY_NOANONYMOUS=false
```

As you can see from this file, we assume that you are running a two-node cluster on the `localhost` address: the first one running the default port settings and the second one using an offset of `200` (just as shown in the second paragraph of the *Starting a cluster of standalone nodes* section).

Replace the `remote.connection.nodeX.host` variable's value with the actual IP or host if you are running your server nodes on different machines from your client.

Deploying and testing high availability

Deploying an application to a cluster can be achieved in several ways; if you prefer automation instead of manually copying each archive into the `deployments` folder, you can reuse the CLI deployment script contained in the previous chapter.

Alternatively, if you are using the WildFly Maven plugin to deploy, you can parameterize its configuration, including the hostname and the port as variables, which will be passed to the command line:

```
<plugin>
    <groupId>org.wildfly.plugins</groupId>
    <artifactId>wildfly-maven-plugin</artifactId>
    <version>1.0.2.Final</version>
    <configuration>
        <filename>${project.build.finalName}.jar</filename>
        <hostname>${hostname}</hostname>
        <port>${port}</port>
    </configuration>
</plugin>
```

Therefore, you will use the following shell to compile the package and deploy the application on the first node:

```
mvn install wildfly:deploy -Dhostname=localhost -Dport=9999
```

For the second node, you will use the following:

```
mvn install wildfly:deploy -Dhostname=localhost -Dport=10194
```

> Deploying the application in the domain node works the same as mentioned in the preceding example, except that you need to add the `domain` tag to your configuration and need to specify at least one server group. Visit `https://docs.jboss.org/wildfly/plugins/maven/latest/examples/deployment-example.html` for more information.

Once you have deployed both the applications on your server node, you should be able to see the cluster view in the server console logs and also see that the Infinispan cache has been started and has discovered other nodes in the cluster. You should see something similar to the following on one of the nodes:

Before you launch your application, update Maven's `exec` plugin information, which should now reference our remote EJB client application as shown in the highlighted section of the following code snippet:

```
<plugin>
    <groupId>org.codehaus.mojo</groupId>
    <artifactId>exec-maven-plugin</artifactId>
    <version>${version.exec.plugin}</version>
    <executions>
      <execution>
          <goals>
              <goal>exec</goal>
          </goals>
      </execution>
    </executions>
    <configuration>
      <executable>java</executable>
      <workingDirectory>${project.build.directory}/
      exec-working-directory</workingDirectory>
```

```
      <arguments>
        <argument>-classpath</argument>
        <classpath>
        </classpath>
        <argument>com.packtpub.wflydevelopment.chapter11.client.
        TicketAgencyClient</argument>
      </arguments>
    </configuration>
  </plugin>
```

You can run it using the following command:

mvn exec:exec

The first part of the client will show the evidence that we have successfully completed the first transaction. On the client console, you will see the return value of the booking transaction and the Seat list, as shown in the following screenshot:

```
Seat [id=15, name=Balcony, price=10, booked=false]

> book
Enter SeatId: 14
Seat booked.
> money
cze 04, 2014 11:30:56 PM com.packtpub.wflydevelopment.chapter11.client.TicketAgencyClient handleMoney
INFO: You have: 90 money left.
>
```

The following screenshot shows the server node where our EJB client landed:

```
standalone.bat -c standalone-full-ha.xml -Djboss.node.name=another            - □ x
23:30:34,257 INFO  [org.wildfly.extension.undertow] (MSC service thread 1-1) JBAS017
d web context: /ticket-agency-cdi
23:30:34,266 INFO  [org.jboss.weld.deployer] (MSC service thread 1-2) JBAS016009: St
ice for deployment ticket-agency-cdi.war
23:30:34,363 INFO  [org.jboss.as.server.deployment] (MSC service thread 1-3) JBAS015
loyment ticket-agency-cdi.war (runtime-name: ticket-agency-cdi.war) in 10112ms
23:30:34,397 INFO  [org.jboss.as.server] (DeploymentScanner-threads - 2) JBAS018558:
ket-agency-cdi.war" (runtime-name: "ticket-agency-cdi.war")
23:30:53,658 INFO  [com.packtpub.wflydevelopment.chapter11.boundary.TheatreBooker] (
 Seat 14 booked.
23:31:00,001 INFO  [com.packtpub.wflydevelopment.chapter11.control.AutomaticSellerSe
ult - 6) Somebody just booked seat number 2
```

Now shut down the preceding server node (*Ctrl* + *C* would suffice if you are starting it as a foreground process) and press *Enter* (or *Return* on a Mac) on the client application.

As you can see from the following screenshot, you should see that the session continues to run on the survivor node and correctly displays the session values (the money left). Your client window should also display the updated cache information.

```
cze 04, 2014 11:32:44 PM com.packtpub.wflydevelopment.chapter11.client.TicketAgencyClient handleMoney
INFO: You have: 90 money left.
> book
Enter SeatId: 13
Seat booked.
> money
cze 04, 2014 11:32:57 PM com.packtpub.wflydevelopment.chapter11.client.TicketAgencyClient handleMoney
INFO: You have: 80 money left.
>
```

Web application clustering

Web application clustering involves two aspects: setting up an HTTP load balancer and telling WildFly to make the application's user sessions as HA. How to do the former depends on what load balancer you would choose (mod_cluster is our suggested choice — it is preconfigured and integrates with WildFly out of the box); the latter could not be simpler — just add the <distributable/>tag to your application's web.xml file. Whenever a node fails, the user's HTTP session will be handled by another one. If everything goes well, the end user will not know that there was a failure — everything will be handled behind the scenes.

Let's see how to action both these steps in concrete terms.

Load balancing your web applications

You have several choices available in order to achieve load balancing of your HTTP requests. You can opt for a hardware load balancer that sits in front of your cluster of servers or you can choose from the many available software solutions for WildFly, which include the following:

- Use Apache Tomcat's mod_jk module to route your requests to your nodes
- Use Apache mod_proxy that configures Apache to act as a proxy server and forwards requests to WildFly nodes
- Use WildFly's built-in solution mod_cluster to achieve dynamic load balancing of your requests

Here, we will illustrate how to get started with `mod_cluster`—a module for the Apache HTTP server. The advantage of using `mod_cluster` against other options can be summarized in the following key points:

- Dynamic clustering configuration
- Server-side pluggable load metrics
- Life cycle notifications of the application status

As a matter of fact, when using a standard load balancer such as `mod_jk`, you have to provide a static list of nodes that is used to spread the load. This is a very limiting factor, especially if you have to deliver upgrades to your configuration by adding or removing nodes; alternatively, you simply need to upgrade software used by single nodes. Besides this, using a flat cluster configuration can be tedious and it is prone to errors, especially if the number of cluster nodes is high.

When using `mod_cluster`, you can dynamically add or remove nodes from your cluster because cluster nodes are discovered through an advertising mechanism.

In practice, the `mod_cluster` libraries on the HTTP side send UDP messages on a multicast group, which is subscribed by WildFly nodes. This allows WildFly nodes to automatically discover HTTP proxies when application life cycle notifications are sent.

The next diagram illustrates this concept better:

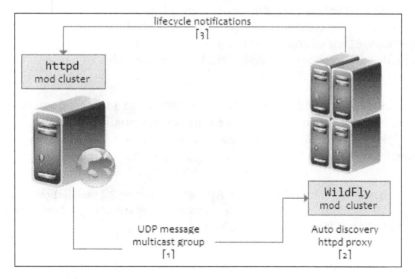

Installing mod_cluster

The mod_cluster module is implemented as a core WildFly module, which is a part of the distribution. On the HTTP side, it is available as a set of libraries installed on the Apache web server.

On the WildFly side, you can find the mod_cluster module's subsystem already bundled as part of the clustered configuration file. You can locate it in either the standalone-ha.xml file or the standalone-full-ha.xml (and of course in the domain.xml file) configuration file:

```
<subsystem xmlns="urn:jboss:domain:modcluster:1.2">
  <mod-cluster-config advertise-socket="modcluster"
  connector="ajp">
   <dynamic-load-provider>
       <load-metric type="cpu"/>
   </dynamic-load-provider>
  </mod-cluster-config>
</subsystem>
```

The subsystem contains just a bare-bones configuration that references its socket binding through the advertise-socket element:

```
<socket-binding name="modcluster" port="0" multicast-
    address="224.0.1.105" multicast-port="23364"/>
```

On the Apache web server side, we have to install the core libraries that are used to interact with mod_cluster. This is a very simple procedure; just point the browser to the latest mod_cluster release at http://www.jboss.org/mod_cluster/downloads. Be sure to choose a version that suits your operating system and architecture (x86 or x64).

Once the binaries are downloaded, extract the archive to a folder; then, navigate to the extracted folder. The mod_cluster binaries essentially consist of a bundled Apache web server with all the required libraries installed. To preconfigure your installation, be sure to run the \httpd-2.2\bin\installconf.bat file.

 It is possible to use your own Apache web server 2.2 installation; just pick up the modules from the mod_cluster bundle and copy them to the modules folder of your Apache web server.

If you choose to use your own Apache web server over the bundled one, you have to load the following libraries into your `httpd.conf` file (the same set is used in the bundled Apache HTTP):

```
LoadModule proxy_module modules/mod_proxy.so
LoadModule proxy_ajp_module modules/mod_proxy_ajp.so
LoadModule proxy_http_module modules/mod_proxy_http.so
LoadModule proxy_cluster_module modules/mod_proxy_cluster.so
LoadModule manager_module modules/mod_manager.so
LoadModule slotmem_module modules/mod_slotmem.so
LoadModule advertise_module modules/mod_advertise.so
```

Each of these modules covers an important aspect of load balancing, listed as follows:

- `mod_proxy`, `mod_proxy_http`, and `mod_proxy_ajp`: These are the core modules that forward requests to cluster nodes using either the HTTP/HTTPS or AJP protocol

- `mod_manager`: This module reads the information from AS 7 and updates the shared memory information in conjunction with `mod_slotmem`

- `mod_proxy_cluster`: This module contains the balancer for `mod_proxy`

- `mod_advertise`: This is an additional module that allows HTTP to advertise via multicast packets — the IP and port — where the `mod_cluster` module is listening

The next part of the configuration that we need to add is the core load balancing configuration:

```
Listen 192.168.10.1:8888

<VirtualHost 192.168.10.1:8888>
<Location />
    Order deny,allow
    Deny from all
    Allow from 192.168.10.
</Location>
  KeepAliveTimeout 60
  MaxKeepAliveRequests 0
  ManagerBalancerName mycluster
  ServerAdvertise On
</VirtualHost>
```

Basically, you have to replace the `192.168.10.1` IP address with the one that your Apache web server listens for requests and the port value of `8888` with the one you want to use to communicate with WildFly.

As it is, the Apache virtual host allows you to have incoming requests from the subnetwork `192.168.10`.

The `KeepAliveTimeout` directive allows you to reuse the same connection within 60 seconds. The number of requests per connection is unlimited since we are setting `MaxKeepAliveRequests` to `0`. The `ManagerBalancerName` directive provides the balancer name for your cluster (defaults to `mycluster`).

What's most important for us is the `ServerAdvertise` directive that is set to `On` and uses the advertise mechanism to tell WildFly whom it should send the cluster information to.

This option is disabled in the bundled server by default. Be sure to uncomment the `ServerAdvertise` directive in its `httpd.conf` file.

Now, restart the Apache web server and the single application server nodes. If you have correctly configured the mode cluster on the HTTP side, you will see that each WildFly node will start receiving UDP multicast messages from `mod_cluster`.

 If you are running on a Windows machine, be sure to run your web server as an administrator.

If everything goes well, you can visit `http://127.0.0.1:6666/mod_cluster_manager` to see the status of your load balancer and the interconnected nodes. Be sure to not use Google Chrome for this because it considers the `6666` port as an unsecure one (it is an IRC port by default). You should see the following information on the simple webpage:

```
mod_cluster/1.2.6.Final

Auto Refresh show DUMP output show INFO output

Node michal-pc (ajp://localhost:8009):

Enable Contexts Disable Contexts
Balancer: mycluster,LBGroup: ,Flushpackets: Off,Flushwait:
10000,Ping: 10000000,Smax: 65,Ttl: 60000000,Status: OK,Elected:
0,Read: 0,Transferred: 0,Connected: 0,Load: 100
```

If you don't have a running WildFly instance now, be sure to start it with one of the full-HA configuration files. Refresh Apache's configuration web page after the server is up.

Clustering your web applications

Clustering web applications requires the least amount of effort to be put in by the developer. As we have just discussed, all you need to do to switch on clustering in a web application is to add the following directive to the web.xml descriptor:

```
<web-app>
  <distributable/>
</web-app>
```

Once your application ships with the distributable stanza in it, the cluster will start, and provided you have correctly designed your session layer, it will be load balanced and fault tolerant as well.

You could check it out by pointing the browser to your HTTP proxy. For the default setup, it would be http://localhost:6666/your_web_application/.

Programming considerations to achieve HA

In order to support in-memory replication of HTTP session states, all servlets and JSP session data must be serializable.

Serialization is the conversion of an object to a series of bytes so that the object can be easily saved to a persistent storage or streamed across a communication link. The byte stream can then be deserialized, converting the stream into a replica of the original object.

Additionally, in an HTTP servlet that implements javax.servlet.http. HttpSession, you need to use the setAttribute method to change the attributes in a session object. If you set the attributes in a session object with setAttribute, by default the object and its attributes are replicated using the Infinispan API. Every time a change is made to an object that is in the session, setAttribute should be called to update that object across the cluster.

Likewise, you need to use removeAttribute to remove an attribute from a session object.

Achieving HA in JSF applications

In the applications included in this book, we have used JSF and the CDI API to manage the web session. In this case, we transparently replicate the other server nodes to the beans, which are marked as @SessionScoped.

Clustering JSF-based applications requires special attention if you are dealing with both HTTP and EJB sessions created by SFSB. In the earlier servlet-centric frameworks, the usual approach was to store references of Stateful Session Beans in `javax.servlet.http.HttpSession`. When dealing with high-level JSF and CDI Beans, it is vital to provide a `@SessionScoped` controller to your application, which gets injected in the SFSB reference; otherwise, you will end up creating a new Stateful Session Beans upon each request.

The following is an example of how to adapt your Ticket CDI application (described in *Chapter 4, Learning Context and Dependency Injection*) to a clustered environment. At first, as we said, we need to include the distributable stanza in your `web.xml` file to trigger clustering modules:

```
<web-app>
    <distributable/>
</web-app>
```

Next, apply the same changes to the `TheatreBox` singleton that we described in the *Turning your cache into a distributed cache* section:

```
@Singleton
@Startup
public class TheatreBox {

    @Resource(lookup="java:jboss/infinispan/container/cluster")
    private CacheContainer container;

    // Apply the same changes described in
    // "Turning your Cache into a distributed cache section

}
```

Since our controller component is bound to a `@SessionScoped` state, you don't need to apply any changes in order to propagate your session across server nodes:

```
@Named
@SessionScoped
public class TheatreBooker implements Serializable {
}
```

Finally, remember to include the Infinispan dependency in your META-INF/ MANIFEST.MF:

```
Dependencies: org.infinispan export
```

Once your application is deployed on both the nodes of your cluster, you can test it by hitting the Apache web server (http://localhost:6666/ticket-agency-cluster in our example) and start booking tickets:

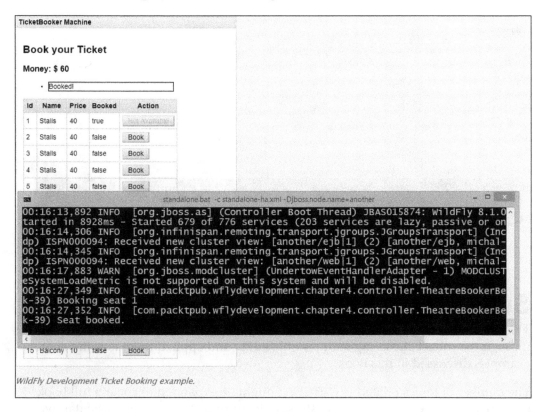

WildFly Development Ticket Booking example.

Since the `mod_cluster` subsystem is configured to use **sticky web sessions** by default, all subsequent requests from the same client will be redirected to the same server node. Therefore, by shutting down the sticky server node, you will get evidence that a new cluster view has been created and you can continue shopping on the other server node.

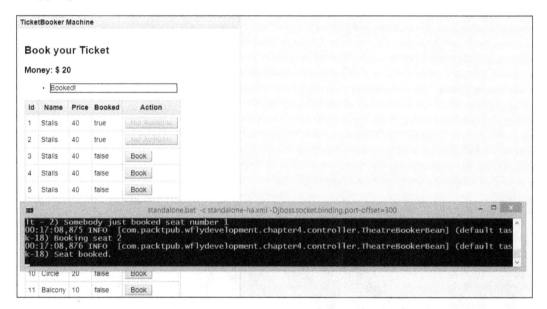

Summary

This chapter was all about the world of clustered applications. Here, we took you through the robust clustering features of WildFly and applied them to some of the examples discussed in this book.

The number of topics related to clustering might be expanded to cover a full book of its own; however, we decided to stress only on some features. In particular, we learned how to cluster EJBs and achieve fault tolerance in case there is a change in the server topology.

Next, we discussed clustering web applications and the integration with load balancing solutions such as the Apache web server and `mod_cluster`.

In the next chapter, we will focus on some new topics added to Java EE 7 related to long-term task execution: batch processing and concurrency utilities' usage.

12
Long-term Tasks' Execution

So far, our applications focused on interaction with the user. This may be the most important aspect of your future projects, but there are some scenarios that require a different approach. Maintenance tasks, importing big sets of data or time-consuming computations are usually addressed in a batch mode instead of an interactive manner. Often, these kinds of jobs are not part of the standard operations and should be invoked only when the server load is at its lowest or periodical.

Before Java EE 7, there was no standardized way to implement batch jobs (operations that do not require user interaction). The deal changed with JSR 352 (`https://jcp.org/en/jsr/detail?id=352`) and the introduction of the batch framework, which uses an XML language to define jobs.

When it comes to processor-intensive tasks, the natural way is to think about parallelization. Modern CPUs have multiple cores, which can be easily utilized by the JVM. The only problem is that in Java EE, using concurrency primitives known from Java SE is discouraged. The programmer may impair the stability and availability of the whole container.

Once more, the new JSR 236 (`https://jcp.org/en/jsr/detail?id=236`) provides new ways to overcome this architectural obstacle. The new specification `ManagedExecutorService` is a container-aware version of `ExecutorService` known from Java SE.

In this chapter, we will cover the following topics:

- How to create and execute batch jobs
- What are the differences between different batch job types
- How to create our custom worker threads inside a Java EE container

The overview of the batching framework

The batching framework defines the concept of a batch **job**, which is a feature of the application that can be executed without user interaction. A single job consists of one or more **steps**, which can be executed sequentially or in parallel. Additionally, a sequence of **steps** can be grouped into a **flow**. The start of a parallel execution is called a **switch**. And finally, if we want to control the sequence of steps using conditional statements, we should use **decisions**. These following five nouns are the basic building blocks of a batch application. To compose such an application, we will use a specification language written in an XML file, as shown in the following code snippet:

```
<job id="jobName">
    <step> … </step>
    <step> … </step>
    <decision> … </decision>
    <flow> … </flow>
    <split> … </split>
</job>
```

A step is the basic unit of work and our main area of interest. The batching framework defines two types of steps, which are as follows:

- **Chunk steps**: These work on chunks of data in three phases: reading, processing, and writing (for each phase, a separate class is created). The chunks can be configured with a number of elements that should be processed in one transaction.
- **Task steps**: These execute a specific block of code created by the programmer, without any special constraints. They are used for most non-data processing errands.

Additionally, the batching framework allows listeners to register for the whole job or specific phases of the tasks.

Now that we've covered the basic vocabulary, it will be best to jump straight to coding.

Our first batch job

WildFly comes with an implementation of JSR 352 called JBeret (`https://github.com/jberet/jsr352`). This means that we can easily extend our ticket application with batch jobs, by simply implementing the required interfaces; no additional dependencies are required. All APIs are already in place in our current samples, so we only need to create some classes and an XML file to specify the job flow.

As a base for our development in this chapter, it would be best to use the code from *Chapter 5, Combining Persistence with CDI*. The persistence layer will allow us to code a sample import batching job. To keep it simple, let's start by defining an artificial external service that will provide us with IDs of tickets that should be booked. We can deploy it as part of our application or as a separate WAR file. This sample is based on a REST endpoint, so be sure to configure JAX-RS in your deployment (for details, check out *Chapter 7, Adding Web Services to Your Applications*). This is shown in the following code snippet:

```
@Singleton
@Startup
@ConcurrencyManagement(ConcurrencyManagementType.BEAN)
@Path("/external")
@Produces(MediaType.TEXT_PLAIN)
public class PendingSeats {

    private final Queue<Integer> seats =
                            new ConcurrentLinkedQueue<>();

    @PostConstruct
    private void setUp() {
        for (int i = 5; i < 10; i++) {
            seats.add(i);
        }
    }

    @GET
    public Integer getNextSeat() {
        return seats.poll();
    }
}
```

As you can see in the preceding code snippet, our sample is initialized with IDs from 5 to 9, and on every GET request, it will provide the ID as the output. When all IDs are emitted, a null value will be returned. This endpoint will serve as a model of a reservation system. For simplicity, it produces plaintext values instead of JSON. Of course, a flat file or any other source of data could also be used for integration.

Creating a chunk-based batch step

Our integration scenario will be pretty straightforward. We need to read all of the reservation IDs from the external system to get the corresponding seats from our database and write the changes back to the database. It would also be great to write a log with the operations made by the import. Let's start with the item reader:

```
package com.packtpub.wflydevelopment.chapter12.batching;

import java.io.Serializable;
import javax.batch.api.chunk.AbstractItemReader;
import javax.inject.Named;
import javax.ws.rs.client.Client;
import javax.ws.rs.client.ClientBuilder;
import javax.ws.rs.client.WebTarget;

@Named
public class ExternalSystemReader extends AbstractItemReader {

    private WebTarget target;

    @Override
    public void open(Serializable checkpoint) throws Exception {
        final Client restclient = ClientBuilder.newClient();
        this.target = restclient.target("http://localhost:8080/ticket-
agency-longterm/rest/external");
    }

    @Override
    public Object readItem() throws Exception {
        return target.request().get(String.class);
    }
}
```

Our reader extends the `AbstractItemReader` class so that we don't have to implement all methods of the `javax.batch.api.chunk.ItemReader` interface. The only two methods we are interested in are `open` and `readItem`. The first one initializes the REST client, which will get the data from the server. The implementation is optional because not every reader needs initialization logic. Note that a checkpoint parameter is passed to the method. It can be used to restart the batch job from a specific point. We will, however, leave out this feature.

The `readItem` method requests the data from an external service and returns a single item to the batch framework. A null value is an indicator that there is no more data. Additional methods of the `ItemReader` interface are responsible for checkpoint handling and closing of the reader.

When we define the XML specification for the batch job, we must use the names of managed beans to refer to the reader, processor, or writer we want (just like in JSF). Therefore, we need the @Named annotation in order to provide a string-based qualifier; by default, it will be a lowercase name of the class on which the annotation is placed. For the ExternalSystemReader bean, we will use the externalSystemReader name.

After an item is read, we may process it. Our SeatProcessor class goes as the following code snippet:

```
package com.packtpub.wflydevelopment.chapter12.batching;

import javax.batch.api.chunk.ItemProcessor;
import javax.inject.Inject;
import javax.inject.Named;
import com.packtpub.wflydevelopment.chapter12.control.SeatDao;
import com.packtpub.wflydevelopment.chapter12.entity.Seat;

@Named
public class SeatProcessor implements ItemProcessor {

    @Inject
    private SeatDao dao;

    @Override
    public Object processItem(Object id) throws Exception {
        Seat seat = dao.find(Long.parseLong((String) id));
        if (seat != null) {
            if (seat.getBooked() == true) {
                return null;
            }
            seat.setBooked(true);
        }
        return seat;
    }
}
```

Our processor retrieves IDs from the reader and finds the corresponding entry in the database. To find the entity, we reuse our SeatDao class known from previous chapters. Because we have CDI working on the batch framework, we can just inject our EJB without caring about transaction handling.

If the seat is found, we check if it's already booked. If yes, we can simply return a null value to omit this item from further processing.

The last step is `SeatWriter`. This is shown in the following code snippet:

```
package com.packtpub.wflydevelopment.chapter12.batching;

import javax.batch.api.chunk.AbstractItemWriter;
import javax.batch.runtime.context.JobContext;
import javax.inject.Inject;
import javax.inject.Named;
import javax.persistence.EntityManager;
import javax.persistence.PersistenceContext;

@Named
public class SeatWriter extends AbstractItemWriter {

    public static final String FILENAME_PARAM = "logFile";

    @Inject
    private JobContext jobContext;

    @PersistenceContext
    private EntityManager em;

    private BufferedWriter writer;

    @Override
    public void open(Serializable ckpt) throws Exception {
        Properties jobProperties = jobContext.getProperties();
        String fileName = jobProperties.getProperty(FILENAME_PARAM);

        writer = new BufferedWriter(new FileWriter(fileName));
        writer.write("Importing...");
        writer.newLine();
    }

    @Override
    public void writeItems(List<Object> items) throws Exception {
        writer.write("Chunk size: " + items.size());
        writer.newLine();

        for (Object obj : items) {
            em.persist(obj);
            writer.write("Persisted: " + obj);
```

```
                writer.newLine();
            }
        }

        @Override
        public void close() throws Exception {
            writer.write("Import finished");
            writer.newLine();
            writer.close();
        }
    }
```

Our `ItemWriter` class starts by defining an `open` method, which gets a file for writing. The name of the newly created logfile is taken from the job properties. Our source of information about the current batch job is the injected `JobContext` class (there is also a `StepContext` object that provides information about a specific step). It gives us the possibility to get the properties defined for a job, its current ID, status, and additional transient data.

The heart of our writer is, of course, the `writeItem` method. It receives a list of items (seats in our case) to be written and its responsibility is to persist them. This method can be invoked multiple times up to the moment when there is no more data to be written. You can configure the number of elements that will be processed in every chunk. What's more, every chunk runs in its own transaction.

Finally, when the last chunk is written, the `close` method writes a summary and closes the file.

All elements are now in place, so we need to create a batch job specification. The file `externalSystem.xml` should be placed in the `src/main/resources/META-INF/batch-jobs` directory in your project. The contents are as follows:

```xml
<job id="externalSystem" xmlns="http://xmlns.jcp.org/xml/ns/javaee"
    version="1.0"> [1]
    <properties>
        <property name="logFile" value="log.txt" /> [2]
    </properties>
    <step id="processData">
        <chunk item-count="2"> [3]
            <reader ref="externalSystemReader" /> [4]
            <processor ref="seatProcessor" />
            <writer ref="seatWriter" />
        </chunk>
    </step>
</job>
```

The structure is pretty straightforward. First, we define a job ID matching the filename [1]. Next, in the properties section, we set a property `logFile` with the `log.txt` value [2] we used it in our `SeatWriter` to create an output file [3]. Then, we define a step with a data chunk. The `item-count` attribute defines the number of items we process in one transaction. Finally, we reference our reader, processor, and writer in their matching tags [4].

Now, when our job is defined, it is time to start it. To do this, we need to the use the BatchRuntime's static method, `getJobOperator`. In order to simplify the solution, we will use a REST endpoint's GET method as a way to invoke our code:

```
package com.packtpub.wflydevelopment.chapter12.batching;

import java.util.Properties;
import javax.batch.runtime.BatchRuntime;
import javax.ejb.Stateless;
import javax.ws.rs.GET;
import javax.ws.rs.Path;

@Stateless
@Path("/job")
public class JobStarter {

    @GET
    public String start() {
        long jobId = BatchRuntime.getJobOperator()
        .start("externalSystem", new Properties());
        return Long.toString(jobId);
    }
}
```

The `JobOperator start` method returns a job ID, which is a representation of the ongoing batch process. We need to provide the name of the file defining the batch job without the XML extension and a set of runtime parameters.

The properties provided during runtime are not the same as we used earlier! These kinds of properties are not bound to a specific job (in contrast to the ones defined in the XML file), but can be accessed from the job execution. The batching framework calls them parameters. If you need this kind of logic in your application, you should just pass them during a job's startup and use the job execution ID to access them:

```
JobOperator operator = BatchRuntime.getJobOperator();
Properties properties = new Properties();
properties.put("propertyName", "propertyValue");

long jobId = operator.start("externalSystem",
properties);

JobExecution execution = operator.
getJobExecution(jobId);
Properties jobParameters = execution.
getJobParameters();
```

You can point your browser to `http://localhost:8080/ticket-agency-longterm/rest/job` and your batch job should start running! Be sure to set up your seats before running the job (the console is available at `http://localhost:8080/ticket-agency-longterm/faces/views/setup.xhtml`).

A sample output file in your WildFly's bin directory would look like the following:

```
Importing...

Chunk size: 2

Persisted: Seat [id=5, booked=true, seatType=com.packtpub.
wflydevelopment.chapter12.entity.SeatType@a55bb6e]

Persisted: Seat [id=6, booked=true, seatType=com.packtpub.
wflydevelopment.chapter12.entity.SeatType@a55bb6e]

Chunk size: 2

Persisted: Seat [id=7, booked=true, seatType=com.packtpub.
wflydevelopment.chapter12.entity.SeatType@440a007]

Persisted: Seat [id=8, booked=true, seatType=com.packtpub.
wflydevelopment.chapter12.entity.SeatType@440a007]

Chunk size: 1

Persisted: Seat [id=9, booked=true, seatType=com.packtpub.
wflydevelopment.chapter12.entity.SeatType@307124b7]

Import finished
```

Of course, you could also start the batch job using a Java EE timer after a specific event in your application or even as an effect of an incoming JMS message. You can also use the retrieved job IDs to monitor the already running jobs or terminate them on demand. The batching framework API gives you many possibilities without too many complications in the area of job management.

Creating a job-based batch step

Our chunk-based job was great to process big data sets. However, what if we only want to perform a specific task? Besides creating chunks, we can also define steps that will simply call a process method of a specific class. These kinds of classes must implement the `Batchlet` interface (or extend the `AbstractBatchlet` class).

In our sample, let's try to contact an external API to ask about the current Bitcoin exchange rate (a decentralized, virtual currency). Then, we will store the current prices of our tickets in a simple flat file. Our batchlet would be as follows:

```
@Named
public class BitcoinTask extends AbstractBatchlet {

    private static final String EXTERNAL_API = "https://api.
bitcoinaverage.com/exchanges/USD";
    public static final String FILENAME_PARAM = "bitcoinFile";

    @Inject
    private SeatTypeDao seatTypeDao;

    @Inject
    private JobContext jobContext;

    @Override
    public String process() throws Exception { // [1]
        WebTarget api = ClientBuilder.newClient()
          .target(EXTERNAL_API);
        Response response = api.request().get();
        JsonObject entity = response.readEntity(JsonObject.class); //
    [2]

        double averageValue = entity.getJsonObject("btce")
          .getJsonObject("rates").getJsonNumber("bid").doubleValue();

        Map<SeatType, Double> pricesInBitcoins = calculeteBitcoinPrice
    s(averageValue, seatTypeDao.findAll()); // [3]
```

```
        writeToFile(pricesInBitcoins); // [4]

        return "OK";
    }

    private Map<SeatType, Double> calculeteBitcoinPrices(double
averageValue, List<SeatType> findAll) {
        return findAll.stream().collect(
                Collectors.toMap(seatType -> seatType, seatType ->
seatType.getPrice() / averageValue));
    }

    private void writeToFile(Map<SeatType, Double> pricesInBitcoins)
throws Exception {
        Properties jobProperties = jobContext.getProperties(); // [5]
        String fileName = jobProperties.getProperty(FILENAME_PARAM);
        try (BufferedWriter writer = new BufferedWriter(
          new FileWriter(fileName))) {
            writer.write(pricesInBitcoins.toString());
            writer.newLine();
        }
    }
}
```

The process method [1] is our entry point to the batchlet. We will start by making a REST request against an external API [2] and use the response to calculate our prices in bitcoins [3]. Finally, we will try to write so as to gathered data into a file. As you can see, once more, we use `JobContext` to get the configuration properties from the batching framework (the filename in this case).

You may wonder, what is the point of the return type in the `process` method? It simply indicates the status of the job, if it has been completed successfully or not.

That's all we wanted to do and we achieved it in a single batch step: reading, processing, and writing. In the chunk-oriented approach, we will have three separate mechanisms for this. Let's add our new step to `externalSystem.xml` from `src/main/resources/META-INF/batch-jobs`:

```
<job id="externalSystem" xmlns="http://xmlns.jcp.org/xml/ns/javaee"
    version="1.0">
    <properties>
        <property name="logFile" value="log.txt" />
        <property name="bitcoinFile" value="bitcoins.txt" /> [1]
    </properties>
    <step id="processData" next="checkBitcoins"> [2]
        <chunk item-count="2">
```

```
                <reader ref="externalSystemReader" />
                <processor ref="seatProcessor" />
                <writer ref="seatWriter" />
            </chunk>
        </step>
        <step id="checkBitcoins"> [3]
            <batchlet ref="bitcoinTask" />
        </step>
    </job>
```

There are three new things to notice in the XML file. First, we added a new property, which we referenced earlier in our batchlet [1]. Next, we defined that after our chunk processing step, we would like to invoke another one, checkBitcoins [2]. Finally, we created a new step in which we referenced our batchlet class.

You can once again start your job, and after it is completed, a bitcoins.txt file should appear in WildFly's bin directory.

We've covered the foundation of the batching framework, which allows you to fulfill most of the frequent requirements defined for enterprise applications. However, there is a lot more inside the specification, such as splits, partitions, and workflow-related elements (statuses and decisions) that you can explore if a more sophisticated mechanism is required by the business processes that you're implementing.

Our next step is to provide some parallelism inside our Java EE container using the new concurrency utilities.

Using concurrency utilities in Java EE

In Java EE 6 (specifically in the EJB container), creation of new threads was discouraged because the application server would not be able to control the stability of the platform nor guarantee any transactional features. This could be a problem for applications that would like to effectively use CPU and execute multiple tasks in parallel. It was possible to overcome this using JCA adapters, but additional effort was required to implement them.

Fortunately, the JSR 236 introduces the `ManagedExecutorService` (along with the `ManagedScheduledExecutorService`), a container-aware version of the `ExecutorService` used in Java SE. The well-known API ported to Java EE was merged in the platform, providing a smooth workflow for concurrent operations in the EJB container. The new managed executor services have the following advantages over the standard ones:

- They rely on the thread pool provided by the container. This means that the server controls have many threads that can be spawned from all deployed applications and you can tweak the configuration in order to ensure the desired quality of service.
- The thread configuration is totally separated from the code, so it is possible to change it without changing the application itself.
- It is possible to propagate the caller context to the created thread. For example, it is possible to use the security principal of the user's request that initiated the new thread.
- The application server allows monitoring of the current thread count.
- Threads started by the managed executors can create new transactions for business components; they cannot, however, participate in transactions from other components.

The main parts of the concurrency utilities are described in the following table:

Component	Description
ManagedExecutorService	This is used to execute submitted tasks in an asynchronous manner. The developer may submit a `Callable` or `Runnable` function and use returned `Future` to check for the result when it is available. The container context will be propagated by the container. This interface extends the standard `ExecutorService` interface.
ManagedScheduledExecutorService	This is similar to `ManagedExecutorService`, but it is used to execute tasks at specific times (cyclic, scheduled, or delayed). The interface extends the standard `ScheduleExecutorService`, but it additionally provides the Trigger feature; the possibility to create a dynamic object, which can decide when a specific event should be fired (see `javax.enterprise.concurrent.Trigger`).

Component	Description
ContextService	This is used to capture the context of the container; it can then be used while submitting a job to the executor service.
ManagedThreadFactory	This is used to create threads by the container. The developer can provide its own thread factory in order to fulfil specific use cases (for instance, setting specific properties on the created objects).

Instances of these components can be obtained using the JNDI lookup or the @Resource injection. The Java EE 7 specification requires that every container provides a set of default resources that should be injectable without any additional configuration. So, in WildFly, the easiest way to get your hands on them would be to just type the following code:

```
@Resource
private ManagedExecutorService executorService;

@Resource
private ManagedScheduledExecutorService scheduledExecutorService;

@Resource
private ContextService contextService;
```

The aforementioned code snippet is shorthand for a lookup of the default instances, which are as follows:

```
@Resource(lookup="java:comp/DefaultManagedExecutorService")
private ManagedExecutorService executorService;
```

You can also find any additional executor services and the configuration of the default ones in the standalone.xml file (and in other variants of the configuration file). A part of the relevant subsystem is presented as follows:

```
<subsystem xmlns="urn:jboss:domain:ee:2.0">
    <spec-descriptor-property-replacement>false</spec-descriptor-property-replacement>
    <concurrent>
        (...)
        <managed-executor-services>
            <managed-executor-service name="default" jndi-name="java:jboss/ee/concurrency/executor/default" context-service="default" hung-task-threshold="60000" core-threads="5" max-threads="25" keepalive-time="5000"/>
```

```
        </managed-executor-services>
        (...)
    </concurrent>
</subsystem>
```

As you can see, the `standalone.xml` file contains the configuration of the default `ManagedExecutorService`. You can add a new custom configuration with another name and JNDI path; you can also create a separate one for every deployed application.

 Note that the default ManagedExecutorService has two JNDI names: the one in the configuration and the one defined in the Java EE specification (`java:comp/DefaultManagedExecutorService`). You can switch to the default executor service (and other components) using the default-bindings tag in the `standalone.xml` file.

Let's take a closer look at some of the properties of the executor service:

- **core-threads**: This defines how many threads should be alive in the thread pool all the time (even if those threads are idle and the server is handling no user requests).

- **max-threads**: This states how many threads the server can start (including the core threads) if necessary, for instance, when under heavy load.

- **keepalive-time**: This defines after how many milliseconds a thread can be idle before the server kills it (it only applies if there are more threads running than the core-threads parameter specified). This configuration value defines how long the server will keep around the additional threads when they are not needed anymore.

- **hung-task-threshold**: This defines after how many milliseconds the server will mark a thread as hung. If set to `0`, a thread will never be marked as hung (the thread will have no execution time limit).

By using these configuration properties and creating additional executor services, the server administrator can gain a fine control over the maximum load that the server can handle at a given time. Be sure to take a closer look at them during an application's performance tuning.

As for development, the default configuration suits us well, so it's time to dive into the code with an example usage of the concurrency utilities!

Introducing threads to enterprise beans

When we were working with the batching framework, we contacted a REST endpoint, which was mocking an external system in our sample. Now, we are going to add some concurrency to it.

An external system may aggregate booking requests from several sources. If every request takes a substantial amount of time, it could be a good idea to make all the requests simultaneously. Let's start with creating Callable, which will return a list of the seat IDs that should be booked. This is shown in the following code snippet:

```
package com.packtpub.wflydevelopment.chapter12.external;

import java.util.concurrent.Callable;
import javax.enterprise.concurrent.ManagedTask;
import javax.enterprise.concurrent.ManagedTaskListener;
import javax.enterprise.inject.Instance;

public class GenerateSeatRequestFromArtificial implements
Callable<List<Integer>>, ManagedTask [1] {

    @Inject
    private Logger logger;

    @Inject
    private Instance<TaskListener> taskListener; [2]

    @Override
    public ManagedTaskListener getManagedTaskListener() {
        return taskListener.get(); [3]
    }

    @Override
    public Map<String, String> getExecutionProperties() {
        return new HashMap<>(); [4]
    }

    @Override
    public List<Integer> call() throws Exception {
        logger.info("Sleeping...");
        Thread.sleep(5000); [5]
        logger.info("Finished sleeping!");

        return Arrays.asList(4, 5, 6);
    }
}
```

Our task implements [1] two interfaces: `Callable` and `ManagedTask`. The `ManagedExecutorService` requires an object that fulfils the contract of a `Callable` or `Runnable` interface known from Java SE.

The `ManagedTask` interface is optional, but it allows us to register a `ManagedTaskListener` along with the task itself and return additional properties from the task. The task listener has a set of life cycle callbacks, which are called during the task's execution. We will use it in order to log additional information about our task. In order to create an instance of the task listener, we used the `Instance<T>` class [2]. It is used to create instances of CDI beans on demand. We return `ManagedTaskListener` in a method from the `ManagedTask` interface [3]. We don't need any additional properties; therefore, we return an empty object in the second method from the `ManagedTask` interface [4].

Finally, we implement the `call` method; the thread will be suspended for 5 seconds (to simulate long work) and return a list of predefined IDs.

Our task listener is simply a bean with a logger, which will get all the information about the task's lifecycle. This is shown in the following code snippet:

```
public class TaskListener implements ManagedTaskListener {

    @Inject
    private Logger logger;

    @Override
    public void taskSubmitted(Future<?> future, ManagedExecutorService
executor, Object task) {
        logger.info("Submitted " + task);
    }

    @Override
    public void taskAborted(Future<?> future, ManagedExecutorService
executor, Object task, Throwable exception) {
        logger.log(Level.WARNING, "Aborted", exception);
    }

    @Override
    public void taskDone(Future<?> future, ManagedExecutorService
executor, Object task, Throwable exception) {
        logger.info("Finished task " + task);
    }

    @Override
```

```
        public void taskStarting(Future<?> future, ManagedExecutorService
executor, Object task) {
            logger.info("Starting " + task);
        }
    }
```

As you can see, most of the implemented methods are getting the executor service, future, and the task itself as parameters. We simply log the current status using an injected logger.

So, we've created one task, which is pretty static. Now, let's try to create another one, which will contact a database. As before, we'll need a `Callable` implementation, which returns a list of integers. This is shown in the following code snippet:

```
public class GenerateSeatRequestsFromDatabase implements
Callable<List<Integer>> {

    private static final int SEATS_TO_RETURN = 3;

    @Inject
    private SeatDao dao; // [1]

    @Inject
    private Logger logger;

    @Override
    public List<Integer> call() throws Exception {
        logger.info("Sleeping...");
        Thread.sleep(5000); // [4]
        logger.info("Finished sleeping!");

        List<Seat> databaseSeats = dao.findAll(); // [2]

          List<Integer> freeSeats = databaseSeats.stream()
          .filter(seat -> !seat.getBooked())
          .limit(SEATS_TO_RETURN)
          .map(seat -> seat.getId().intValue())
          .collect(Collectors.toList()); // [3]

        if (freeSeats.isEmpty()) {
            logger.info("No seats to book");
        } else {
            logger.info("Requesting booking for " + freeSeats);
        }
        return freeSeats;
    }
}
```

The main difference between this task and the previous one is that we injected an EJB [1], which will start an underlying transaction. In the `call` method, a database request is issued [2]. The returned list of seats is then filtered and transformed into a list of IDs [3].

Additionally, as mentioned earlier, we will stop the thread for 5 seconds so that we can observe the execution later [4].

We've got our building blocks in place. Now, it is time to combine them into a working example. We can revisit our `PendingSeats` class from the beginning of this chapter, as shown in the following code:

```
package com.packtpub.wflydevelopment.chapter12.external;

@Singleton
@Startup
public class PendingSeats {

    private final Queue<Long> seats =
                                new ConcurrentLinkedQueue< >();

    @Resource
    private ManagedExecutorService executorService; // [1]

    @Inject  // [2]
    private Instance<GenerateSeatRequestsFromDatabase>
            databaseCollector;

    @Inject
    private Instance<GenerateSeatRequestFromArtificial>
            artificalCollector;

    @Inject
    private Logger logger;

    @PostConstruct
    private void setUp() {
        try {
            List<Future<List<Integer>>> futures = executorService.
invokeAll(Arrays.asList(
            databaseCollector.get(), artificalCollector.get()
)); // [3]

            List<Integer> requestedIds = futures.stream().
flatMap(future -> get(future).stream()).distinct()
```

```
                    .collect(Collectors.toList()); // [4]

            logger.info(requestedIds.toString());
        } catch (InterruptedException e) {
            logger.log(Level.SEVERE, e.getMessage(), e);
        }

    }

    private List<Integer> get(Future<List<Integer>> future) {
        try {
            return future.get();
        } catch (InterruptedException | ExecutionException e) {
            logger.log(Level.SEVERE, e.getMessage(), e);
            return new ArrayList<>();
        }
    }
}
```

We start by obtaining an instance of `ManagedExecutorService` using the `@Resource` annotation [1]. Next, the previously created tasks are injected using the CDI's `Instance<T>` class pattern [2]. Thanks to this, the are managed beans and have their dependencies injected. With the dependencies in place, we use the `invokeAll` method [3] of `executorService` in order to start all our tasks at once (we could also use multiple calls of the `submit` method). The return values represent a set of future results, which can be used to retrieve the collected data when it is ready.

At this point, our tasks are already running so we can simply make a blocking `get` call on the future results and wait for the data [4]. When it is ready, we remove any duplicates, and collect the results in a single list using the `flatMap` operation. As you remember, our previous two tasks were waiting 5 seconds each. Thanks to the fact that they are executed simultaneously, we expect that they will both finish after 5 seconds.

Because our bean is a singleton with a startup annotation, the whole process will be invoked during the deployment of our application. Feel free to try it out now!

Of course, the database task requires some data in the `seats` table or it will yield empty results (that's not a big issue for us). If you want the application to automatically seed some data to the database, you can create another singleton bean, for instance:

```
@Startup
public class DatabaseInitializer {

    @PersistenceContext
```

```
    private EntityManager em;

    @PostConstruct
    public void setup() {
        SeatType seatType = new SeatType();
        seatType.setPosition(SeatPosition.BALCONY);
        seatType.setDescription("Test Data");
        seatType.setQuantity(10);
        seatType.setPrice(10);
        em.persist(seatType);

        Seat seat = new Seat();
        seat.setSeatType(seatType);
        em.persist(seat);

    }
}
```

Be sure to add a @DependsOn("DatabaseInitializer") annotation on the PendingSeats bean, so that the initializer runs before our database collector.

If everything goes well, you should see something like this on your console:

```
23:42:48,455 INFO  [TaskListener] (ServerService Thread Pool -- 54)
Submitted GenerateSeatRequestFromArtificial@4256cb0c

23:42:48,456 INFO  [GenerateSeatRequestsFromDatabase] (EE-
ManagedExecutorService-default-Thread-1) Sleeping... (1)

23:42:48,456 INFO  [TaskListener] (EE-ManagedExecutorService-default-
Thread-2) Starting GenerateSeatRequestFromArtificial@4256cb0c

23:42:48,456 INFO  [GenerateSeatRequestFromArtificial] (EE-
ManagedExecutorService-default-Thread-2) Sleeping... (2)

23:42:53,457 INFO  [GenerateSeatRequestsFromDatabase] (EE-
ManagedExecutorService-default-Thread-1) Finished sleeping!

23:42:53,461 INFO  [GenerateSeatRequestFromArtificial] (EE-
ManagedExecutorService-default-Thread-2) Finished sleeping!

23:42:53,461 INFO  [TaskListener] (EE-ManagedExecutorService-default-
Thread-2) Finished task GenerateSeatRequestFromArtificial@4256cb0c

23:42:53,617 INFO  [GenerateSeatRequestsFromDatabase] (EE-
ManagedExecutorService-default-Thread-1) Requesting booking for [1]

23:42:53,621 INFO  [PendingSeats] (ServerService Thread Pool -- 54) [1,
4, 5, 6] (3)
```

As you can see, both tasks started at the same time (1 and 2) in two separate threads (notice the `EE-ManagedExecutorService-default-Thread-1` and `...-Thread-2` entries in the log). The final result is yielded after roughly 5 seconds, and it contains data from both the collectors, and additionally, is collected in the thread that originally submitted the tasks (`ServerService Thread Pool -- 54`).

You can also use the Java VisualVM tool to visualize your threads in the application server. The tool is available in your JDK installation in the `bin` directory (the `jvisualvm` executable). After running it, you should see JBoss in the left tree and the **Threads** tab after clicking on the JBoss node. This is shown in the following screenshot:

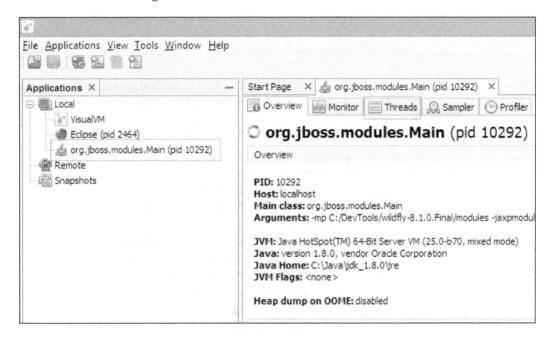

If you switch to the **Threads** tab during your application deployment, you will see a graph, as shown in the following screenshot:

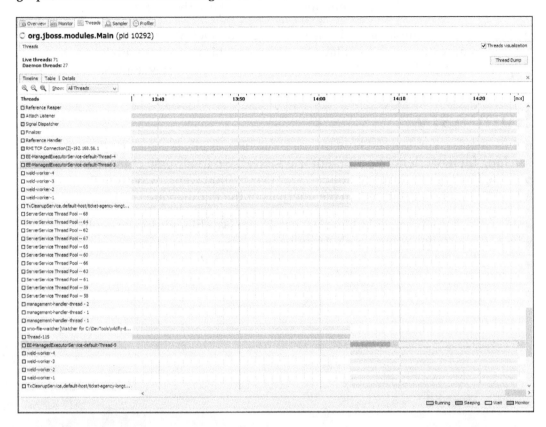

The purple color denotes a sleeping thread and the two highlighted threads with a purple part of the timeline are our tasks during execution. You can use a detailed thread view to additionally examine your worker threads. This is shown in the following screenshot:

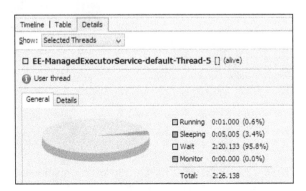

Java VisualVM offers many more features useful for every developer, such as resource monitoring of the virtual machine, profiler, sampler, and others that are implemented as dedicated plugins. Be sure to check them out!

In this section, we implemented a use case that was a lot harder to cover in a proper manner in previous versions of Java EE. We were able to do this with less code, thanks to the high-level API that was made available to the developers.

Summary

In this chapter, you learned how to create batching applications using the new batching framework in two different ways. Next, we tried some of the mechanisms provided by the concurrency utilities. Our exploration went away from the user interaction and concentrated on the internals of the middleware layer.

In the next chapter, we will fill the last gap in the Java EE developer's toolbox, which is integration testing with Arquillian.

13
Testing Your Applications

In previous chapters, we covered the most important technologies of the Java EE platform. However, every professional developer knows that software development should begin from writing tests. At first, it does not sound easy to be able to verify the correctness of the execution of EJBs, database-related code, or, for example, REST services but it appears really straightforward when using the right tools! In this chapter, we will present the fundamental testing framework used for Java EE applications testing: the Arquillian. Additionally, we will take a look at its extensions and related libraries.

In this chapter, we will focus on the following topics:

- An introduction to enterprise testing, from mock objects to the Arquillian framework
- How to integrate an Arquillian test case for our ticket machine application
- How to use the Eclipse IDE and Maven shell to run Arquillian tests
- The most important Arquillian extensions and how to use them

Test types

The word *tests* can be interpreted in multiple ways. Most often, tests perform the validation and verification of the application requirements. Tests can be performed on multiple levels, covering single methods to whole business features. Tests can also cover nonfunctional aspects such as security or performance.

First, let's introduce categories of tests that validate the functional requirements. Mike Cohn has introduced a concept of the test pyramid, which is shown here:

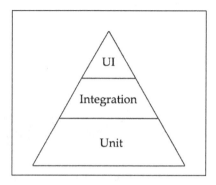

As you can see, the majority of tests in an application are usually tests that cover units of code. A unit can be a single method, the most basic feature. Because of this scope, these type of tests are called **unit tests**. They can be defined as tests written by a programmer to verify that a relatively small piece of functionality is doing what it is intended to do. Because the unit is rather small, the number of these tests increases rapidly, so they become the fundament of application testing appearing on the lowest level of the pyramid.

The next type of tests concerns bigger areas of code. They cover whole services or business features. This means they cover multiple units of code and concern different modules and libraries. The number of such tests would be lower than the number of unit tests. This type of test is often called an **integration test**. Integration tests are done to demonstrate that different pieces of the system work together; since they cover entire applications, they require much more effort to be put together. For example, they usually require resources such as database instances and hardware to be allocated for them. Integration tests do a more convincing job of demonstrating how the system works (especially to nonprogrammers); at least to the extent that the integration test environment resembles the production environment.

The last type of tests are UI tests, which can also be called acceptance tests. Their number is the smallest in the project; they are usually the most troublesome to write to simulate the user interacting with the application. They cover whole requirements and features.

Let's leave the topic of nonfunctional tests. For now, you have to only remember that they can cover topics related to performance, security, and so on.

Instruments used for testing

As you can imagine, each kind of testing uses a different approach and often requires different testing libraries.

When you're writing unit tests, you have to just provide some method input parameters, and validate if their outcome covers the expectations. To do this in Java, you probably already use **JUnit**, **TestNG**, or **Spock**. When you're moving from bigger parts of code to testing whole services, some problems may appear. It's often hard to separate the code you'd like to test, to make it testable without running all the other services. You usually create some mock objects that simulate behavior of modules you don't want to include in your test. If you have an object whose methods you want to test, and if these methods depend on another object, you can create a mock of the dependency rather than an actual instance of that dependency. This allows you to test your object in isolation.

As an example, one common use case might be in database applications, where you would like to test, for example, the user registration process but you don't want to run the whole database (which means that you will set its schema, some initial data, and finally clean its state manually after the test is complete). You can mock just the database interaction and define the behavior of some methods execution, for example, your stub will always return four users, which will be hardcoded in your test code.

This kind of approach, although very immediate to understand and put into practice, has several limitations. Firstly, it relegates you into an artificial environment, where you will often make invalid assumptions about the behavior and stability of that environment.

Secondly, you will end up with a hard-to-maintain mock code, which will allow your tests to pass and give you the warm feeling of having done a great job.

Thirdly, sometimes it's very hard to isolate a service you'd like to test, and code mocking all its interactions can be larger than the code of the meaningful tests.

So, even if mock objects may still provide some benefits to start systems, where you don't have full implementations of a particular subsystem, it might be good to stay as close as possible to the target environment that the code is supposed to run in. At some point, The No Mock Movement (**Not Only Mocks Movement**) was launched pointing out that mocking often takes too much time, and makes you focus on writing mocks instead of writing tests.

Arquillian tries to solve these problems. It is a platform that simplifies integration testing for Java middleware. It deals with all the plumbing of container management, deployment, and framework initialization so that you can focus on the task of writing your tests — real tests. Arquillian minimizes the burden on you — for the developer — by covering aspects surrounding test execution; some of these aspects are as follows:

- Managing the life cycle of the container (start/stop)
- Bundling the test class with the dependent classes and resources into a deployable archive
- Enhancing the test class (for example, resolving the `@Inject`, `@EJB`, and `@Resource` injections)
- Deploying the archive to test applications (deploy/undeploy), and capturing results and failures

Arquillian also has extensions that enhance its features, for example, allowing it to perform UI tests or some nonfunctional tests.

In the next section, we will discuss which instruments are required to run your integration tests using Arquillian.

Getting started with Arquillian

Although Arquillian does not depend on a specific build tool, it is commonly used with Maven; it offers dependency management and thus simplifies the task of including the Arquillian libraries in the application since they are distributed in the Central Maven repository.

Depending on the type of archetype you used for generation, you might have a different folder structure in your project; this is not an issue. What is really important is that you provide the following structure under your `src` folder:

- `main/java/`: Place all application Java source files here (under the Java package)
- `main/resources/`: Place all application configuration files here
- `test/java/`: Place all test Java source files here (under the Java package)
- `test/resources/`: Place all test configuration files here (for example, `persistence.xml`)

So by now, we will be working under `test/java`, which is where we will place our first Arquillian test class.

Writing an Arquillian test

If you have been working with JUnit (`http://www.junit.org`), you will find a similar Arquillian test, with some extra spice in it.

In order to do this, we will use Eclipse and Maven, just as we have done so far. If you are about to add test classes to your project, there is obviously no need to create a new project for this purpose. However, for learning purposes, we delivered this example in a separate project so that you can see exactly what to add in order to run Arquillian tests.

In order to avoid recreating the whole project from scratch, you could simply clone the `ticket-agency-jpa` project and name it `ticket-agency-test`, moving the root package from `com.packtpub.wflydevelopment.chapter5` to `com.packtpub.wflydevelopment.chapter13`. If this still seems like too much work, you could simply import the `Chapter13` project from the book sample.

Configuring the pom.xml file

The first thing that is necessary to include in order to run an Arquillian test is the `junit` dependency, which is required to run our unit tests:

```
<dependency>
    <groupId>junit</groupId>
    <artifactId>junit</artifactId>
    <scope>test</scope>
    <version>4.11</version>
</dependency>
```

In earlier chapters, we introduced the term **Bill of Materials (BOM)**. Now, we will use the Arquillian BOM in order to import versions of all Arquillian-related dependencies:

```
<dependencyManagement>
    <dependencies>
        <dependency>
            <groupId>org.jboss.arquillian</groupId>
            <artifactId>arquillian-bom</artifactId>
            <version>1.1.5.Final</version>
            <scope>import</scope>
            <type>pom</type>
        </dependency>
    </dependencies>
</dependencyManagement>
```

We're using Arquillian with JUnit (like mentioned before other possibilities are `TestNG`, `Spock`, `JBehave`, and `Cucumber`) so we need to include the appropriate dependency:

```
<dependency>
    <groupId>org.jboss.arquillian.junit</groupId>
    <artifactId>arquillian-junit-container</artifactId>
    <scope>test</scope>
</dependency>
```

After being done with the basic dependencies, we now have to specify the container against which the tests will be run. Container adapters are available for the more important Java EE Application Servers (WildFly, Glassfish, WebLogic, and WebSphere), as well as for some servlet containers such as Tomcat or Jetty. Here, we want to use WildFly so we will use an appropriate container adapter. However, we have a few possible choices. Container adapters can be divided into three basic groups:

- **Embedded**: This is the mode in which a container is run on the same JVM instance the tests are running. Often, a container run in this mode is not an original one, but packed to a single JAR limited version.

- **Managed**: In this mode, the real application server is run on a separate JVM. As the name implies, it's possible to manage the state of the container, run it, stop it, and so on. By default, when you run the test, the server is started, tests are run against it, and then it is stopped. However, it is possible to configure Arquillian to run tests on the already running instance.

- **Remote**: In this mode, we just connect to some existing server instance and run tests against it.

The most universal choice to run tests is the managed container. Tests are run on the real server, same as on the production environment, and additionally, it is possible to manage its state, allowing for some more advanced tests such as testing features related to high-availability or communication between two applications that run on different instances. Now, we need to add the appropriate container adapter to our `pom.xml` file. To do this, we will create a Maven profile:

```
<profile>
    <id>arq-wildfly-managed</id>
    <dependencies>
        <dependency>
            <groupId>org.wildfly</groupId>
            <artifactId>wildfly-arquillian-container-managed</artifactId>
            <scope>test</scope>
```

```
        </dependency>
    </dependencies>
</profile>
```

There might be situations in which you'd like to run tests against different application servers. It's possible to just define a few Maven profiles and run tests a few times, each time activating other profiles. Keep in mind that some application servers don't provide all types of the adapters.

There is one more container-related topic. Our Arquillian tests use a protocol to communicate with the micro deployment on the application server. If we don't specify the protocol, the container will choose the default one. In order to specify it manually, we will need to add the `org.jboss.arquillian.protocol` dependency (named so as it's compatible with Servlet 3.0 specifications):

```
<dependency>
    <groupId>org.jboss.arquillian.protocol</groupId>
    <artifactId>arquillian-protocol-servlet</artifactId>
    <scope>test</scope>
</dependency>
```

Writing your first Arquillian test

Once the configuration is complete, we will finally code our test. So, create a Java class named `TicketTest` under the package `com.packtpub.wflydevelopment.chapter13.test`. The first thing that you will add to this class is the following annotation that tells JUnit to use Arquillian as the test controller:

```
@RunWith(Arquillian.class)
public class TicketServiceTest {

}
```

Arquillian then looks for a static method with the `@Deployment` annotation; it creates a micro deployment including all the specified classes and resources (instead of deploying the whole application), allowing to test only part of the system:

```
@Deployment
public static Archive<?> createTestArchive() {
    return ShrinkWrap.create(WebArchive.class)
        addPackage(SeatType.class.getPackage())
        .addPackage(TicketService.class.getPackage())
        .addPackage(LoggerProducer.class.getPackage())
        .addAsResource("META-INF/persistence.xml")
        .addAsWebInfResource(EmptyAsset.INSTANCE, "beans.xml");
}
```

The fluent API provided by the **ShrinkWrap** project (http://www.jboss.org/shrinkwrap) makes this technique possible using the create method, which accepts the type of deployment unit (WebArchive) as the argument and all the resources are included in this archive. In our case, instead of including all the single classes, we use the addPackage utility method that adds all the classes that are contained in a class package (for example, by adding the SeatType.class.getPackage() method, we will include all the classes that are in the same package as the SeatType class). Our project uses the JPA, so we also add persistence configuration; here, we specify a path to the .xml file, so we can point, for example, to some other test configuration using some other non-production database. And, of course, we also have to add the empty beans.xml file in order to enable the CDI.

Finally, we inject the service we would like to test (yes, it's possible to inject services to test classes) and add one test method:

```
@Inject
TicketService ticketService;

@Test
public void shouldCreateSeatType() throws Exception {
    // given
    final SeatType seatType = new SeatType();
    seatType.setDescription("Balcony");
    seatType.setPrice(11);
    seatType.setQuantity(5);

    // when
    ticketService.createSeatType(seatType);

    // then
    assertNotNull(seatType.getId());
}
```

Here, the shouldCreateSeatType method will create a new SeatType attribute using the createSeatType method from the TicketService class. Note how we inject TicketService just as we would if we were running this code on the server side.

Our first test case is now ready. We will just need to add an Arquillian configuration file named arquillian.xml in our project, under src/test/resources:

```
<?xml version="1.0" encoding="UTF-8"?>
<arquillian xmlns="http://jboss.org/schema/arquillian"
            xmlns:xsi="http://www.w3.org/2001/XMLSchema-instance"
            xsi:schemaLocation="http://jboss.org/schema/arquillian
```

```
http://jboss.org/schema/arquillian/arquillian_1_0.xsd">

<container qualifier="jboss-managed" default="true">
    <!-- Additional configuration -->
</container>

</arquillian>
```

You have to configure the container adapter. In this example, we assume that you have set the JBOSS_HOME environment variable to the WildFly main directory. In this case, no more configurations are required. However, if you want to run something non-standard, for example, connect to a remote container with altered management ports, then this file is the appropriate place to modify this. When you don't specify JBOSS_HOME, you can set the WildFly location using property as follows:

```
<container qualifier="jboss-managed" default="true">
    <configuration>
        <property name="jbossHome">C:\wildfly</property>
    </configuration>
</container>
```

However, this method may be hard to maintain when more than one person is working on the project. In order to avoid problems, you can use the system property resolution, for instance, ${jbossHome}.

If you configure the remote container, the configuration would look just like this:

```
<container qualifier="jboss-remote" default="true">
    <configuration>
        <property name="managementAddress">localhost</property>
        <property name="managementPort">9999</property>
    </configuration>
</container>
```

Running Arquillian TicketTest

It's possible to run Arquillian tests both from Maven and your IDE. You have to remember that we declared the container adapter in the Maven profile, so in order to run the full build, you have to run the following command line:

```
mvn clean package -Parquillian-wildfly-managed
```

If you want to run the test from Eclipse, you have to navigate to the project properties and select the **Maven** property. In the **Active Maven Profiles** field, enter `arquillian-wildfly-managed` (as shown in the following screenshot), which we declared earlier in the `pom.xml` file:

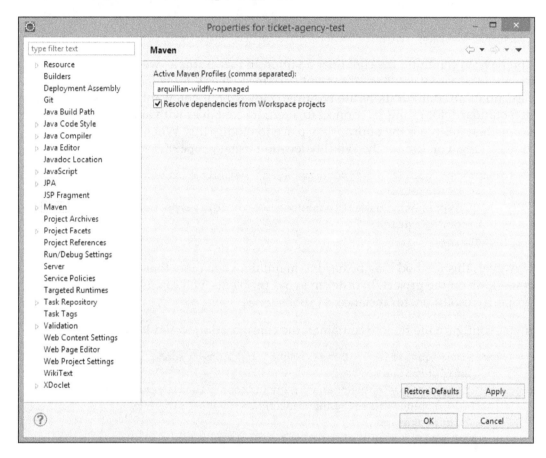

Now all you have to do is right-click on your `TicketServiceTest` class and select **Run As JUnit Test**. The Arquillian engine will start, producing the outcome of the test in the JUnit view (you can make it visible by navigating to **Menu | Window | Show View | JUnit**).

Congratulations! The JUnit console accounts for the first test that was run successfully.

If you want to use only one container in your test, then a good idea would be to set the default Maven profile, by adding the following lines to it in the `pom.xml` file:

```
<activation>
    <activeByDefault>true</activeByDefault>
</activation>
```

Running Arquillian tests using Spock

Arquillian is not limited to only JUnit. As we mentioned earlier, there are already containers, for example, TestNG and Spock; let's focus on the second one.

Spock is a modern testing framework written in Groovy and uses some of the Groovy language features to make your tests more readable and easier to write. Spock's primary goal is to test the Groovy code but it is perfect to write all kinds of tests for the Java code. Spock introduces a few additional semantics with its **Domain Specific Language (DSL)** in order to make testing even more easier and developer friendly.

Let's rewrite our previous test example using Spock:

```
@RunWith(ArquillianSputnik.class)
class TicketServiceTest extends Specification {

    @Deployment
    def static WebArchive createTestArchive() {
        return ShrinkWrap.create(WebArchive.class)
            .addPackage(SeatType.class.getPackage())
            .addPackage(TicketService.class.getPackage())
            .addPackage(LoggerProducer.class.getPackage())
            .addAsResource('META-INF/persistence.xml')
            .addAsWebInfResource(EmptyAsset.INSTANCE, 'beans.xml');
    }

    @Inject
    TicketService ticketService;


    def "should create SeatType"() {
        given:
        def seatType = new SeatType(description: "Balcony",
                                    price: 11, quantity: 6)

        when:
```

```
            ticketService.createSeatType(seatType);

            then:
            seatType.getId() != null
        }
    }
```

You can notice a few differences. First of all, it's really Groovy! Secondly, the test uses a different runner, `ArquillianSputnik`. What's more, you can already notice some Spock DSL here, such as the **given**, **when**, and **then** constructions, which come from **behavior-driven development (BDD)**. The **given** construction is expected to put the system in a specific state, **when** describes an action, and **then** contains assertions that verify the outcome of an action performed.

This fully working Spock example with the complete `pom.xml` configuration can be found in this chapter's example project named `ticket-agency-spock`. More information concerning the Arquillian Spock test runner, its features, and usage instructions can be found on GitHub at `https://github.com/arquillian/ arquillian-testrunner-spock`. More information concerning Spock can also be found on GitHub at `https://github.com/spockframework/spock`.

ShrinkWrap Resolver

In almost every Arquillian test, you will probably use ShrinkWrap to create micro deployments. After working with it for a bit, you will probably notice some shortcomings. You might be wondering what happens when you've got a test that relies on some external library; do you need to add all packages from that library? The answer is no. **ShrinkWrap Resolver** offers integration with Maven and basic Gradle support is also available. You can just write in your test what dependency you'd like to include in the archive and it will be deployed with the micro deployment.

Let's look at the basic example of the ShrinkWrap Resolver Maven integration:

```
    Maven.resolver().resolve("G:A:V").withTransitivity().asFile();
```

The preceding line means that we want to resolve an artifact with the given group ID, artifact ID, and version (Maven coordinates in canonical form) from Maven's central repository with all its dependencies, and convert it to a list of files.

However, with this example, you have to maintain the artifact version both in the test code and build file. You can improve this! Just import some dependencies data from your `pom.xml` file, so that ShrinkWrap Resolver resolves artifacts of the same versions the main project is using:

```
Maven.resolver().loadPomFromFile("/path/to/pom.xml").
resolve("G:A").withTransitivity().asFile();
```

So now, first of all, the `pom.xml` data is loaded, including all depending management sections and artifacts versions. Also, the artifact coordinates do not have to include the version.

These are the most basic features. You can fully configure the resolver manually, the repositories you want to use, Maven profiles to be applied, and much more. Let's now grab an example.

Let's say you're testing your project using JUnit and some fancy assertion library. **AssertJ** (successor of **FEST** assertions) is a fluent assertions library that allows you to write your project in a more human-readable form:

```
assertThat(frodo.getName()).isEqualTo("Frodo");
```

Using such a library in every test means you have to include it in every micro deployment. There is another thing you will always need: the `beans.xml` file. So let's create some utility classes:

```
public class ArquillianWarUtils {

    private static final String BEANS_XML = "beans.xml";
    private static final String ASSERTJ_COORDINATE =
                                 "org.assertj:assertj-core";

    private static File[] ASSERTJ_ARTIFACT = Maven.resolver()
      .loadPomFromFile("pom.xml").resolve(ASSERTJ_COORDINATE)
      .withTransitivity().asFile();

    public static WebArchive getBasicWebArchive() {
        return ShrinkWrap.create(WebArchive.class)
            .addAsLibraries(ASSERTJ_ARTIFACT)
            .addAsWebInfResource(EmptyAsset.INSTANCE, BEANS_XML);
    }
}
```

Also, now in each test case, you'd have just to write the following code:

```
@Deployment
public static WebArchive createDeployment() {
    return ArquillianWarUtils.getBasicWebArchive()
                    .addPackage(SomePackage.class.getPackage();
}
```

At some point, you might want to do one more thing; instead of adding all your libraries manually, you can import them on runtime dependencies:

```
Maven.resolver().loadPomFromFile("pom.xml")
                .importRuntimeDependencies().resolve()
            .withTransitivity().asFile();
```

There are some unfortunate cases in which isolation of a part of the project for the micro deployment is not possible. You just add more and more classes to it and there is no end. This means that your project might have a poor design, but let's say you want to introduce Arquillian in some existing legacy project and you had no influence on its structure. In that case, you might want to import not just some classes or packages, but the whole project to your integration test. Some people do tricks; they just use the basic ShrinkWrap and import a `.jar` or `.war` file using the `ZipImporter` ShrinkWrap:

```
ShrinkWrap
    .create(ZipImporter.class)
    .importFrom(new File("/target/myPackage.war"))
    .as(WebArchive.class);
```

The problem is what is really in this archive? You probably import an archive created during the previous build since it is created after finishing the tests! What's more, it cannot even exist when you're just working from the IDE and not running the full Maven build! It's the place where you can use the `MavenImporter` class. Refer to the following code:

```
ShrinkWrap.create(MavenImporter.class)
    .loadPomFromFile("/path/to/pom.xml")
    .importBuildOutput()
    .as(WebArchive.class);
```

That's it! Internally, it runs the simplified build, gathering compiled classes and resources and packing it to the archive. It does not run inside the complete Maven build using some embedded instance, since that would be much too slow. You might want to add such a method to your test utilities:

```
public class ArquillianWarUtils {

    // already presented code

    public static WebArchive getBasicWebArchive() { . . . }

    public static WebArchive importBuildOutput() {
        return ShrinkWrap.create(MavenImporter.class)
                .loadPomFromFile("pom.xml")
                .importBuildOutput()
                .as(WebArchive.class);
    }
}
```

There exists a similar feature for the Gradle project included since ShrinkWrap Resolver 2.2.0-alpha-1. However, it uses the Gradle Tooling API internally:

```
ShrinkWrap.create(EmbeddedGradleImporter.class)
    .forProjectDirectory("/path/to/dir")
    .importBuildOutput()
    .as(WebArchive.class);
```

At some point, you might be surprised that this last example did not work. The reason might be that `arquillian-bom` does not include this ShrinkWrap Resolver version. However, it is possible to override the BOM imported versions with another BOM. It's pretty easy; just insert the more important BOM first:

```
<dependencyManagement>
    <!-- shrinkwrap resolvers import must be before arquillian bom!
-->
    <dependency>
        <groupId>org.jboss.shrinkwrap.resolver</groupId>
        <artifactId>shrinkwrap-resolver-bom</artifactId>
        <version>${version.shrinkwrap-resolver}</version>
        <scope>import</scope>
        <type>pom</type>
```

```
    </dependency>
    <dependency>
        <groupId>org.jboss.shrinkwrap</groupId>
        <artifactId>shrinkwrap-bom</artifactId>
        <version>${version.shrinkwrap}</version>
        <scope>import</scope>
        <type>pom</type>
    </dependency>
</dependencyManagement>
```

More info about ShinkWrap Resolver can be found on its GitHub repository at `https://github.com/shrinkwrap/resolver`.

ShrinkWrap Descriptors

There is one more ShrinkWrap family project. A little less popular and not known by many people, it is called **ShrinkWrap Descriptors**. Its goal is to provide a fluent API for the creation of descriptor resources you usually create and insert inside your micro deployments.

Let's start with an example. Let's say you're writing a persistence framework extension. While doing this, you use an incredible amount of `persistence.xml` files such as the following code:

```xml
<persistence>
    <persistence-unit name="myapp">
        <provider>org.hibernate.ejb.HibernatePersistence</provider>
        <jta-data-source>java:/DefaultDS</jta-data-source>
        <properties>
            <property name="hibernate.dialect"
                      value="org.hibernate.dialect.HSQLDialect"/>
            <property name="hibernate.hbm2ddl.auto" value="create-drop"/>
        </properties>
    </persistence-unit>
</persistence>
```

With ShrinkWrap Descriptors, instead of putting all these files in `src/test/resources` and then referencing them from particular tests, you can just put some code in the test itself:

```java
final PersistenceDescriptor persistence = Descriptors
  .create(PersistenceDescriptor.class)
        .createPersistenceUnit()
            .name("myapp")
            .provider("org.hibernate.ejb.HibernatePersistence")
```

```
.jtaDataSource("java:/DefaultDS")
.getOrCreateProperties()
   .createProperty().name("hibernate.dialect")
       .value("org.hibernate.dialect.HSQLDialect").up()
   .createProperty().name("hibernate.hbm2ddl.auto")
       .value("create-drop").up()
.up().up()
```

Such a `PersistenceDescriptor` class can be exported as `String` or just be added to the `ShrinkWrap` archive.

By default, the project contains descriptors ready for all the most important `.xml` of Java EE platform. However, it also allows for code generation using XSD and DTD files. Be cautious, it's still in alpha stage. It is stable, but the API might already be changed.

Persistence testing

Real challenges start when you have to include other systems in your testing process. Troubles might be caused even by the necessity of testing interactions with a relational database. In *Chapter 5, Combining Persistence with CDI*, we introduced the JPA. Now it's time to describe how you can test your interactions with it.

There are a few issues that have to be considered when testing database-related code:

- How to verify that data was really inserted to the database?
- How to maintain the database state between tests and how to automatically clean it?

Arquillian persistence extension allows you to test both these things. Before running a test, you can seed your database from `.xml`, `.xls`, `.yaml`, `.json`, or custom SQL scripts. It's done by just annotating the test case using the `@UsingDataSet("path-to-seeding-file")` annotation. After the test execution, you can compare the database state against another file, this time using the `@ShouldMatchDataSet("path-to-dataset")` annotation. Let's look at an example:

```
@Test
@UsingDataSet("datasets/seats.yml")
@ShouldMatchDataSet("datasets/expected-seats.yml")
public void shouldMakeACleanup() throws Exception {
    // given
    // from annotation

    // when
```

```
        ticketService.doCleanUp();

        // then
        // from annotation
    }
```

The `seats.yml` and `expected-seats.xml` files are just simple YAMLs placed in `/src/test/resources/datasets`. The first file contains `SeatType`:

```
Seat_Type:
  - description: test
    position: "box"
    price: 10
    quantity: 10
```

The second file contains:

```
Seat_Type:
```

Since we're executing a cleanup. Note that the names and values used here are the SQL names, not the JPA names.

JPA allows you to use a second-level cache in order to improve the operations performance. With this, not all of the operations are instantly reflected on the database state. During the tests running, you might be interested in the `@JpaCacheEviction` annotation, which makes a cache to evict after every test run. Each test is also wrapped in a separate transaction so that it won't influence the execution of other tests

Of course, there are some dependencies you need to make this extension work. There are exactly three of them as follows:

```
<dependency>
    <groupId>org.jboss.arquillian.extension</groupId>
    <artifactId>arquillian-persistence-dbunit</artifactId>
    <version>1.0.0.Alpha7</version>
    <scope>test</scope>
</dependency>
```

Arquillian in 1.1.4.Final version has a bug that passes all persistence tests even when they should not. The 1.1.5.Final version works correctly.

A fully configured example project for this chapter is named `ticket-agency-test-ape`.

The Arquillian Persistence Extension manual is available on GitHub at `https://github.com/arquillian/arquillian-extension-persistence`.

Arquillian Warp

The last Arquillian extension that we will discuss here is **Warp**. Authors say that it allows you to write client-side tests that assert server-side logic. To be more descriptive, it allows for execution of client side requests, and then to execute server side tests. This fills the gap between client-side and server-side testing.

In order to fully understand the Warp, we have to introduce the `@RunAsClient` annotation. It can be placed on a test class or test method and it mentions that tests will be executed on the client side and not on the server side. The second important annotation is `@Deployment`, which you have already met on method creating the archives. However, it can take some parameters that are Boolean value testable. If a testable is `false`, it is also executes on the client side, not repacking the deployment and so on. However, Warp mixes these two modes and requires `@Deployment(testable=true)` and `@RunAsClient` annotations. The test class has to be annotated additionally with `@WarpTest`:

```
@RunWith(Arquillian.class)
@WarpTest
@RunAsClient
public class BasicWarpTest {

    @Deployment(testable = true)
    public static WebArchive createDeployment() {
        ...
    }

    @Test
    public void test() {
        // Warp test
    }
}
```

Every Warp test uses the following construction:

```
Warp
    .initiate(Activity)
    .inspect(Inspection);
```

An activity is the client part that makes the requests. Inspection is a server-side assertion. It's also possible to filter some requests by additional specification of the Observer:

```
Warp
    .initiate(Activity)
    .observer(Observer)
    .inspect(Inspection);
```

An Observer can, for example, filter HTTP addresses.

Let's take a look at something more concrete. Arquillian Warp also has some extensions. Currently, all of them are HTTP oriented; however, it is possible to extend Warp to cover non-HTTP use cases. The extensions add some special classes for testing:

- JSF
- JAX-RS
- Spring MVC

Now we're going to look at the JAX-RS part. To do this, we will use the code from *Chapter 7, Adding Web Services to Your Applications*. We want to test our REST service. First of all, we need to add all the standard Arquillian-related dependencies and the `arquillian.xml` file. For the Warp itself, we will need the following dependency:

```
<dependency>
    <groupId>org.jboss.arquillian.extension</groupId>
    <artifactId>arquillian-warp</artifactId>
    <version>1.0.0.Alpha7</version>
    <type>pom</type>
    <scope>test</scope>
</dependency>
```

For the JAX-RS extension, we will need the following dependency:

```
<dependency>
    <groupId>org.jboss.arquillian.extension</groupId>
    <artifactId>arquillian-rest-warp-impl-jaxrs-2.0</artifactId>
    <version>1.0.0.Alpha2</version>
    <scope>test</scope>
</dependency>
```

Additionally, we will use the JAX-RS client:

```
<dependency>
    <groupId>org.jboss.resteasy</groupId>
    <artifactId>resteasy-client</artifactId>
    <version>3.0.9.Final</version>
    <scope>test</scope>
</dependency>
```

Our test will look like this:

```java
@RunWith(Arquillian.class)
@WarpTest
@RunAsClient
public class SeatsResourceTest {

    @Deployment(testable = true)
    public static WebArchive deployment() {
        return ShrinkWrap.create(MavenImporter.class)
                    .loadPomFromFile("pom.xml")
                    .importBuildOutput()
                    .as(WebArchive.class);
    }

    @ArquillianResource
    private URL contextPath;                // [1]

    private ResteasyWebTarget target;

    @Before
    public void setUp() {
        final ResteasyClient client =
                new ResteasyClientBuilder().build();
        this.target = client.target(contextPath + "rest/seat");
    }

    @Test
    public void testasd() {
        Warp.initiate(new Activity() {
            @Override
            public void perform() {
                final String response = target
                  .request(MediaType.APPLICATION_JSON_TYPE)
                  .get(String.class);   // [2]
                assertNotNull(response);            // [3]
            }
        }).inspect(new Inspection() {

            private static final long serialVersionUID = 1L;
```

```
        @ArquillianResource
        private RestContext restContext;

        @AfterServlet
        public void testGetSeats() {
            assertEquals(200, restContext.getHttpResponse().
              getStatusCode());
            assertEquals(MediaType.APPLICATION_JSON,
              restContext.getHttpResponse().getContentType());
            assertNotNull(restContext.getHttpResponse().
              getEntity());  // [4]
        }
    });
  }
}
```

First of all, you can see all the annotations mentioned earlier. We use the `ShrinkWrap Resolver MavenImporter` class here to get the whole project in the deployment. The [1] object is the injection of the application URL. In [2], we execute a client request to get the seats and in [3], we do some basic client-side assertion. In [4], we test the server side, to check if the appropriate HTTP code was returned and so on. In more complex scenarios, we can execute some beans logic to confirm that the appropriate state change was performed on the server side. This last thing distinguishes the Arquillian Warp from running tests in the client mode (a `@RunAsClient` annotation) and doing assertions with `ResteasyWebTarget`.

Some more information concerning this extension can be found at `https://github.com/arquillian/arquillian-extension-warp`.

WebSockets testing

We introduced the topic of WebSockets in the earlier chapters. Now let's see how we can test them. To do this in plain Java, we will need a WebSocket client implementation; be sure to add **Tyrus** to your `pom.xml` file:

```xml
<dependency>
    <groupId>org.glassfish.tyrus.bundles</groupId>
    <artifactId>tyrus-standalone-client</artifactId>
    <scope>test</scope>
    <version>1.8.3</version>
</dependency>
```

For this example, we will use Tyrus as a base code from *Chapter 8, Adding WebSockets*. Our test realizes a simple scenario. Using the REST API, we reserve a seat, and as a WebSocket client, we wait for a message broadcasting information concerning new reservations. Let's look at the code:

```
@RunAsClient
@RunWith(Arquillian.class)
public class TicketServiceTest {

    private static final String WEBSOCKET_URL = "ws://localhost:8080/
ticket-agency-test-websockets/tickets";
    private static final String SEAT_RESOURCE_URL = "http://
localhost:8080/ticket-agency-test-websockets/rest/seat";

    @Deployment
    public static Archive<?> createTestArchive() { // [1]
        return ShrinkWrap.create(MavenImporter.class).
loadPomFromFile("pom.xml").importBuildOutput()
            .as(WebArchive.class);
    }

    @Test
    public void shouldReceiveMessageOnBooking() throws Exception {
        // given
        final int seatNumber = 4;
        final Deque<JsonObject> messages =
          new ConcurrentLinkedDeque<>(); // [2]
        final CountDownLatch messageLatch =
          new CountDownLatch(1); // [3]
        final MessageHandler.Whole<String> handler = // [4]
          new MessageHandler.Whole<String>() {
            @Override
            public void onMessage(String message) {
                messages.add(Json
                  .createReader(new StringReader(message))
                  .readObject());
                messageLatch.countDown();
            }
        };

        ContainerProvider.getWebSocketContainer()   // [5]
                        .connectToServer(new Endpoint() {
```

```
        @Override
        public void onOpen(Session session,
                           EndpointConfig endpointConfig) {
            session.addMessageHandler(handler);
        }
    }, new URI(WEBSOCKET_URL));

    // when
    RestAssured.when()
            .post(SEAT_RESOURCE_URL + "/" + seatNumber)
            .then().statusCode(200); // [6]
    messageLatch.await(10, TimeUnit.SECONDS); // [7]

    // then [8]
    assertThat(messages.size(), equalTo(1));
    final JsonObject message = messages.poll();
    assertThat(message.getInt("id"), equalTo(seatNumber));
    }
}
```

The test is run as described in this chapter's client mode and uses Tyrus: the WebSocket client reference implementation under the hood. The perfect deployment for this test is our whole application, so we are going to use MavenImporter [1]. In the test, we declared a concurrent deque to gather a received messaged [2] and a latch [3], which we will use to wait in [7]. In order to handle WebSockets on the client side, we have to declare a handler [4], which specifies the behavior on receiving the message. Here, we just add a message to our deque and perform a latch countdown. In [5], we have to register the handler so that it will be used for an open session. The REST call is executed using a rest-assured library, which provides a fluent API to test REST APIs. Finally, in [8], we perform some basic assertions concerning the received messages.

The fully configured pom.xml file and a whole working project can be found under ticket-agency-test-websockets.

Enhancing your Arquillian test

You might have noticed that we, on purpose, created just a part of the integration tests we needed. We did not reach the last mile, that is, creating seats and reserving one. As a matter of fact, if you remember, our ticket application uses ConversationScope to track the user's navigation. Thus, we need to bind ConversationScope into our test as well.

Luckily, the `Weld` container provides all that you need with `org.jboss.weld.context.bound.BoundConversationContext`, which needs to be injected into your test class:

```
@Inject BoundConversationContext conversationContext;

@Before
public void init() {
    conversationContext.associate(
    new MutableBoundRequest(new HashMap<String, Object>(),
                            new HashMap<String, Object>()));
    conversationContext.activate();
}
```

Note that the `@Before` annotation is invoked before each test method and after injections have occurred. In our case, it is used to associate `conversationContext` with `MutableBoundRequest` before being activated by `conversationContext.activate`. This is needed to mimic the conversation behavior from within the Arquillian test bed.

Just for completeness, you must be aware that `BoundRequest` interfaces are defined in the Weld API to hold a conversation that spans multiple requests, but are shorter than a session.

So here's the full `TicketTest` class, which contains a theatre creation and booking seat reservation in the `testTicketAgency` method:

```
@RunWith(Arquillian.class)
public class TicketTest {

    @Inject BoundConversationContext conversationContext;

    @Before
    public void init() {
        conversationContext.associate(
        new MutableBoundRequest(new HashMap<String, Object>(),
            new HashMap<String, Object>()));
        conversationContext.activate();
    }

    @Deployment
    public static Archive<?> createTestArchive() {
        return ShrinkWrap.create(WebArchive.class, "ticket.war")
            .addPackage(SeatProducer.class.getPackage())
```

```
                    .addPackage(Seat.class.getPackage())
                    .addPackage(TicketService.class.getPackage())
                    .addPackage(DataManager.class.getPackage())
                    .addAsResource("META-INF/persistence.xml")
                    .addAsWebInfResource(EmptyAsset.INSTANCE, "beans.xml");
        }

        @Inject
        TicketService ticketService;

        @Inject
        BookerService bookerService;

        @Inject
        Logger log;

        @Test
        public void testTicketAgency () throws Exception {

            SeatType seatType = new SeatType();
            seatType.setDescription("Balcony");
            seatType.setPrice(20);
            seatType.setQuantity(5);

            ticketService.createSeatType(seatType);
            log.info("Created Seat Type");
            assertNotNull(seatType.getId());

            List<SeatType> listSeats = new ArrayList();
            listSeats.add(seatType);
            ticketService.createTheatre(listSeats);

            log.info("Created Theatre");
            log.info(seatType.getDescription() + " was persisted with id "
+ seatType.getId());

            bookerService.bookSeat(new Long(seatType.getId()), seatType.
getPrice());
            log.info("Created Theatre");
            log.info("Money left: " +bookerService.getMoney());
            assertTrue(bookerService.getMoney() <100);
        }
    }
```

Additional information

The Arquillian project is an evolving framework with many other interesting topics. Describing all its extensions, however, is out of the scope of this book. However, the other interesting areas to look into are **Drone** and **Graphene**, which bring the **WebDriver** and **Page Object** patterns to Arquillian testing.

At some point, you may find yourself creating separate deployment methods in each test case. You can change this behavior by the usage of **Arquillian Suite Extension**, which allows specifying a deployment for a set of test cases.

Arquillian is fully open source, so you can learn more about it from the online documentation that is available at `http://arquillian.org/`. When you need some help, or you have an awesome idea for a new feature, you can contact the Arquillian community on forums or IRC (`http://arquillian.org/community/`). Remember that if you find a bug, don't complain; just file an issue on JBoss JIRA at `https://issues.jboss.org`.

One of the Arquillian contributors John D. Ament has already published a book on this topic called *Arquillian Testing Guide*, *Packt Publishing*.

Summary

In this chapter, we went through a critical part of enterprise systems: integration testing. Historically, one main downside of Java EE is its testability, but Arquillian has really solved this issue to a great extent.

Used as an extension to the JUnit framework, Arquillian excels in checking the integration layer that exposes the business logic in an enterprise Java application.

Arquillian hooks into your testing framework to manage the container's life cycle. It also bundles the `test` class into a deployable archive with dependent classes and resources.

This is the last chapter covering basic Java EE and WildFly features. We started with a few session beans, and ended up with web sockets, an asynchronous messaging system, RESTful API, and even a little bit of JavaScript. During the course of this book, we saw how the newest edition of Java EE provided us with tools to create modern and scalable applications. The platform's goal is to help the developer to focus on the business logic. This means removing the boilerplate code through the whole application stack from the backend to the view layer. In most areas, we only covered the most important features of the multiple technologies provided by Java EE. There is still plenty to explore!

In the appendix, we will learn a few things about the JBoss Forge tool, which can greatly increase the productivity when working with Java EE.

Rapid Development Using JBoss Forge

In the appendix of this book, we will give you an overview of JBoss Forge, which is a powerful, rapid application development (aimed at Java EE) and project comprehension tool. With Forge, you can start a new project from scratch and generate the skeleton for your application just with a few commands. However, it can also be used for incremental enhancements for your existing projects using extra plugins.

Installing Forge

In order to install Forge, you need to perform the following steps:

1. Download and unzip Forge from `http://forge.jboss.org/` into a folder on your hard disk; this folder will be your `FORGE_HOME`.

2. Add `FORGE_HOME/bin` to your path (Windows, Linux, and Mac OS X).

In Unix-based operating systems, this typically means editing your `~/.bashrc` or ~/.profile; you will need to enter the following code snippet:

```
export FORGE_HOME=~/forge/
export PATH=$PATH:$FORGE_HOME/bin
```

In Windows systems, you will need to open the **Control Panel** window, then navigate to **System Properties** | **Advanced** | **Environment Variables**, and add these two entries visually. It is recommended to set user variables for Forge, unless you have placed the unzipped distribution in a folder where all users can access it.

In case of any problem, check out the online installation guide available at `http://forge.jboss.org/document/installation`.

Starting Forge

In order to start Forge, there is a script named `forge.bat` (or the equivalent Forge for Unix). Run the following script:

```
forge.bat
```

This will launch the Forge console, as shown in the following screenshot:

The console accepts a large set of commands, such as commands to navigate and manipulate the filesystems, to create new projects, to operate on the Forge environment and UI generation, and scaffolding commands. It also offers the autocomplete feature.

In order to learn the following available commands in current context, press the *Tab* key twice:

[bin] $	
alias	echo
unalias	edit
export	exit
about	git-clone
addon-build-and-install	grep
addon-install	less
addon-install-from-git	ls
addon-list	man
addon-remove	mkdir
archetype-add	more
archetype-list	open
archetype-remove	pl-cmil-forge-ecore-ui
cat	project-new

cd	pwd
clear	rm
command-list	run
config-clear	system-property-get
config-list	system-property-set
config-set	touch
connection-create-profile	track-changes
connection-remove-profile	transaction-start
cp	version
date	wait

> Besides the standard commands, it is possible to enrich the syntax of the Forge command line with add-ons, which adds superior capabilities to your project creation. On http://forge.jboss.org/addons, you can find a list of available plugins. For example, we are going to use the angular-js plugin in order to create a GUI for our application.

In the following section, we will demonstrate how to use some of the available commands in order to create a Java EE 7 application.

Creating your first Java EE 7 application with JBoss Forge

So, Forge installation is quite easy; however, creating your first Java EE 7 application will be even faster! Although, we can create rather advanced applications with Forge, for the purpose of learning, we will just use a simple schema that contains a user table, which can be built using the following command:

```
CREATE TABLE users (
  id serial PRIMARY KEY,
  name varchar(50),
  surname varchar(50),
  email varchar(50)
);
```

The first thing that we need to do is to create a new project using the project-new command. Execute the following commands from within the Forge shell:

```
[bin]$ project-new --named forge-demo --topLevelPackage com.packtpub.
wflydevelopment.appendix –projectFolder forge-demo
```

Now, you have a new Forge project, which is based on a Maven project structure. Arguably, generating a new project isn't Forge's greatest value—the same can be achieved with Maven archetypes. The sweet part of Forge is that now you have the luxury of defining your own application skeleton interactively after it has already been generated. This means that you can create the project using the Maven archetype first and then extend it using Forge's intuitive suggestions.

When the project is created, you can then enter command-list from the shell, as shown in the following screenshot, which enlists all the basic commands that you can use in Forge 2.12.1 Final:

If you want to learn more about the single commands, you can use man followed by the command name, as shown in the following screenshot:

```
                  C:\Windows\system32\cmd.exe                    _  □  ✕

SYNOPSIS
   project-new [-] [--buildSystem] ProjectProvider [--named] String [
ectType

DESCRIPTION
   Create a new project (multi-step wizard - some options may not be
ted in this man page.)
      --buildSystem
   Build system - [ProjectProvider] (required) Valid choices:
   ["Maven" ]

      --finalName
   Final name - [String]

      --named
   Project name - [String] (required)

      --overwrite
   Overwrite existing project location - [Boolean] defaults to:
   [false]

      --targetLocation
   Project location - [DirectoryResource] defaults to:
   [C:Usersmich]

      --topLevelPackage
   Top level package - [String] defaults to: [org.example]

      --type
   Project type - [ProjectType] (required) Valid choices: ["war"
   "jar" "parent" "addon" "resource-jar" "ear" "from-archetype"
   "from-archetype-catalog" ]

      --version
   Version - [String] defaults to: [1.0.0-SNAPSHOT]



RESOURCES
   forge: <http://forge.jboss.org/>
Manual page project-new(1) line 1 (press h for help or q to quit)
```

When you have learned how to get help using Forge, let's get back to our application.

In the first step, we need to specify what Java and Java EE version we want to use:

```
[forge-demo]$ project-set-compiler-version --sourceVersion 1.8
--targetVersion 1.8
[forge-demo]$ javaee-setup --javaEEVersion 7
***SUCCESS*** JavaEE 7 has been installed.
```

At this point, our project already contains Java EE 7 API dependency. Now, since we will need to reverse-engineer our database table into Java entities, the next step will be to configure the **Java Persistence API (JPA)** layer for your application. This application will be based on WildFly JPA implementation, which is based on the Hibernate provider, referencing a database named Forge. This database is reachable at the **Java Naming and Directory Interface (JNDI)** named `java:jboss/datasources/PostgreSqlDS`. This is shown in the following command line:

```
[forge-demo]$ jpa-setup --jpaVersion 2.1 --provider HIBERNATE --container
WILDFLY --dbType POSTGRES --dataSourceName java:jboss/datasources/
PostgreSqlDS
```

The `persistence.xml` file was generated, and currently the console indicates that we are editing it. We can check its content by using the `cat` command:

```
[persistence.xml]$ cat .

<?xml version="1.0" encoding="UTF-8" standalone="yes"?>

<persistence xmlns="http://xmlns.jcp.org/xml/ns/persistence"
xmlns:xsi="http://w

ww.w3.org/2001/XMLSchema-instance" version="2.1"
xsi:schemaLocation="http://xmln

s.jcp.org/xml/ns/persistence http://xmlns.jcp.org/xml/ns/persistence/
persistence

_2_1.xsd">
  <persistence-unit name="forge-demo-persistence-unit" transaction-
type="JTA">

    <description>Forge Persistence Unit</description>

    <provider>org.hibernate.ejb.HibernatePersistence</provider>

    <jta-data-source>java:jboss/datasources/PostgreSqlDS</jta-data-
source>

    <exclude-unlisted-classes>false</exclude-unlisted-classes>

    <properties>

      <property name="hibernate.hbm2ddl.auto" value="create-drop"/>

      <property name="hibernate.show_sql" value="true"/>

      <property name="hibernate.format_sql" value="true"/>

      <property name="hibernate.transaction.flush_before_completion"
value="true

"/>

      <property name="hibernate.dialect" value="org.hibernate.dialect.
PostgreSQL
```

```
Dialect"/>
   </properties>
  </persistence-unit>
</persistence>
```

Next, we will use the `jpa-generate-entities-from-tables` command in order to generate your `Entity` class. You will need to provide the following **Java Database Connectivity (JDBC)** connection information:

- The JDBC URL
- The username and password
- The SQL dialect
- The JDBC driver class name
- The path in the filesystem where the JDBC driver is located
- The package where the entities will be generated

You can specify all the parameters in a one-line command or complete it interactively. The final command would look like this (line breaks added for readability):

```
[persistence.xml]$ jpa-generate-entities-from-tables  \
--jdbcUrl jdbc:postgresql://localhost:5432/forge \
--hibernateDialect org.hibernate.dialect.PostgreSQLDialect \
--userName jboss \
--userPassword jboss \
--driverLocation c:\\forge\\postgresql-9.3-1101.jdbc41.jar \
--driverClass org.postgresql.Driver \
--databaseTables users
```

After completing the persistence layer, we will now create the GUI application using the `scaffold` command, which can be associated with several providers such as the AngularJS one. First, let's install the add-on using the following shell command (note that it should be executed in your system's shell, not in the Forge CLI):

```
forge --install org.jboss.forge.addon:angularjs
```

After the installation is complete, we need to issue three more commands. First, we will prepare the scaffolding framework:

```
[forge-demo]$ scaffold-setup --provider AngularJS
```

Our application now is a web app with AngularJS libraries. Next, we will define that we would like to generate a UI for the Users entity:

```
[forge-demo]$ scaffold-generate --provider AngularJS --targets com.
packtpub.wflydevelopment.appendix.model.Users
```

Finally, we create an JAX-RS endpoint:

```
[forge-demo]$ rest-generate-endpoints-from-entities --targets com.
packtpub.wflydevelopment.appendix.model.Users
```

And we are done! The application is now a complete Java EE application with REST endpoints, JPA, and an AngularJS UI.

When these samples were written, JBoss Forge did not fully support all Java EE 7 dependencies. This can be fixed by manually modifying the pom.xml file of the generated project. You should just remove all the dependencies besides the one shown in the following code snippet:

```
<dependency>
    <groupId>javax</groupId>
    <artifactId>javaee-api</artifactId>
    <version>7.0</version>
    <scope>provided</scope>
</dependency>
```

Additionally, if your Users entity doesn't have an @javax.persistence.GeneratedValue annotation in its ID field, make sure you add it manually (there is currently a bug in the JPA add-on):

```
@Id
@Column(name = "id", unique = true, nullable = false)
@GeneratedValue(strategy=GenerationType.IDENTITY)
public int getId() {
    return this.id;
}
```

Building and deploying the application

Now, it is time to build your application using the build command, which will compile and package your application in a web application archive (forge-demo.war):

```
[forge-demo]$ build
***SUCCESS*** Build Success
```

The `Maven build` command has created an artifact `forge-demo-1.0.0-SNAPSHOT.war` in the `target` folder of your project. You can now either manually copy the archive into the `deployments` folder of your application server or use the `management` interfaces.

Remember that the server should have the `java:jboss/datasources/PostgreSqlDS` data source defined!

Your Forge-demo application in action

You can access your application at the default URL, `http://localhost:8080/forge-demo-1.0.0-SNAPSHOT/`.

The main application screen will contain the list of entities on the left menu. If you choose the **Users** position, then you should see a list of users that have been added, a **Search** button which can be used to filter across the users, and a **Create** button, which obviously will insert some data. This is shown in the following screenshot:

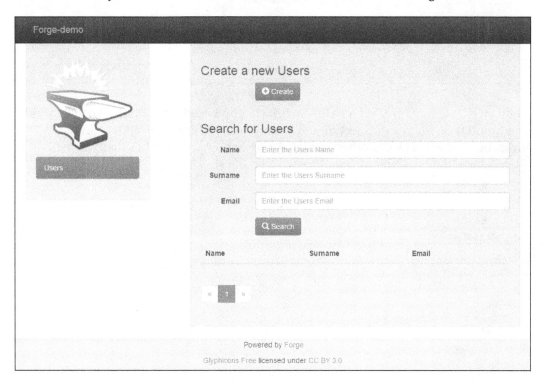

By clicking on the **Create** button, you will be taken to the screen that allows the insertion of a new user to the database (remember that we have configured this application to run against a PostgreSQL database). This is shown in the following screenshot:

In this way, we have created a basic AngularJS app based on Java EE. It can be used as a foundation for your project or just a sandbox in which you can try out new ideas. Be sure to check out other available add-ons, and remember that you will always have the possibility to create your own ones!

Index

message producer 172
message selectors
  specifying 187-189
module-name element 81
multicast 312

N

name attribute 52, 145
named beans 104, 105
Native SQL 150
NetBeans
  URL 27
new user
  creating, details 37
No-interface view 59
nondurable subscription 170
nonpersistent delivery mode 171
notations, resource address
  node-name 256
  node-type 256

O

observer 113
operations
  performing, on resources 257, 258
overriding pools, beans
  URL 180

P

Page Object 389
passwords
  encrypting 290, 291
path attribute 52
Path Relative to attribute 52
persistence
  adding, to application 135
  configuring 144, 145
  controller, adding to drive
        user requests 154-156
  database, setting up 135, 136
  example, running 165-168
  JDBC driver, installing in WildFly 136, 137
  JSF view, coding 157-164
  producer classes, adding 146-148

queries, coding for application 149-151
services, adding to application 151-154
testing 379, 380
persistent delivery mode 171
Picketbox 279
plugin, for JBoss
  URL 273
point-to-point (PTP) 172
POJOs
  about 134, 173, 243
  transforming, to JSON 249-252
POJO web service
  developing 206, 207
pom.xml file
  configuring 367-369
PostgreSQL database
  URL 135
PostgreSQL JDBC driver
  URL 136
producer classes
  adding 146-148
profiles, WildFly domain
  default 314
  full 314
  full-ha 314
  ha 314
programmatic security 281
programmatic timers 93
project object module, client
  configuring 82-84
public-key cryptography 298
Puppet
  URL 254

Q

queries
  coding, for application 149-151
queues 172

R

rar-info command shell 192
raw management API
  management model descriptions,
        reading via 270, 271
  resource watches creating, detyped API
        used 271-273

Thank you for buying

Java EE 7 Development with WildFly

About Packt Publishing

Packt, pronounced 'packed', published its first book, *Mastering phpMyAdmin for Effective MySQL Management*, in April 2004, and subsequently continued to specialize in publishing highly focused books on specific technologies and solutions.

Our books and publications share the experiences of your fellow IT professionals in adapting and customizing today's systems, applications, and frameworks. Our solution-based books give you the knowledge and power to customize the software and technologies you're using to get the job done. Packt books are more specific and less general than the IT books you have seen in the past. Our unique business model allows us to bring you more focused information, giving you more of what you need to know, and less of what you don't.

Packt is a modern yet unique publishing company that focuses on producing quality, cutting-edge books for communities of developers, administrators, and newbies alike. For more information, please visit our website at www.packtpub.com.

About Packt Enterprise

In 2010, Packt launched two new brands, Packt Enterprise and Packt Open Source, in order to continue its focus on specialization. This book is part of the Packt Enterprise brand, home to books published on enterprise software – software created by major vendors, including (but not limited to) IBM, Microsoft, and Oracle, often for use in other corporations. Its titles will offer information relevant to a range of users of this software, including administrators, developers, architects, and end users.

Writing for Packt

We welcome all inquiries from people who are interested in authoring. Book proposals should be sent to author@packtpub.com. If your book idea is still at an early stage and you would like to discuss it first before writing a formal book proposal, then please contact us; one of our commissioning editors will get in touch with you.

We're not just looking for published authors; if you have strong technical skills but no writing experience, our experienced editors can help you develop a writing career, or simply get some additional reward for your expertise.

Java 7 New Features Cookbook

ISBN: 978-1-84968-562-7   Paperback: 384 pages

Over 100 comprehensive recipes to get you
up-to-speed with all the exciting new features
of Java 7

1. Comprehensive coverage of the new features of
   Java 7 organized around easy-to-follow recipes.

2. Covers exciting features such as the try-with-
   resources block, the monitoring of directory
   events, asynchronous IO and new GUI
   enhancements, and more.

3. A learn-by-example based approach that focuses
   on key concepts to provide the foundation to
   solve real-world problems.

JBoss EAP6 High Availability

ISBN: 978-1-78328-243-2   Paperback: 166 pages

Leverage the power of JBoss EAP6 to successfully
build high-availability clusters quickly and efficiently

1. A thorough introduction to the new domain
   mode provided by JBoss EAP6.

2. Use mod_jk and mod_cluster with JBoss EAP6.

3. Learn how to apply SSL in a
   clustering environment.

Please check **www.PacktPub.com** for information on our titles

Java EE 5
Development with NetBeans 6

ISBN: 978-1-84719-546-3   Paperback: 400 pages

Develop professional enterprise Java EE 5
applications quickly and easily with this popular IDE

1. Use features of the popular NetBeans IDE to
    improve Java EE development.

2. Careful instructions and screenshots lead you
    through the options available.

3. Covers the major Java EE APIs such as JSF,
    EJB 3, and JPA, and how to work with them
    in NetBeans.

Java EE 6 with GlassFish 3
Application Server

ISBN: 978-1-84951-036-3   Paperback: 488 pages

A practical guide to install and configure the
GlassFish 3 Application Server and develop Java EE 6
applications to be deployed to this server

1. Install and configure the GlassFish 3
    Application Server and develop Java EE 6
    applications to be deployed to this server.

2. Specialize in all major Java EE 6 APIs, including
    new additions to the specification such as CDI
    and JAX-RS.

3. Use GlassFish v3 application server and gain
    enterprise reliability and performance with
    less complexity.

Please check **www.PacktPub.com** for information on our titles

www.ingramcontent.com/pod-product-compliance
Lightning Source LLC
Chambersburg PA
CBHW081500050326
40690CB00015B/2873